# 3

**PROJECT COORDINATION**
Sonja Altmeppen, Cologne

**EDITORIAL COORDINATION**
Julia Krumhauer, Cologne

**PRODUCTION**
Horst Neuzner, Cologne

**DESIGN**
Sense/Net, Andy Disl and
Birgit Reber, Cologne

**GERMAN TRANSLATION**
Karin Haag, Vienna

**FRENCH TRANSLATION**
Jacques Bosser, Paris

**PRINTED IN SINGAPORE**
ISBN 978–3–8365–0314–3

© **2008 TASCHEN GMBH**
Hohenzollernring 53
D – 50672 Cologne
**www.taschen.com**

Original Edition
© **2004 TASCHEN GMBH**

# ARCHITECTURE NOW!

*Architektur heute / L'architecture d'aujourd'hui*
*Philip Jodidio*

**TASCHEN**

HONG KONG  KÖLN  LONDON  LOS ANGELES  MADRID  PARIS  TOKYO

# CONTENTS

# INTRODUCTION

## DEATH OF THE MODERN

What is the direction of contemporary architecture? Are there discernible trends that allow the future to be predicted with any degree of certainty? Who are the form givers and the creators who are leaving their mark on our time or, more important still, showing the way to the future? Creativity is known to be difficult to judge in its own time. The art most widely admired today is likely to be the product of an earlier era. Looking forward, almost like looking into a crystal ball, is a question of extrapolating, or of being sensitive to what moves and shapes the art of designing and building architecture. Thus, the computer has opened new horizons, but perhaps not those originally imagined. Used at the outset by some as a way to visualize ever more extravagant structures, digital technology is today rapidly approaching a kind of maturity that is having a much deeper and long-lasting effect on architecture than any "crazy little buildings", as Arata Isozaki once labeled the experimental designs in Japan. The new freedom that suggested the computer could morph architecture out of its Euclidean, modernist box has surely not run its course, as many of the projects published in this book attest. Yet at the same time, computers are in the process of transforming not only the design process, but also production. And this is where the keyboard and the screen become really interesting. An exhibition organized at the end of 2003 at the Centre Pompidou by the talented curator Frédéric Migayrou under the title "Non-Standard Architecture" highlighted some of these deeper changes. What if the standardization born of nothing less than the Industrial Revolution were to come to an end? What if it became just as cheap to manufacture thousands of unique components for a building as it long has been to churn out identical boxes? Under the catchall description of "revolutionary" change, a brave band of architects set out from New York and Italy to declare the end of modernism sometime in the early 1970s. Theirs was the "post-modern" world. Architecture would be free to make reference to the past and to set aside the tabula rasa decreed by Walter Gropius and others in the heady days of the Bauhaus. A few years passed and the new king was quite naked. Philip Johnson's ATT Headquarters in New York (1979), hailed at the time as a symbol of the new, on closer inspection revealed itself as no more than an aging modernist tower in drag.

And what if today's revolution was not at all in the proliferation of exotic blobs seen from Paris to Beijing, but rather inside sometimes very "normal" looking buildings? Progressing toward a seamless process connecting the architect's design computer to digitally controlled production, new technology is making possible the end of the modern. For the modern was a dream of standardization, of assembly-line perfection, like that imagined by Henry Ford when he declared that his Model-T would be available "in any color as long as it is black." Nor does this mean that stylistic trends such as the already well-worn neo-modernism of recent years are forcibly relegated to the past. This revolution is not one of appearances; it is not a question of the length of this season's skirt. It happens inside, where an architect can make a thousand different pieces of wood for a low-cost Paris fashion showroom, where a door handle can be a unique piece, where even a stone can be as unlike its neighbor as the hand-carved blocks of the past. Before the Industrial Revolution, architecture was inevitably hand-made, each piece a unique testimony to its maker. The cost-driven logic of machines made it necessary to abandon the unique in favor of the identical, of the standardized unit of production. Today and tomorrow, the machine will not be set aside, rather it is the machine itself that has changed. Robotics allow lasers or other precision-guided tools to carve out a block of stone for Renzo Piano's Padre Pio Pilgrimage Church (San Giovanni Rotondo, Foggia, Italy, 1995–2003) unlike any other in the building for the same price as identical cubes. This is a real revolution and one that is not a matter of fashion or cosmetics. This is the end of the "modernist" logic that hid cookie-cutter blocks under the occasional curve or fillip, but which offered no real conceptual alternatives. An office or apartment in any shape as long as it was square might have been the rallying call of the true modernist. That day is already gone. Euclidean shapes will surely continue to exist in architecture, but the mold has been broken.

## SYMBOLS FOR A DIGITAL WORLD

A town of 9 000 inhabitants on the southern Japanese island of Kyushu is hardly the place where one might look for significant expressions of public architecture, and yet the Reihoku Community Hall by Hitoshi Abe is proof that such designs have their place in today's world. At the origin of this commission, a project called Artpolis, initiated in 1988 under the authority of the governor of Kumamoto Prefecture by the architect Arata Isozaki, had already shown that major architects could be brought to work in almost rural Kyushu areas. Now under the control of Toyo Ito and Teiichi Takahashi, Artpolis chose Hitoshi Abe for Reihoku and he promptly engaged in long consultations with the local population. The result of these discussions was that nobody could agree on the precise function of a community facility. The architect designed a flexible space appropriate to this indecision, but what is important is that he nonetheless succeeded in making an accepted symbol for the town, a place that really has become the center of Reihoku. The billowing dark folds of the building are not what anyone might expect and yet the structure, with its woodwork, surely recalls Japanese temple architecture. It also brings to mind a great tent, erected just to draw in the townsfolk, and come they do.

Also in Japan, but on quite a different scale, the new Yokohama International Port Terminal designed by Foreign Office Architects (FOA) has gotten a large share of recent architectural publications, if only because of its unexpected appearance and heady reliance on advanced techniques of computer-assisted design. Located so close to Tokyo that it is almost part of the same urban mass, Yokohama is officially the second largest city in Japan, and the place, incidentally, where Admiral Perry landed in 1853, opening the modern era for Japan. Seen from certain angles the facility, which draws large numbers of the curious, looks almost like a kind of natural formation. It might be noted in passing that several contemporary Japanese architects, like Itsuko Hasegawa, have imagined that the role of architecture should be to create a kind of artificial nature. Here, where urban development has run rampant, the curiously tranquil jetty conceived by FOA goes a step in the direction of imagining architecture as a surrogate "Mother Nature," while not reaching at all into the imagery of "organic" design.

## BLINK AND IT'S GONE

While corporate clients, in particular those involved in the ephemeral fashion industry, have sought out the more "permanent" values of quality architecture, there are also excellent reasons to bring good design and avowedly temporary events together. Much like previous corporate attitudes, the organizers of fairs or national exhibitions have often looked to "practical" solutions in designing temporary pavilions. Undistinguished architecture does not necessarily draw in the crowds. Though they have been roundly criticized for the apparent profligacy, the organizers of Switzerland's Expo.02 made no secret of their desire to attract some of the best architects in the world for the structures erected on temporary jetties in the lakes around Neuchâtel. Thus Jean Nouvel was called on to occupy the attractive community of Morat. He did this with a highly visible monolithic block of rusting steel, sitting offshore in the lake. Another perhaps even more unusual participation in

Expo.02 was that of the New York architects Diller + Scofidio. Their Blur Building was intended to resemble nothing so much as a cloud hovering over Lake Neuchâtel. 100 m wide by 60 m deep and 25 m high, the "cloud" effect rising above the water was obtained through the use of filtered lake water "shot as a fine mist through a dense array of 31 500 high-pressure water nozzles integrated into a large cantilevered tensegrity structure." When wind and weather conditions permitted, the effect achieved by the Blur Building was exactly that imagined by the architects. Theirs was an effort to actually make architecture disappear, to be as light as a cloud, yet to be an environment where a kind of sensory deprivation would make visitors lose all notion of "real" space or time. If Nouvel was "artistic" in his approach to Expo.02, then Diller + Scofidio were by far the most radical participants, daring to question the very nature of the built form. Many agreed that they solved the riddle of inherently ephemeral fair architecture. What could be more ephemeral than a cloud?

The link between art and architecture was also blurred by the stunning installation for the sculptor Anish Kapoor in London's Tate Modern. His Marsyas was comprised of three steel rings joined by a single span of red PVC membrane stretched along the length of the 155-meter-long Turbine Hall. Visible in its entirety from no one vantage point, Marsyas clearly challenged conventional perceptions of space and architecture. Emptiness and fullness, standard features of any architecture, here flowed from one into the other without any discernible boundary. Actually, this enigmatic play on space was not at all contradictory to the work of Herzog & de Meuron on Tate Modern itself. Their own approach often consists in blurring the limits between reflection and unobstructed vision, for example, or more frequently lightness and heaviness. The American sculptor Richard Serra has said very pointedly that the "difference between art and architecture is that architecture serves a purpose." It may not be appropriate to call Kapoor's Marsyas a work of architecture, and yet it dealt most adroitly with perceptions of space, light and color, reconfiguring the massive Turbine Hall in a way that no other artwork has before. Perhaps it was not architecture, but it did serve to look at space and volume in a new way.

### BIG TIME FOR THE CULTURE VULTURES
As has been the case for many years, one of the privileged fields of intervention for quality architecture is that of culture. Although it is true that in the United States and elsewhere grandiose plans for new museums have been abandoned, other facilities such as concert halls have flourished. Even as the Los Angeles County Museum abandoned its ambitious reconstruction plans scheduled with Rem Koolhaas, the city completed the new Disney Concert Hall, Frank Gehry's first major public building in his hometown. Although it is not certain that any architect will precisely follow in his footsteps, Frank Gehry has done more than almost any other living architect to liberate his profession. With his billowing clouds of titanium he has confirmed the artistic liberty and status of the architect. This makes it easier for younger designers to seek new forms, even if they do not adhere to the esthetic choices of Gehry.

Might it be that the choice of Zaha Hadid to build the Lois & Richard Rosenthal Center for Contemporary Art in Cincinnati has some relation to the acclaim given Gehry? After all, a place like Cincinnati could use some of the good publicity earned by Bilbao after all. Well-known in architectural circles for her drawings and radical schemes, it seems that Zaha Hadid has now entered a new phase in her career, where major projects are coming her way. It is indeed astonishing that she is the first woman architect to build a museum in America, but in this too she is a pioneer. In Cincinnati, she shows that her exuberant drawings can indeed take built form, and that contemporary art and architecture can mix in the very city that saw the painful efforts to censor the work of Robert Mapplethorpe a few years ago.

## ENGINEERED FOR LIVING

Housing is among the most clear and present needs met by architecture. When an enlightened client meets a talented architect, the result can be a real step ahead for architecture that may influence esthetics and more practical matters for years to come. The residences published in this book are selected precisely for their innovative qualities and for the advances they represent. Architect David Adjaye has gained quite a reputation in London, perhaps because he has had the good fortune to have a number of clients who became famous after he worked for them. He converted a 1930s East London warehouse into a home for artists Tim Noble and Sue Webster in a most surprising way. Although the name "Dirty House" is not explained, the artists are known amongst other things for literally making works out of trash. East London is not best known for its luxurious residences, a fact that neither Adjaye nor the clients objected to. In its radical use of space, light and surfaces, the Dirty House reacts to its location in a way appropriate to a city that is used to seeing the beauty in an industrial environment.

Shigeru Ban's Glass Shutter House in Tokyo is another matter altogether. Located in a relatively fashionable area of Tokyo, it is a combined house and restaurant designed for the specific needs of a well-known Japanese chef. Ban is of course known for his research into flexibility in architecture, both in his choice of materials like paper and in his desire to question such fundamental elements as walls. In the Glass Shutter House, Ban has made it possible for the owner to open two walls entirely, rolling them into the roof. This is particularly useful for the chef in the summer months when he can open his restaurant directly out onto his terrace. Above all, it is an inventive solution to the very solidity of architecture. What if a building could just dissolve when we want it to? "Oh that this too too solid flesh would melt." Ban seeks practical solutions to truly radical ideas and in that he is one of the foremost architects active in the world today.

## BRAVE NEW WORLD

Perhaps the most interesting area of architecture is its capacity to dream, to imagine solutions that have never existed before. Intended as a survey of architecture since 2000, this book gives an overview of the extraordinary wealth of creativity that has been unleashed by a combination of technological advances and conceptual openness. There is no one style today, nor should there be. Architecture has always been influenced first and foremost by practical considerations. Architecture, unlike art, as Richard Serra says, serves a purpose. The most significant development that has begun to reshape architecture is the real possibility of design-to-production integration using computers and robotics. This has already made the production of unique components possible, overturning the esthetics and deeper logic of nearly a century of "modern" architecture. The Modern that demanded that every Model-T should be black or every window the same size and shape is dead. Esthetics may still lead architects to indulge in neo-modernism or neo-minimalism, but they no longer see their real choices fundamentally limited by the economics of the standardized production line. Computer-assisted design is quickly changing from a kind of circus act trained to produce irregular blobs into a real tool of the future, driving cutting-edge processes that will produce a new freedom in architecture.

# EINLEITUNG

## DAS ENDE DES MODERNISMUS

Welche Richtung nimmt die zeitgenössische Architektur? Lassen sich Trends ausmachen, die es ermöglichen, die Zukunft der Architektur vorauszusagen? Wer sind die Formgebenden und Kreativen, die unserer Zeit ihren Stempel aufdrücken, oder – was noch wichtiger ist – die den Weg in die Zukunft weisen? Dies lässt sich bekanntermaßen schwer in der eigenen Zeit beurteilen. Kunstformen, die heute allgemein anerkannt und geschätzt werden, sind in der Regel in einer früheren Ära entstanden. Um in die Zukunft der Architektur zu blicken, muss man das, was heute die Kunst des Gestaltens und Bauens bewegt und formt, weiterdenken oder auch nur dafür empfänglich sein. Während die digitale Technologie von einigen Planern anfänglich eingesetzt wurde, um immer extravagantere Formen und Strukturen zu visualisieren, nähert sie sich heute einem Grad der Ausgereiftheit, der wesentlich tiefer gehende und anhaltendere Auswirkungen auf die Architektur hat als alle „verrückten kleinen Gebäude", wie Arata Isozaki einmal die in Japan entstandenen experimentellen Bauformen genannt hat. Die neue Freiheit, die suggeriert hatte, der Computer könne die Architektur aus ihrer euklidischen, modernistischen Beengtheit befreien, hat sich mit Sicherheit noch nicht verbraucht, wie viele der in diesem Buch vorgestellten Projekte beweisen. Gleichzeitig jedoch verändern Computer nicht nur den Gestaltungsprozess selbst, sondern auch die Produktionsabläufe. Eine Ende 2003 von Frédéric Migayrou am Centre Pompidou geleitete Ausstellung mit dem Titel „Architectures non standard" lenkte die Aufmerksamkeit auf einige dieser tiefgreifenden Veränderungen. Was, wenn die Standardisierung, deren Ursprung in der industriellen Revolution liegt, an ihrem Ende angelangt wäre? Was, wenn sich Tausende individuell gestalteter Einzelteile für ein Gebäude ebenso billig produzieren ließen wie die massenhafte Herstellung identischer Boxen? Unter der alle in einen Topf werfenden Bezeichnung der „revolutionären" Veränderung machte sich in den frühen 1970er Jahren eine mutige Schar von Architekten in New York und Italien daran, das Ende der Moderne zu verkünden. Sie propagierten die Postmoderne, in der die Architektur die Freiheit haben sollte, auf die Vergangenheit Bezug zu nehmen und damit die von Walter Gropius und anderen in der Blütezeit des Bauhaus geforderte *tabula rasa* zu verwerfen. Nach ein paar Jahren stand der Kaiser jedoch ziemlich nackt da. Philip Johnsons ATT Zentrale in New York von 1979, zu ihrer Zeit als ein Symbol des Neuen bejubelt, entpuppte sich bei genauerer Betrachtung lediglich als modernistisch aufgemotzter Turm.

Was, wenn auch die Revolution unserer Tage sich in zuweilen ganz „normal" aussehenden Gebäuden abspielte? Weil die neue Technologie auf einen Prozess zusteuert, in dem sich das computergenerierte Gestalten nahtlos mit einer digital gesteuerten Produktionsweise verbindet, macht sie das Ende der Moderne möglich. Schließlich hatte die Moderne den Traum von einer allgemeinen Standardisierung, von einer fließbandmäßigen Perfektion, wie sie Henry Ford im Sinn hatte, als er erklärte, sein Model-T sei „in jeder Farbe erhältlich, solange sie schwarz sei". Bei der neuen Form von Revolution handelt es sich nicht um eine äußere Erscheinung. Sie findet vielmehr im Innenraum statt, wo ein Architekt 1 000 unterschiedliche Holzteilchen für eine gar nicht so teure Pariser Modeboutique einsetzen, wo ein Türgriff ein Unikat sein und wo sich sogar ein Stein vom andern so stark unterscheiden kann wie die handgemeißelten Quadersteine der Vergangenheit. Vor der industriellen Revolution war jede Architektur zwangsläufig handgemacht und jeder Bestandteil war ein einzigartiges Zeugnis für die Fertigkeit seines Erzeugers. Die kostenorientierte Logik der Maschinen dagegen machte eine Vereinheitlichung der Produktion notwendig, womit das Individuelle zugunsten des Identischen aufgegeben wurde. Weder heute noch morgen wird man die Maschinen abschaffen. Es ist vielmehr so, dass sich die Maschinen selbst gewandelt haben. So macht es zum Beispiel die Robotertechnik möglich, dass alle Steinquader für Renzo Pianos Wallfahrtskirche Padre Pio (San Giovanni Rotondo, Foggia, Italien, 1995–2003) mit Laser und anderen Präzisionsgeräten ohne Mehrkosten vollkommen unterschiedlich gemeißelt werden. Darin besteht die eigentliche Revolution. Sie bedeutet das Ende der „modernistischen" Logik, mit der zwar funktionale Merkmale unter einer Bogenlinie oder anderen Spielereien versteckt wurden, die aber keine reale konzeptionelle Alternative zu bieten hatte. Ein Büro oder eine Wohnung „in jeder beliebigen Form, so lange sie quadratisch ist", mag der Schlachtruf der eingefleischten Modernisten gewesen sein. Diese Zeiten sind vorbei. Zwar werden die euklidischen Formen mit Sicherheit auch in der Architektur der Zukunft fortbestehen, die Gussform aber ist zerbrochen.

## SYMBOLE FÜR EINE DIGITALE WELT

Eine kleine Stadt mit 9 000 Einwohnern auf der südjapanischen Insel Kyushu ist nicht gerade der Ort, an dem man bedeutende Bauten erwarten würde. Und doch ist das von Hitoshi Abe gestaltete Gemeindezentrum in Reihoku ein Beweis dafür, dass Bauten dieser Art auch in der Welt von heute ihren Platz haben. Der Bauauftrag ergab sich aus einem Projekt namens Artpolis, das 1988 von dem Architekten Arata Isozaki im Auftrag des Gouverneurs der Präfektur Kumamoto begonnen wurde und bereits einige namhafte Architekten in die ländlichen Gegenden von Kyushu gebracht hat. Toyo Ito und Teiichi Takahashi, die jetzigen Leiter von Artpolis, wählten Hitoshi Abe für das Reihoku Projekt, woraufhin sich dieser eingehend mit der lokalen Bevölkerung beriet. Am Ende der Diskussionen stand fest, dass sich die Bewohner nicht auf eine genaue Funktion des Gemeindezentrums einigen konnten, und so entwarf der Architekt einen flexiblen Raum, der dieser Unentschiedenheit Rechnung trägt. Die dunklen, sich türmenden Falten des Gebäudes mögen Verblüffung hervorrufen und doch bezieht sich das Haus mit seinem Gebälk eindeutig auf die traditionelle japanische Tempelarchitektur.

Das ebenfalls in Japan, jedoch in einer ganz anderen Größenordnung angesiedelte, neue Gebäude für den internationalen Hafen von Yokohama erhielt viel Aufmerksamkeit in den Medien. Vermutlich in erster Linie wegen seines verblüffenden Äußeren und der Tatsache, dass sein Design von der Gruppe Foreign Office Architects (FOA) in hohem Maß auf den neuesten Techniken des computergestützten Gestaltens beruht. Yokohama, nahe Tokio ist die zweitgrößte Stadt Japans. Hier legte Admiral Perry im Jahr 1853 an und leitete damit den Eintritt Japans in das moderne Zeitalter ein. Das Gebäude sieht aus bestimmten Blickwinkeln wie ein Naturgebilde aus. In diesem Zusammenhang sei erwähnt, dass nach Ansicht einiger zeitgenössischer japanischer Architekten, wie Itsuko Hasegawa, die Rolle der Architektur darin besteht, eine Art künstliche Natur zu schaffen. Und gerade an diesem Ort, wo eine rückhaltlose Verstädterung betrieben wird, geht FOA mit ihrer seltsam unbewegt gestalteten Hafenmole einen Schritt in Richtung einer Architektur, die als ein Ersatz für „Mutter Natur" imaginiert wird, ohne sich allerdings der Bildsprache des „organischen" Designs zu bedienen.

## FLÜCHTIGE AUGENBLICKE

Auch wenn bei den Bauherren aus der Wirtschaft, besonders solchen aus der kurzlebigen Modeindustrie, zur Zeit eher die „dauerhaften" Qualitäten hochwertiger Architektur gefragt sind, gibt es triftige Gründe, gutes Design auch auf Ereignisse oder Veranstaltungen anzuwenden, die erklärtermaßen temporärer Natur sind. Obwohl sie für ihre angebliche Verschwendung gehörig kritisiert wurden, bestanden die Veranstalter der Schweizer Expo.02 auf ihrer Absicht, einige der besten Architekten der Welt für die Entwürfe zu gewinnen, die für die Dauer der Ausstellung in den Seen und dem Gebiet um Neuenburg (Neuchâtel) realisiert werden sollten. Folglich wurde auch Jean Nouvel eingeladen, der einen spektakulären monolithischen Block aus rostigem Stahl in einiger Entfernung vom Ufer auf die Wasseroberfläche des reizvollen Murtensees setzte. Ein weiterer, vielleicht sogar noch ungewöhnlicherer Beitrag zur Expo.02 stammte von den New Yorker Architekten Diller + Scofidio. Ihr Blur Building, das aussah wie eine über dem Neuenburger See schwebende Wolke, war eine 100 m lange und 60 m breite Konstruktion, die sich 25 m über den Wasserspiegel erhob. Der Wolken-Effekt wurde durch den Einsatz gefilterten Seewassers erzielt, das als feiner Nebel aus 31 500 in dichter Folge angeordneten Hochdruck-Wasserdüsen versprüht wurde, die in eine große, freitragende Seilnetz-Konstruktion eingebaut waren. Das Bestreben der Architekten war hier, die Architektur im eigentlichen Sinne zum Verschwinden zu bringen, und so leicht werden zu lassen wie eine Wolke. Gleichzeitig sollte dadurch eine Umgebung entstehen, in der eine Art sinnliche Deprivation die Besucher jedes Gefühl für den „realen" Raum und die Zeit verlieren ließ. Hatte Nouvel einen „künstlerischen" Zugang zur Expo.02 gewählt, so lieferten Diller + Scofidio den weitaus radikalsten Beitrag, indem sie es wagten, das eigentliche Wesen der gebauten Form in Frage zu stellen.

Die Grenze zwischen Kunst und Architektur wurde auch durch eine beeindruckende Installation des Bildhauers Anish Kapoor in der Londoner Tate Modern verwischt. Sie trug den Titel „Marsyas" und bestand aus drei Stahlringen, die durch eine rote, sich durch die gesamte, 155 m lange Turbinenhalle spannende PVC-Folie verbunden waren. Diese von keinem einzigen Punkt in ihrer Gänze überschaubare Installation stellte die konventionellen Wahrnehmungen von Raum und Architektur in Frage. Leere und Fülle, zwei maßgebende Elemente jeder architektonischen Gestaltung, gingen hier vollkommen nahtlos ineinander über. Tatsächlich befand sich dieses enigmatische Spiel mit dem Raum durchaus im Einklang mit der Arbeit von Herzog & de Meuron an der Tate Modern selbst. Schließlich besteht auch deren Zugang häufig darin, die Grenzen zwischen Reflektion und ungehinderter Sicht oder die zwischen Leichtigkeit und Schwere zu verwischen. Der Unterschied zwischen Kunst und Architektur liegt darin, wie der amerikanische Bildhauer Richard Serra einmal pointiert sagte, dass die Architektur immer einem Zweck dient. Auch wenn man Kapoors „Marsyas" nicht als Architektur bezeichnen kann, so setzte sich dieses Werk doch mit der Wahrnehmung von Raum, Licht und Farbe auseinander und gab der riesigen Turbinenhalle eine räumliche Struktur wie noch kein anderes Kunstwerk zuvor.

## DIE GROSSE ZEIT DER KULTURGEIER

Seit vielen Jahren ist der Kulturbereich eines der bevorzugten Aufgabengebiete für hochwertige Architektur. Zwar wurden nicht nur in den Vereinigten Staaten großartige Pläne für neue Museen wieder verworfen, aber andere Kultureinrichtungen, wie etwa Konzerthallen, gedeihen dafür umso prächtiger. Während das Los Angeles County Museum seine ehrgeizigen Modernisierungspläne aufgab, für deren Ausführung Rem Koolhaas vorgesehen war, ist im Zentrum von Los Angeles die Disney Concert Hall von Frank O. Gehry fertig gestellt worden, das erste große, öffentliche Gebäude in seiner Heimatstadt. Mit seinen aufgetürmten Wolken aus Titan hat Gehry für sich und alle anderen Architekten die Freiheit als Künstler beansprucht. Das macht die Suche nach neuen Formen für die jüngeren Gestalter einfacher. Könnte es sein, dass ein Zusammenhang zwischen der Wahl von Zaha Hadid zur Planerin des Lois & Richard Rosenthal Center for Contemporary Art in Cincinnati und der öffentlichen Begeisterung für Gehrys Bauten besteht? Die in Architekturkreisen seit langem für ihre radikalen Konzepte berühmte Zaha Hadid ist die erste Frau, die ein Museum in den Vereinigten Staaten baut. In Cincinnati demonstriert sie, dass sich ihre dynamischen Zeichnungen tatsächlich materialisieren lassen, und dass zeitgenössische Kunst und Architektur selbst in jener Stadt eine Verbindung eingehen können, in der der peinliche Versuch unternommen wurde, das Werk von Robert Mapplethorpe zu zensieren.

## KONSTRUIERT ZUM LEBEN UND WOHNEN

Der Wohnungsbau gehört zu den eindeutigsten und aktuellsten Aufgaben der Architektur. Trifft ein aufgeklärter Bauherr auf einen talentierten Architekten, so kann das Resultat einen Fortschritt für die Architektur bedeuten, der die ästhetischen und auch die praktischen Seiten des Bauens auf Jahre hinaus beeinflusst. Die in diesem Buch präsentierten Wohnhäuser wurden aufgrund ihrer innovativen Merkmale und der sich in ihnen manifestierenden fortschrittlichen Aspekte ausgewählt. Der Architekt David Adjaye hat sich in London einen Namen gemacht, vielleicht auch deswegen, weil er das Glück hatte, dass eine Reihe von Auftraggebern berühmt wurde, nachdem er für sie gearbeitet hatte. So baute er beispielsweise ein im Londoner East End gelegenes Lagerhaus aus den 1930er Jahren zu einem höchst ungewöhnlichen Wohnhaus für das Künstlerpaar Tim Noble und Sue Webster um. Die Tatsache, dass das East End nicht gerade als luxuriöse Wohngegend gilt, schreckte weder Adjaye noch seine Auftraggeber ab. In seiner radikalen Behandlung von Raum, Licht und Oberflächen geht das Dirty House in einer Weise auf seinen Standort ein, wie es einer Stadt entspricht, in der man imstande ist, das Schöne auch in einer industriellen Umgebung zu erkennen.

Ganz anders dagegen Shigeru Bans Glass Shutter House in Tokio. In einer relativ schicken Gegend von Tokio gelegen, handelt es sich hierbei um eine Kombination von Wohnhaus und Restaurant eines japanischen Starkochs. Ban ist bekannt für seine beständige Auseinandersetzung mit dem Thema Flexibilität in der Architektur, was sich sowohl in der Wahl seiner Baumaterialien wie Papier, als auch in seinem Drang niederschlägt, so fundamentale Elemente wie Wände in Frage zu stellen. So ermöglicht Ban in seinem Glass Shutter House dem Hausherrn, zwei Wände, die in das Dach hinein eingerollt werden können, komplett zu öffnen, so dass das Restaurant im Sommer nahtlos in die Terrasse übergehen kann. Vor allem ist es jedoch eine ausgesprochen originale Alternative zu der herkömmlichen Solidität von Architektur.

## SCHÖNE NEUE WELT

Die vielleicht interessanteste Eigenschaft der Architektur ist ihre Fähigkeit, zu träumen und noch nie da gewesene Lösungen zu ersinnen. Dieses Buch vermittelt im Rahmen eines Überblicks über die seit 2000 entstandene Architektur einen plastischen Eindruck von dem enormen Kreativitätsschub, der durch eine Kombination aus technologischem Fortschritt und inhaltlicher Unvoreingenommenheit ausgelöst wurde. Es gibt heutzutage nicht mehr den einen Stil und das soll es auch gar nicht. Die Architektur ist immer schon in erster Linie von praktischen Erwägungen bestimmt worden. Im Gegensatz zur Kunst dient die Architektur, wie Richard Serra sagt, einem Zweck. Die bedeutendste Veränderung, die sich in der Architektur derzeit bemerkbar macht, ist die reale Möglichkeit einer Integration sämtlicher Prozesse von Entwurf bis Produktion durch Computer und Robotertechnik. Dies hat bereits die Herstellung individueller Einzelteile ermöglicht, was eine Überwindung der Ästhetik und wirtschaftlichen Logik eines knappen Jahrhunderts „moderner" Architektur bedeutet. Jene Moderne, die verlangte, dass jedes Model-T Auto schwarz sein und jedes Fenster die gleiche Größe und Farbe haben müsse, ist tot. Zwar mögen Architekten aus ästhetischen Gründen nach wie vor auf die Formensprache eines „Neo-Modernismus" oder „Neo-Minimalismus" zurückgreifen, ihre Umsetzungen sind jedoch nicht länger durch die ökonomischen Grenzen einer standardisierten Produktionsweise limitiert. Computergestütztes Design wandelt sich derzeit von einer Art Zirkusnummer, mit der seltsame Gebilde produziert werden, zu einem praktikablen Instrumentarium der Zukunft, das eine neue Freiheit für die Gestaltungsmöglichkeiten der Architektur mit sich bringen wird.

# INTRODUCTION

## LA MORT DU MODERNISME

Dans quelle direction s'oriente aujourd'hui l'architecture contemporaine ? Peut-on repérer des tendances claires qui permettent d'entrevoir le futur avec quelque degré de certitude ? Qui sont les créateurs de formes ? Qui va laisser sa marque sur notre temps ou, plus important encore, qui nous montre la voie de l'avenir ? On sait que toute époque éprouve des difficultés à juger de sa propre créativité. L'art le plus admiré aujourd'hui est vraisemblablement le produit de périodes antérieures. Regarder vers l'avant – un peu comme dans une boule de cristal – est un problème d'extrapolation, de sensibilité à ce qui mobilise et formalise l'art de la conception et de la construction architecturales. L'ordinateur nous a ouvert de nouveaux horizons, qui ne sont pas forcément ceux auxquels on avait pensé à l'origine. Utilisée au départ par certains comme un mode de visualisation de structures de plus en plus extravagantes, la technologie numérique approche rapidement d'une relative maturité qui exercera un effet beaucoup plus profond et durable sur l'architecture que toutes ces « petites constructions folles », comme Arata Isozaki qualifiait certains projets japonais expérimentaux. La nouvelle liberté que suggère un ordinateur capable de faire sortir l'architecture de sa boîte euclidienne et moderniste n'a certainement pas encore atteint son but, comme beaucoup de projets publiés dans cet ouvrage en attestent. Cependant les ordinateurs sont en passe de transformer non seulement le processus de conception, mais aussi de production. C'est justement à ce niveau que le clavier et l'écran commencent à devenir vraiment intéressants. Une exposition organisée au Centre Pompidou à Paris, fin 2003, par le talentueux commissaire Frédéric Migayrou, intitulée « Une architecture non standard » a identifié quelques-uns de ces changements importants. Que va-t-il se passer si la standardisation, née de la Révolution industrielle, disparaît ? Qu'arrivera-t-il s'il est aussi économique de fabriquer des milliers de composants uniques que des pièces identiques ? Sous l'appellation attrape-tout de changement « révolutionnaire », un groupe d'architectes new-yorkais et italiens avait annoncé la fin du modernisme vers le début des années 1970. Leur monde était celui du postmodernisme. Pour eux, l'architecture devait être libre de faire référence au passé et de laisser de côté la *tabula rasa* décrétée par Walter Gropius et autres à la grande époque du Bauhaus. Quelques années se sont écoulées et le nouveau roi s'est révélé un peu nu. Vu de plus près, le siège d'ATT par Philip Johnson à New York (1979), salué en son temps comme le symbole de la nouveauté, est-il autre chose qu'une tour moderniste déguisée ?

Et si la révolution que nous connaissons s'observait plus dans certaines constructions à l'air tout à fait « normal » que dans la prolifération de *blobs* exotiques de Paris à Pékin ? En favorisant la progression d'un processus apparemment lisse, qui va du logiciel de conception architecturale à une production contrôlée par informatique, la nouvelle technologie rend possible la fin du modernisme. Car celui-ci était aussi un rêve de standardisation, celui de la perfection de la ligne de montage imaginée par Henry Ford qui déclarait que son modèle T était disponible « dans toutes les couleurs à condition que ce soit le noir ». La révolution actuelle n'est pas une révolution d'apparence. Il ne s'agit pas de la longueur de jupe à la mode cette saison. Elle est intériorisée, intégrée. C'est le cas lorsqu'un architecte peut faire fabriquer un millier de pièces de bois différentes pour un show-room parisien de vêtements bon marché, lorsqu'une poignée de porte peut être une pièce unique, lorsque même une pierre peut être aussi différente de sa voisine que les blocs taillés jadis à la main. Avant la Révolution industrielle, l'architecture était inévitablement quelque chose de manuel. Chaque pièce était un témoignage de la main de son créateur. La logique économique des machines pousse à l'abandon de l'unique au profit de l'identique et de l'unité standardisée de production. Aujourd'hui et demain, la machine ne sera certes pas écartée, mais elle aura évolué. La robotique permet aux lasers et autres outils guidés avec précision, un découpage spécifique de chaque bloc de pierre, différent de tous les autres, pour un prix semblable à celui de blocs identiques (église du pèlerinage de Padre Pio, San Giovanni Rotondo, Foggia, Italie, 1995–2003). Il s'agit bien d'une vraie révolution, qui n'a rien à voir avec la mode ou les solutions cosmétiques. C'est la fin de la logique « moderniste » qui cachait les parpaings de béton dans une courbe ou sous un remplissage, mais n'offrait aucune alternative conceptuelle réelle. Un bureau ou un appartement de n'importe quelle forme, pourvu qu'elle soit orthogonale, a pu être le cri de ralliement des modernistes purs et durs. Cette époque est terminée. Les formes euclidiennes perdureront certainement, mais leur moule a été brisé.

## SYMBOLES POUR UN MONDE NUMÉRIQUE

Une ville de 9 000 habitants sur une île du sud du Japon, Kyushu, n'est sans doute guère le lieu où l'on pourrait s'attendre à trouver des expressions significatives d'une grande architecture publique. Néanmoins, le Hall communautaire de Reihoku, par Hitoshi Abe, prouve que ce type de projet a toute sa place dans le monde actuel. À l'origine de cette commande, un programme intitulé Artpolis, initié par l'architecte Arata Isozaki en 1988 sous l'autorité du gouverneur de la préfecture de Kumamoto, avait montré que de grands architectes pouvaient avoir envie de travailler dans ces contrées quasi rurales de Kyushu. Aujourd'hui sous le contrôle de Toyo Ito et de Teiichi Takahashi, Artpolis a sélectionné Hitoshi Abe pour le projet de Reihoku. L'architecte a rapidement lancé de longues consultations avec la population locale, mais personne n'était d'accord sur la fonction précise de ce type d'équipement communautaire. Abe a conçu un espace flexible adapté à cette indécision, mais réussit néanmoins à en faire un symbole bien accepté par Reihoku, un lieu devenu réellement le centre de la cité. Les sombres plis en forme de vague du bâtiment ne ressemblent à rien de connu, et cependant cette structure et son travail du bois évoquent l'architecture des temples japonais, un peu comme une grande tente dressée pour attirer le public. Et celui-ci vient.

Au Japon également, mais à une échelle assez différente, le nouveau terminal international du port de Yokohama conçu par Foreign Office Architects (FOA) a été abondamment reproduit dans de multiples publications architecturales récentes, ne serait-ce que pour son aspect inattendu et son recours aux techniques de CAO les plus avancées. Située si près de Tokyo qu'elle fait presque partie de la même mégalopole, Yokohama est officiellement la seconde ville du Japon et, pour mémoire, le lieu du débarquement de l'amiral Perry en 1853, qui allait ouvrir les portes de la modernisation au Japon. Vu sous certains angles, cet équipement qui attire de nombreux curieux, fait presque penser à une formation naturelle. On peut noter, au passage, que plusieurs architectes japonais contemporains, comme Itsuko Hasegawa, pensent que le rôle de l'architecture devrait être de créer une sorte de nature artificielle. Ici, dans le cadre d'un développement urbain inexorable, la simple et curieuse jetée conçue par FOA va dans le sens de cette architecture qui serait une « Mère-Nature » subrogée, sans pour autant faire appel à une imagerie « organique ».

## DISPARU EN UN CLIN D'ŒIL

Si les grandes entreprises, en particulier celles du domaine éphémère de la mode, sont à la recherche des valeurs plus « permanentes » d'une architecture de qualité, de bonnes raisons militent également en faveur de l'application du *Good Design* à des événements temporaires par nature. Un peu comme les grandes institutions, les organisateurs d'expositions universelles ou nationales ont souvent recherché des solutions « pratiques » pour leurs pavillons éphémères. Mais une architecture banale n'attire pas les foules. Bien qu'ils aient été globalement critiqués pour l'ampleur de leurs dépenses, les organisateurs de l'Expo nationale suisse 02 n'ont pas caché leur souhait d'attirer les meilleurs architectes du monde pour concrétiser des projets prévus sur des jetées provisoires en bordure des lacs de Neuchâtel et de Morat. Jean Nouvel a été chargé de Morat. Il a imaginé un monolithe en acier rouillé amarré à quelques encablures de la rive et que l'on ne pouvait manquer de voir. Une autre participation très remarquée était signée des New-yorkais Diller + Scofidio. Leur Blur Building se proposait tout simplement de ressembler à un nuage en arrêt au-dessus du lac de Neuchâtel. De 100 m de large, 60 de profondeur et 25 de haut, cet effet de « nuage » était obtenu par la production d'une « fine brume générée par un réseau de 31 500 buses haute-pression intégrées à une grande ossature en porte-à-faux et tenségrité ». L'eau était celle du lac, filtrée bien sûr. Lorsque les conditions météorologiques le permettaient, l'effet obtenu était exactement celui imaginé. Leur propos était de faire disparaître leur architecture, aussi légère qu'un cumulus, et de susciter une sorte de privation sensorielle pour que les visiteurs perdent toute notion d'espace ou de temps « réels ». Si Nouvel a été « artistique » dans son approche d'Expo.02, la proposition de Diller + Scofidio fut de loin la plus radicale, car elle osait remettre en question la nature même de la forme construite. Beaucoup de visiteurs ont pensé qu'ils avaient résolu la quadrature d'une architecture de foire par nature éphémère. Quoi de plus éphémère en effet qu'un nuage ?

Les rapports entre l'art et l'architecture ont été brouillés par l'étonnante installation du sculpteur Anish Kapoor à la Tate Modern de Londres. Son *Marsyas* composé de trois anneaux d'acier réunis par une membrane de PVC rouge s'étirait sur les 155 mètres du Hall de la turbine. Cette pièce – visible dans son intégralité d'un point unique –, remettait en cause les perceptions conventionnelles de l'espace et de l'architecture. Le plein et le vide, éléments standard de toute architecture, alternaient dans un flux continu, sans frontière visible. Ce jeu énigmatique sur l'espace n'était en rien contradictoire avec le travail de Herzog & de Meuron sur la Tate Modern elle-même. Leur approche consiste souvent à brouiller les limites entre le reflet et la vision directe, par exemple, ou plus fréquemment encore le poids et la légèreté. Le sculpteur américain Richard Serra a noté avec pertinence que « la différence entre l'art et l'architecture est que l'architecture répond à un objectif ». S'il ne convient pas de qualifier *Marsyas* d'œuvre d'architecture, elle traite néanmoins avec beaucoup d'habileté les perceptions de l'espace, de la lumière et de la couleur, et reconfigure le hall de la turbine d'une façon qu'aucune œuvre d'art n'avait approché jusqu'alors. Ce n'est peut-être pas de l'architecture, mais cette sculpture contribue à faire regarder l'espace et le volume d'un œil nouveau.

## LA CONSOMMATION DE LA CULTURE

Comme c'est le cas depuis de nombreuses années, un des champs d'intervention privilégiés de l'architecture de qualité reste le domaine de la culture. Bien qu'aux États-Unis comme ailleurs de grandioses projets de nouveaux musées aient été abandonnés, d'autres types d'équipements culturels comme les salles de concerts se sont multipliés. Si le Los Angeles County Museum a abandonné ses ambitieux plans de reconstruction sous la houlette de Rem Koolhaas, la ville a enfin achevé le Disney Concert Hall, première commande publique d'importance de Frank Gehry dans sa ville de résidence. Ses vagues de titane ont affirmé la liberté artistique et le statut de Gehry. Ceci aide des praticiens plus jeunes à rechercher des formes nouvelles, même s'ils n'adhèrent pas aux choix esthétiques du maître. Le choix de Zaha Hadid pour le Lois & Richard Rosenthal Center for Contemporary Art à Cincinnati a-t-il un rapport avec les triomphes de Gehry ? Une ville comme

Cincinnati aurait sans doute bien besoin de la publicité dont a bénéficié Bilbao. Très connue pour ses dessins et ses projets radicaux, Zaha Hadid semble entrer aujourd'hui dans une phase nouvelle de sa carrière qui voit affluer les projets majeurs. Première femme à édifier un musée en Amérique – elle est une pionnière à cet égard –, elle montre à Cincinnati que son mode de dessin exubérant est réalisable et que l'art et l'architecture d'aujourd'hui peuvent fusionner, y compris dans la ville qui voulait censurer l'œuvre de Robert Mapplethorpe.

### L'INGÉNIERIE DE LA VIE QUOTIDIENNE

L'habitat fait partie des besoins actuels les plus pressants auxquels doit répondre l'architecture. De la rencontre entre un client éclairé et un architecte de talent peut naître une avancée architecturale qui influencera l'esthétique et la vie quotidienne pendant des années. Les résidences publiées ici sont choisies pour les innovations et les progrès qu'elles représentent. L'architecte David Adjaye s'est acquis une certaine réputation à Londres, parce qu'il a eu la chance de voir un certain nombre de ses clients devenir célèbres après qu'il ait travaillé pour eux. Dans l'est de Londres, il a converti un entrepôt des années 1930 en maison pour les artistes Tim Noble et Sue Webster. L'East London n'est pas réputé pour le luxe de son habitat. Dans son utilisation de l'espace, de la lumière et des surfaces, la Dirty House répond au site d'une façon adaptée à une ville qui sait apprécier la beauté dans les environnements industriels.

La Glass Shutter House (maison à volet de verre) de Shigeru Ban à Tokyo est tout autre. Située dans un quartier relativement élégant de la capitale japonaise, c'est une combinaison de maison et de restaurant conçue pour un chef japonais très connu. Ban est réputé pour ses recherches sur la flexibilité en architecture, dans ses choix de matériaux, et dans son désir de remettre en question des éléments fondamentaux comme le mur. Dans cette maison, le propriétaire peut faire disparaître deux des murs, qui s'enroulent dans le toit. C'est pratique en été pour ouvrir le restaurant sur la terrasse, c'est une solution inventive en termes de matérialité de l'architecture.

### BEAU NOUVEAU MONDE

L'un des aspects fascinants de l'architecture est sa capacité à rêver, et à imaginer des solutions totalement neuves, à travers de nouvelles technologies ou une manière de pensée différente. Survol de l'architecture depuis 2000, cet ouvrage offre une vision globale de l'extraordinaire richesse d'une créativité libérée par une combinaison de progrès technologiques et d'ouverture conceptuelle. Nous ne sommes plus confrontés à un seul style. L'architecture a toujours été influencée par des considérations pratiques. À la différence de l'art, comme le disait Richard Serra, elle est au service d'un but. Les développements significatifs qui commencent à donner une forme nouvelle tiennent à la possibilité d'une intégration conception-production via les ordinateurs et la robotique. Ce phénomène a déjà permis la production de composants uniques, qui bouleversent l'esthétique et la logique profonde d'un siècle d'architecture « moderne ». Le modernisme qui voulait que chaque Ford Model-T soit noire et chaque fenêtre de la même taille est mort. Des raisons esthétiques peuvent pousser certains architectes à se complaire dans le néo-modernisme ou le néo-minimalisme, mais leurs choix concrets ne sont plus limités par l'économie de chaînes de production standardisées. La conception assistée par ordinateur va passer de la performance de cirque consistant à produire des *blobs* pleins de fantaisie à un outil concret, qui pilotera des outils offrant à l'architecture une nouvelle liberté.

# HITOSHI ABE

*Atelier Hitoshi Abe*
*3-3-16 Oroshimachi,*
*Wakabayashi-ku, Sendai*
*Miyagi, 984-0015*
*Japan*

*Tel: +81 22 784 3411*
*Fax: +81 22 782 1233*
*e-mail: house@a-slash.jp*
*Web: http://www.a-slash.jp/*

*Reihoku Community Hall*

Hitoshi Abe was born in 1962 in Sendai. He worked from 1988 to 1992 in the office of COOP HIMMELB(L)AU and obtained his Master of Architecture degree from the Southern California Institute of Architecture (SCI-Arc) in 1989. He created his own firm, Atelier Hitoshi Abe, in 1992. From 1994 he directed the Hitoshi Abe Architectural Design Laboratory at the Tohoku Institute of Technology. He has been a Professor in the same Institute since 2002. His work includes the Miyagi Water Tower (Rifu, Miyagi, Japan, 1994), the Gravel-2 House (Sendai, Miyagi, Japan, 1998), the Neige, Lune, Fleur Restaurant (Sendai, Miyagi, Japan, 1999), the Miyagi Stadium (Rifu, Miyagi, Japan, 2000), the Michinoku Folklore Museum (Kurikoma, Miyagi, Japan, 2000) and the A-House (Sendai, Miyagi, Japan, 2000). More recently, he has been working on the JB House, the S-Orthopedics Factory and Office Building, all located in Sendai. He won the 2003 Architectural Institute of Japan Award, for the Reihoku Community Hall, published here.

Hitoshi Abe, 1962 im japanischen Sendai geboren, arbeitete von 1988 bis 1992 im Büro von COOP HIMMELB(L)AU und erwarb 1989 seinen Master of Architecture am Southern California Institute of Architecture (SCI-Arc). 1992 gründete er seine eigene Firma, das Atelier Hitoshi Abe. Seit 1994 leitet er die Hitoshi Abe Werkstätte für Architekturdesign am Institut für Technologie in Tohoku und ist seit 2002 Professor an diesem Institut. Zu seinen Bauwerken, die alle in der japanischen Präfektur Miyagi entstanden sind, gehören: der Miyagi Water Tower in Rifu (1994), das Haus Gravel-2 in Sendai (1998), das Restaurant Neige-Lune-Fleur in Sendai (1999), das Miyagi-Stadium in Rifu (2000), das Volkskundemuseum Michinoku in Kurikoma (2000) und das A-House in Sendai (2000). In jüngster Zeit plante er das Haus JB und die Fabrik und Bürogebäude für die orthopädische Klinik Sasaki, alle in Sendai. 2003 wurde er für das hier vorgestellte Gemeindezentrum in Reihoku mit dem Preis des japanischen Architekturinstituts ausgezeichnet.

Hitoshi Abe est né en 1962 à Sendai. Obtient son Master of Architecture au South California Institute of Architecture (SCI-Arc) en 1989, il travaille de 1988 à 1992 chez COOP HIMMELB(L)AU. Il crée sa propre agence, Atelier Hitoshi Abe, en 1992. Depuis 1994, il dirige le Hitoshi Abe Architectural Design Laboratory à l'Institut de technologie Tohoku, où il enseigne également depuis 2002. Parmi ses réalisations, toutes au Japon : le château d'eau de Miyagi (Rifu, Miyagi, 1994) ; la maison Gravel-2 (Sendai, Miyagi, 1998) ; le restaurant Neige-Lune-Fleur (Sendai, Miyagi, 1999) ; le stade de Miyagi (2000) ; le Musée du folklore Michinoku (Kurikoma, Miyagi, 2000) et la Maison A (Sendai, Miyagi, 2000). Plus récemment, il a travaillé sur la Maison JB et les bâtiments d'orthopédie Sasaki, tous à Sendai. Il a remporté le Prix 2003 de l'Institut d'architecture du Japon, pour le Centre communautaire de Reihoku, publié ici.

# REIHOKU COMMUNITY HALL

*Reihoku, Kumamoto, Japan, 2001–02*

*Client: Town of Reihoku, Kumamoto. Ground area: 993 m². Costs: not specified.*

This community hall and 207-seat theater for a town of 9 000 persons is a 993-square-meter laminated lumber structure built on a reinforced concrete base. The two-story building is 9.95 meters high. The site area is 3 830 square meters. As part of the Kumamoto Artpolis originated in 1988 under the authority of Kumamoto Governor Morihiro Hosokawa and the architect Arata Isozaki, the project is the result of three years of close consultations between the architect and the local population. Set apart from the town by a green area, the structure has an unusual billowing exterior appearance. Though it appears rather closed, in part because of its dark local cedar cladding, it is quite open to outside light. Despite the complex exterior curves, the structure was designed so that local craftsmen could place the glazing and its horizontal wooden supports. Inside corridors are limited to a strict minimum and an intentional ambiguity is maintained in the division between one space and another. In a sense, this ambiguity, a frequent feature of Japanese architecture, also corresponds to the case of the Reihoku Community Hall in a more specific way – despite the lengthy consultations, townspeople could not agree on a precise use for the building and the architect opted for giving them the most flexible space possible.

Das Gemeindezentrum und Theater mit 207 Sitzen wurde für eine Kleinstadt mit 9 000 Einwohnern entworfen. Es besteht aus einer 993 m² messenden Schichtholzkonstruktion, die auf einem Fundament aus Stahlbeton ruht. Das Grundstück, auf dem der zweigeschossige, knapp 10 m hohe Bau errichtet wurde, umfasst 3 830 m². Das Gebäude ist Teil des Artpolis-Projekts, das 1988 vom Gouverneur der Präfektur Kumamoto, Morihiro Hosokawa, und dem Architekten Arata Isozaki ins Leben gerufen wurde. Der Entwurf ist das Ergebnis eingehender Befragungen, die der Planer Hitoshi Abe über einen Zeitraum von drei Jahren mit der lokalen Bevölkerung durchführte. Von außen fällt das durch eine Grünfläche von der Stadt abgesetzte Bauwerk durch seine wellenartig geschwungenen Formen auf. Und obwohl der Bau recht geschlossen wirkt, was teilweise auf seine Fassadenverkleidung aus dunklem Zedernholz zurückzuführen ist, lässt er viel Tageslicht ein. Trotz der komplexen Bogenlinien der Fassaden wurde der Entwurf so konzipiert, dass lokale Handwerker die Verglasungen und horizontalen Holzstützen ohne Schwierigkeiten anbringen konnten. Im Innern wurde die Zahl der Flure auf ein absolutes Minimum begrenzt und die Trennlinien zwischen den einzelnen Räumen blieben bewusst unklar. Diese Ambivalenz, ein häufiges Merkmal in der japanischen Architektur, hat im Fall des Gemeindezentrums von Reihoku noch einen besonderen Grund: Auch nach den ausführlichen Diskussionen konnten sich die Bewohner nicht auf einen genauen Zweck des Gebäudes einigen, so dass sich der Architekt für eine Raumgestaltung entschied, die eine möglichst flexible Nutzung zulässt.

Édifié pour une ville de 9 000 habitants, ce bâtiment municipal de 993 m² sur un terrain de 3 830 m² regroupe une salle de réunion et un théâtre de 207 places. Il fait appel à une structure en bois lamellé-collé sur soubassement en béton armé, et compte deux niveaux pour une hauteur totale de 9,95 m. Réalisé dans le cadre du projet Kumamoto Artpolis lancé en 1988 sous l'autorité du gouverneur de Kumamoto, Morihiro Hosokawa, et de Arata Isozaki, il est l'aboutissement de trois années de consultations approfondies entre l'architecte et la population locale. Le bâtiment qui est séparé de la ville par un espace vert présente un curieux aspect sinusoïdal. Bien qu'il semble assez fermé, en partie parce qu'il est habillé de cèdre local foncé, il reste ouvert à la lumière naturelle. Malgré ses courbes extérieures complexes, la précision de sa conception a permis aux artisans locaux de poser facilement les vitrages. À l'intérieur, les corridors sont limités à un strict minimum et l'ambiguïté entretenue entre les volumes est voulue. Fréquente dans l'architecture japonaise, elle correspond également à la situation locale puisque, malgré les longues consultations, les habitants n'ont pu se mettre d'accord sur l'utilisation précise du bâtiment. L'architecte s'est donc efforcé de leur offrir un espace qui permette l'utilisation la plus souple possible.

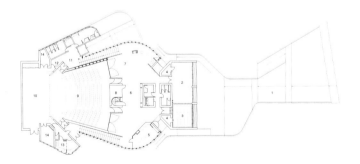
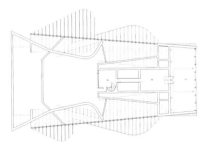

*Plans show the relatively simple disposition of the interior spaces with the unexpected billowing volumes flanking each side of the structure.*

*Die Grundrisse zeigen die relativ einfache Anordnung der Innenräume mit den Ausbuchtungen, die das Gebäude zu beiden Seiten flankieren.*

*Les plans montrent la disposition relativement simple des espaces intérieurs et les volumes gonflés qui flanquent chaque côté du bâtiment.*

Mixing the concrete base with wood and glazing, the architect animates the exterior surfaces without sacrificing an intentional austerity.

In der Kombination aus Betonsockel mit Holz und Glas lockert der Architekt die Außenfassaden auf, ohne die gewollte Strenge aufzuheben.

L'architecte a animé les façades au moyen du soubassement en ciment, du bardage en bois et du vitrage, sans rien perdre de l'austérité voulue.

Seen from certain angles, the
Reihoku Community Hall appears to
be almost blank and windowless. In
this respect, and due to its black-
ness, it does recall some Japanese
temple structures.

Aus bestimmten Blickwinkeln wirkt
das Gemeindezentrum von Reihoku
nahezu undurchbrochen und fenster-
los. Darin und in seinem schwarzen
Äußeren erinnert es an einige japanische Tempelbauten.

Sous certains angles, cette salle
polyvalente semble presque aveugle
et dénuée de fenêtres. Elle rappelle
à cet égard, et par sa couleur noire,
certains temples japonais.

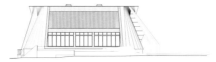

# VITO ACCONCI

*Acconci Studio*
*70 Washington Street, #501, Brooklyn, NY 11201, USA*
*Tel: +1 718 852 6591, Fax: +1 718 624 3178*
*e-mail: studio@acconci.com, Web: www.acconci.com*

*Idea developed by: Robert Punkenhofer*
*ART & IDEA, Morizgasse 8/12, 1060 Vienna, Austria*
*Tel: +43 1 596 4736, Fax: +43 1 596 4738*
*e-mail: punkenhofer@art-idea.com, Web: www.art-idea.com*

Born in the Bronx in 1940, Vito Acconci lives and works in Brooklyn. Vito Acconci's early work was in the area of fiction and poetry. In the late 1960s and early 1970s, his first artworks used performance, photos, film and video as instruments of self-analysis. His audio and video installations of the mid-70s turned exhibition spaces into community meeting places. His "architectural games" of the early 80s made performance spaces for viewers, whose activity resulted in the construction and deconstruction of house prototypes. In the mid-80s his work crossed over into architecture, landscape and industrial design. In 1988 he created the Acconci Studio, a theoretical-design and building workshop. The Studio treats architecture as an "occasion to make spaces fluid, changeable, portable." The Studio has recently completed an artificial island in Graz, published here; a plaza for a Performing Arts Center in Memphis; an art gallery (Kenny Schachter's contTEMPorary Adjustable gallery in New York); and a clothing store for United Bamboo in Tokyo. The Acconci Studio is working on a skate park in San Juan, a park on a street median in Vienna, and a spiraling-ramped house in Kalamata, Greece. Their past projects include a screened walkway for a station in Tokyo, 2000; a movable landscape in Munich, 2000; and the Renovation of the Storefront for Art & Architecture (New York, in collaboration with Steven Holl, 1994).

Vito Acconci, geboren 1940 in der Bronx, lebt und arbeitet heute in Brooklyn. Seine ersten Arbeiten stammten aus den Bereichen Literatur und Poesie. In den späten 1960er und frühen 1970er Jahren widmete er sich den Kunstformen Performance, Fotografie, Film und Video, die er als Instrumente der Selbstanalyse einsetzte. Mitte der 1970er Jahre verwandelten seine Audio- und Videoinstallationen die Galerien in Versammlungsräume. Seine „architektonischen Spiele" aus den frühen 1980er Jahren schufen Präsentationsräume für Besucher, deren Aktivitäten in der Konstruktion und Dekonstruktion von Prototypen für Häuser bestanden. Mitte der 1980er Jahre wechselten seine Arbeiten in die Bereiche Architektur, Landschafts- und Industriedesign. 1988 gründete er das Acconci Studio, eine Denkwerkstatt für Design und Bauen. Die Mitarbeiter des Studios behandeln Architektur als eine „Gelegenheit, Räume fließend, veränderbar, tragbar zu machen". Zu ihren früheren Projekten gehören ein Gehweg mit Schutzblende für einen Bahnhof in Tokio (2000), eine bewegliche Landschaft in München (2000) und die gemeinsam mit Steven Holl durchgeführte Renovierung der Geschäftsfassade für Art & Architecture in New York (1994). In jüngster Zeit hat das Studio die hier vorgestellte künstliche Mur-Insel in Graz, einen öffentlichen Platz für das Performing Arts Center in Memphis, die Kunstgalerie Kenny Schachter's contTEMPorary Adjustable gallery in New York und eine Modeboutique für United Bamboo in Tokio fertig gestellt. Zur Zeit arbeitet das Acconci Studio Team an einem Park für Skater in San Juan, einem Park auf einer Allee in Wien sowie einem mit einer Spiralrampe ausgestatteten Haus in Kalamata, Griechenland.

Né dans le Bronx en 1940, Vito Acconci vit et travaille à Brooklyn. Ses premiers essais créatifs portent sur la fiction et la poésie. À la fin des années 1960 et au début des années 1970, ses premières interventions artisytiques utilisent la performance, la photographie, le film et la vidéo comme instruments d'auto-analyse. Ses installations audio et vidéo du milieu des années 1970 transforment les espaces d'exposition en lieux communautaires. Ses «jeux architecturaux» du début des années 1980 proposent des espaces de performance aux spectateurs, autour de la construction et de la déconstruction de prototypes de maisons. À cette époque, son travail aborde l'architecture, le paysage et le design industriel. En 1988, il crée le Acconci Studio, atelier de conception théorique et de construction qui traite l'architecture comme une «occasion de rendre l'espace fluide, modifiable, portatif.» Le Studio a récemment achevé une île artificielle à Graz, publiée ici, une place pour le Performing Arts Center de Memphis, une galerie d'art à New York (contTEMPorary Adjustable gallery de Kenny Schachter) et un magasin de vêtement pour United Bamboo à Tokyo. Il travaille également sur un parc pour la pratique du skate board à San Juan, un parc au milieu d'une rue à Vienne et une maison en rampe spiralée à Kalamata (Grèce). Parmi ses projets passés : une passerelle à écrans pour une gare à Tokyo (2000), un paysage déplaçable à Munich (2000) et la rénovation. En dehors du projet sur la Mur, Vito Acconci est intervenu sur des «Écrans pour une passerelle entre bâtiments, bus et voitures» (Passage d'entrée, gare de Shibuya, Tokyo, Japon, 2000) ; la rénovation du Storefront for Art & Architecture (en collaboration avec Steven Holl, New York, 1994).

# MUR ISLAND PROJECT

*Mur Island, Graz, Austria, 2003*

*Client: Graz 2003 – Cultural Capital of Europe GmbH. Length: 46.6 m, width 16.6 m. Costs: € 5 000 000.*

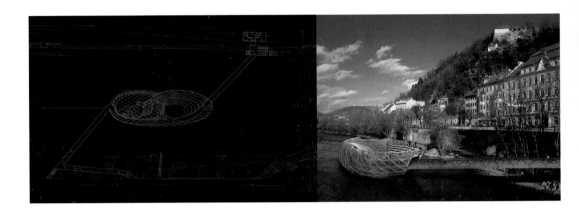

"Project: A twist in the river, a node in the river, a circulation-route in the middle of the river. The circulation-route is an island; the island is a dome that morphs into a bowl that morphs into a dome." This is the way that Vito Acconci describes the floating island he built near the Mariahilferplatz and the old city of Graz. Built in the Mur River to celebrate Graz's selection as European Capital of Culture in 2003, the 7 x 17 x 47 m structure was made of "steel, glass, rubber, asphalt, water, and light" as Acconci put it. The bowl-like space was intended for meetings or to serve as a theater, while the dome was a café/restaurant. "Where dome and bowl intersect," says Acconci, "and where the dome is transformed into a bowl and vice versa, a playground is formed by the collision and by the melting. This in-between space is a three-dimensional grid, like a space frame; the grid functions as monkey bars, a field to climb up and crawl through and hang onto; slides are cut through the grid." The project was originally an idea of Robert Punkenhofer. Born 1965 in Austria, Punkenhofer founded Art & Idea, "a not for profit institution devoted to promoting and facilitating a cultural dialogue by organizing contemporary arts programs of international scope." As he states, "my aim was to break the prevailing isolation between the river and the city by establishing a multifunctional, futuristic platform that offers a new public space for communication, adventure and artistic creation. Housing an open-air theater, a children's playground and a café, the island should take the city into the river and the river into the city."

„Das Projekt: eine Biegung im Fluss, ein Knoten im Fluss, eine Umlaufroute in der Mitte des Flusses. Die Umlaufroute ist eine Insel; die Insel ist eine Kuppel, die zu einer Schale wird, welche sich wiederum zu einer Kuppel formt." So beschreibt Vito Acconci die schwimmende Insel, die er nahe dem in der Altstadt von Graz gelegenen Mariahilferplatz in die Mur gesetzt hat. Die 7 x 17 x 47 m messende Konstruktion, die anlässlich der Ernennung von Graz zur Europäischen Kulturhauptstadt 2003 errichtet wurde, bestand – so Acconci – aus „Stahl, Glas, Gummi, Asphalt, Wasser und Licht". Der schalenartige Raum war für Zusammenkünfte oder als Theater gedacht, während die Kuppel als Café und Restaurant diente. Dazu Acconci: „Wo sich Kuppel und Schale überschneiden, entsteht durch die Kollision und die Verschmelzung ein Spielplatz. Dieser Zwischen-Raum bildet ein dreidimensionales Gitter, das wie ein Klettergerüst funktioniert: man kann daran hochklettern, hindurch kriechen oder sich dranhängen. Auch Rutschen wurden durch das Gitter gelegt." Das Projekt geht auf eine Idee des 1965 geborenen Österreichers Robert Punkenhofer zurück, dem Begründer von Art & Idea, „einer Non-Profit-Institution, die einen kulturellen Dialog ermöglichen und fördern will, indem sie aktuelle Kunstprogramme von internationaler Reichweite organisiert." Wie Punkenhofer erklärt, war es sein Ziel, die bestehende Isolierung zwischen Fluss und Stadt durch eine multifunktionale, futuristische Plattform aufzubrechen, die einen neuen öffentlichen Raum für Kommunikation, Abenteuer und künstlerische Kreativität bietet.

« Projet : un toron dans la rivière, un nœud dans la rivière, une voie de circulation au milieu de la rivière. La voie de circulation est une île ; l'île est un dôme qui se transforme en vasque qui se transforme en dôme. » Telle est la manière dont Vito Acconci décrit l'île flottante ancrée dans la Mur près de la Mariahilferplatz dans la vieille ville de Graz. Cette structure de 7 x 17 x 47 m en « acier, verre, caoutchouc, asphalte, eau et lumière », selon Acconci, célébrait la désignation de Graz comme « Capitale européenne de la culture 2003 ». Le volume en forme de vasque était prévu pour accueillir des manifestations publiques ou servir de théâtre, le dôme étant un café-restaurant. « Là où le dôme et la vasque se coupent », explique Acconci, « là où le dôme se transforme en vasque et vice-versa, un terrain de jeu se dessine en profitant de cette collision et de cette fusion. Cet espace ‹ entre-deux › est une trame tridimensionnelle, une structure spatiale ; la trame sert d'espalier de gymnastique, de terrain d'escalade que l'on traverse en rampant et auquel on peut s'accrocher ; des fentes sont découpées dans sa grille. » Le projet vient d'une idée de Robert Punkenhofer. Né en Autriche en 1965, Punkenhofer a fondé Art & Idea, « organisme sans but lucratif qui se consacre à la promotion et à la facilitation du dialogue culturel par l'organisation de manifestations artistiques contemporaines, de niveau international ». Il précise : « Mon objectif était de rompre la coupure entre la rivière et la ville en établissant une plate-forme futuriste multifonctions qui offre un nouveau lieu de communication, d'aventure et création artistique. »

*To say that the Mur Island project is unexpected in the traditionally minded city of Graz would be an understatement.*

*Ohne Untertreibung war das Mur-Insel-Projekt für eine traditionell eingestellte Stadt wie Graz eine ganz unerwartete Architektur.*

*Dire que le « Mur Island Project » a surpris dans une ville aussi traditionnelle que Graz est une litote.*

Lighting makes the project an integral part of the city, even at night. Although intended to float on the river, it also seems to emerge from the waters.

*Das Lichtdesign macht das Projekt zu einem integralen Bestandteil der Stadt, sogar bei Nacht. Auch wenn die Konstruktion auf dem Fluss schwebt, scheint sie gleichzeitig aus dem Wasser aufzutauchen.*

*L'éclairage intègre totalement le projet à la ville, même la nuit. L'île flotte à la surface de la rivière, tout en semblant en émerger.*

The intersecting ovals are turned up in one instance and down in the other, creating covered and open spaces.

Die ineinander greifenden Ovale sind einmal nach oben und einmal nach unten gekehrt, was eine Abfolge bedeckter und offener Räume ergibt.

Les ovales qui s'entrecoupent sont l'un tourné vers le haut, l'autre vers le bas, pour créer des volumes couverts et découverts.

The hilly landscape around Graz is reflected in the stainless steel design, and through Nirosta steel lattices and glass windows the surroundings can even be seen from within the artificial island.

*Die hügelige Umgebung von Graz spiegelt sich im Design aus rostfreiem Stahl. Durch die Nirostastahlgitter und Glasfenster kann sie sogar vom Innern der künstlichen Insel aus betrachtet werden.*

L'environnement montagneux de Graz se reflète dans l'acier inoxydable, les lattis en acier Nirosta et les vitrages. Il se perçoit aussi de l'intérieur de cette île artificielle.

The shell contains an open-air theater, and the whole of the island can hold about 300 persons at any one time.

Die muschelförmige Schale umschließt ein Freilufttheater. Die gesamte Inselkonstruktion bietet circa 300 Personen Platz.

La vasque contient un théâtre en plein air et l'ensemble de l'île peut accueillir simultanément 300 personnes environ.

Underneath the dome, the "Insel Café," run by the traditional Graz bakery Sorger, was designed by the Acconci Studio and the Graz-based architecture studio purpur.

Das von der Grazer Traditionskonditorei Sorger betriebene „Insel Café" wurde vom Acconci Studio in Zusammenarbeit mit dem Grazer Architekturbüro studio purpur gestaltet.

Sous le dôme, le « Insel Café », géré par une célèbre pâtisserie de Graz, Sorger, a été conçu par le Acconci Studio et l'agence d'architecture locale, purpur.

Set between the historic city center and Mariahilferplatz the "Island in the Mur" has been described as "a small concentration of urban life in a place that has never been part of the city."

Zwischen historischem Stadtkern und Mariahilferplatz gelegen, ist die „Insel in der Mur" als eine „kleine Ansammlung urbanen Lebens an einem Ort, der nie ein Teil der Stadt gewesen war", beschrieben worden.

Entre le centre historique de la ville et la Mariahilferplatz, « L'île sur la Mur » a pu être décrite comme « un petit concentré de vie urbaine en un lieu qui n'avait jamais fait partie de la cité. »

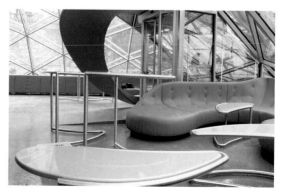

# DAVID ADJAYE

*Adjaye Associates*
*23-28 Penn Street*
*London N1 5DL*
*UK*

*Tel: +44 20 7739 4969*
*Fax: +44 20 7739 3484*
*e-mail: info@adjaye.com*
*Web: www.adjaye.com*

David Adjaye was born in 1966 in Dar-Es-Salaam, Tanzania. He studied at the Royal College of Art (Masters in Architecture 1993), and worked in the offices of David Chipperfield and Eduardo Souto de Moura before creating his own firm in London in 2000 (Chassay Architects, 1988–1990; David Chipperfield Architects, 1991; Eduardo Souto de Moura Architects, 1991; Adjaye & Russell, 1994–2000). He has been widely recognized as one of the leading architects of his generation in the UK, in part because of the talks he has given in various locations such as the Architectural Association, the Royal College of Art and Cambridge University, as well as Harvard, Cornell, and the Universidad de Luisdad in Lisbon. He was also the co-presenter of the BBC's six part series on modern architecture "Dreamspaces." His Idea Store library in East London was selected by Deyan Sudjic for the exhibition highlighting 100 projects that are changing the world at the 8th Venice Biennale of Architecture in 2002. His offices currently employ a staff of 35, and some of his key works are: Studio/home for Chris Ofili (London, 1999); Extension to house (St. John's Wood, 1998); Siefert Penthouse (London, 2001); Elektra House (London, 2001); Studio/gallery/home for Tim Noble and Sue Webster (London, 2003); and the SHADA Pavilion (London, 2000, with artist Henna Nadeem). Current work includes: The Nobel Peace Center, Oslo (2002–2005); Bernie Grant Centre, Tottenham, London (2001–2006); Stephen Lawrence Centre, Deptford, London (2004–2006); and the Museum of Contemporary Art/Denver, Denver, Colorado, USA (2004–2006).

David Adjaye, geboren 1966 in Daressalam, Tansania, studierte am Londoner Royal College of Art, wo er 1993 seinen Master of Architecture erwarb. Von 1988 bis 1990 arbeitete er im Architekturbüro Chassay Architects, 1991 bei David Chipperfield und bei Eduardo Souto de Moura und von 1994 bis 2000 bei Adjaye & Russell, bevor er noch im selben Jahr seine eigene Firma in London gründete. Er ist weithin anerkannt als einer der führenden britischen Architekten seiner Generation. Dies ist zum Teil auf die Vorträge zurückzuführen, die er an so renommierten Institutionen wie der Architectural Association, dem Royal College of Art sowie den Universitäten Cambridge, Harvard, Cornell und Lissabon gehalten hat. Außerdem war er Co-Moderator der sechsteiligen BBC-Serie „Dreamspaces" über moderne Architektur. Seine „Idea Store"-Bibliothek in East London wurde von Deyan Sudjic in die Ausstellung der 100 Projekte, die die Welt verändert haben, aufgenommen, die 2002 im Rahmen der 8. Architekturbiennale in Venedig gezeigt wurde. Zu den wichtigsten Arbeiten seines Büros, das derzeit 35 Mitarbeiter beschäftigt, gehören: ein Hausanbau in St. John's Wood (1998), ein Studio mit Wohnung für Chris Ofili in London (1999), der SHADA Pavillon (2000) – in Zusammenarbeit mit der Künstlerin Henna Nadeem, das Elektra House (2001), das Penthouse Siefert (2001) sowie eine Kombination aus Studio, Galerie und Wohnung für Tim Noble und Sue Webster (2003), alle in London. Zu den aktuellen Arbeiten zählen: Das Nobel Friedenszentrum in Oslo (2002–2005), das Bernie Grant Centre in Tottenham, London (2001–2006), das Stephen Lawrence Centre in Deptford, London (2004–2006) und das Museum of Contemporary Art in Denver, Colorado (2004–2006).

David Adjaye, né en 1966 à Dar-Es-Salam (Tanzanie), étudie au Royal College of Art (Master of Architecture, 1993), puis travaille dans les agences de David Chipperfield et d'Eduardo Souto de Moura avant de créer sa propre structure à Londres en 2000 (Chassay Architects, 1988–1990 ; David Chipperfield Architects, 1991 ; Eduardo Souto de Moura Architects, 1991 ; Adjaye & Russell, 1994–2000). Il est généralement reconnu comme un des plus brillants architectes de sa génération au Royaume-Uni, en partie pour ses conférences données devant divers publics dont l'Architectural Association, le Royal College of Art et la Cambridge University, ainsi qu'Harvard, Cornell ou l'Universidad de Luisdad à Lisbonne. Il a été coprésentateur d'une série de la BBC sur l'architecture. Sa bibliothèque Idea Store dans l'East Londres a été sélectionnée par Deyan Sudjic pour la grande exposition « 100 projets qui ont changé le monde » présentée à la 8ème Biennale d'architecture de Venise en 2002. Son agence emploie actuellement 35 collaborateurs. Parmi ses principales réalisations : maison-atelier pour Chris Ofili (Londres, 1999) ; extension d'une maison (St. John's Wood, 1998) ; Siefert Penthouse (Londres, 2001) ; Maison Elektra (Londres, 2001) ; l'atelier-galerie-maison de Tim Noble et Sue Webster (Londres, 2003) et le SHADA Pavilion (Londres, 2000 avec l'artiste Henna Nadeem). Ses chantiers actuels comprennent le Centre Nobel de la paix (Oslo, 2002–2005) ; le Bernie Grant Centre (Tottenham, Londres, 2001–2006) ; le Stephen Lawrence Centre (Deptford, Londres, 2004–2006) et le Museum of Contemporary Art (Denver, Colorado, 2004–2006).

# DIRTY HOUSE

*East London, UK, 2003*

*Client: Tim Noble and Sue Webster. Building area: 350 m². Costs: £ 300 000.*

David Adjaye converted a 1930s East London warehouse into a home for artists Tim Noble and Sue Webster in a most surprising way. Ground-floor windows surfaced in mirrored glass lie flush with the façade, while the upper story windows are deeply recessed. A high glass wall to the rear of the building brings daylight into the upper-floor bedrooms, but again offers no possible view into the house. The lightness of this glass wall is in sharp contrast to the voluntary heaviness of the lower part of the house. As Sue Webster has said, "we love the contradictions the glass wall creates, the feeling of an inside-outside space. We feel very exposed yet there's a sense of being protected." Removing interior columns and the first floor of the warehouse to create double-height space for the artists, the architect intentionally used industrial and inexpensive off-the-shelf products for the finishing. White concrete was chosen for the kitchen work surfaces for example, and standard strip lights were used for much of the interior lighting. Although the name "Dirty House" is not explained, the artists are known amongst other things for literally making works out of trash.

David Adjaye gelang es, ein im Londoner East End gelegenes, ehemaliges Lagergebäude aus den 1930er Jahren auf sehr originelle Weise in ein Zuhause für die beiden Künstler Tim Noble und Sue Webster zu verwandeln. Während die mit Spiegelglas ausgestatteten Fenster im Erdgeschoss eine Ebene mit der Fassade bilden, sind die Fenster im oberen Stockwerk stark zurückversetzt. Die hohe Glaswand an der Hinterseite des Gebäudes lässt Tageslicht in die Räume im Obergeschoss, ohne jedoch Einblicke von außen zuzulassen. Die Leichtigkeit, die diese Glaswand ausstrahlt, steht in scharfem Kontrast zu dem bewusst massiv gestalteten unteren Teil des Hauses. Dazu Sue Webster: „Wir lieben die Widersprüchlichkeit, die durch die Glaswand entsteht, dieses Gefühl, gleichzeitig drinnen und draußen zu sein. Wir fühlen uns sehr exponiert und dennoch geschützt." David Adjaye ließ im Inneren Säulen und eine Zwischendecke entfernen, um Räume zu schaffen, die sich über zwei Stockwerke erstrecken. Für die Ausstattung wurden kostengünstige und gebrauchsfertige Industrieerzeugnisse verwendet. So wurden beispielsweise weißer Beton für die Arbeitsflächen in der Küche und Standardneonlampen für den Großteil der Beleuchtung gewählt. Wenn auch der Name „Dirty House" vom Architekten nicht erklärt wird, sind die beiden Künstler dafür bekannt, dass sie im wahrsten Sinne des Wortes aus Müll Kunst machen.

Pour les artistes Tim Noble et Sue Webster, David Adjaye a transformé en maison cet entrepôt de l'East End londonien, datant des années 1930, d'une manière qui ne manque pas de surprendre. Les fenêtres du rez-de-chaussée en verre argenté sont montées à fleur de façade, tandis que celles de l'étage sont en retrait marqué. À l'arrière, un haut mur de verre éclaire les chambres de l'étage, sans laisser pour autant le regard pénétrer dans la maison. La légèreté de ce mur de verre contraste nettement avec la lourdeur voulue de la partie inférieure. Comme l'explique Sue Webster : « Nous aimons les contradictions que crée le mur de verre, le sentiment d'un espace dedans-dehors. Nous nous sentons très exposés et très protégés à la fois. » L'architecte a supprimé des colonnes intérieures et le premier niveau de l'entrepôt afin de créer un volume double hauteur pour les artistes, et a volontairement choisi des matériaux et des équipements industriels et bon marché pour les finitions. Par exemple, il a retenu le béton pour les plans de travail de la cuisine, et des bandeaux de néon standard pour la plupart des éclairages intérieurs. Bien que le nom de « Dirty House » (maison sale) ne soit pas explicite, les artistes sont connus, entre autres, pour utiliser des déchets dans leurs œuvres.

*In its rather harsh East London surroundings, the Dirty House stands out because of its austerity and lighting that appears to make the roof float over the dark cubic shape of the structure.*

*Das Dirty House fällt aus seiner ziemlich rauen Ostlondoner Umgebung heraus, aufgrund seiner Strenge und einer Beleuchtung, die das Dach scheinbar über der dunklen, kubischen Form des Gebäudes schweben lässt.*

*Dans le contexte assez brutal de l'East London, la Dirty House se remarque par son austérité et son éclairage, qui donnent l'impression que le toit flotte au dessus de la forme cubique et sombre de la maison.*

The austerity visible from the outside of the house is reflected in these interior views where light and volume play as much of a role as the stark furniture and kitchen installation (above).

Die äußere Strenge des Hauses spiegelt sich in den Innenansichten wider, in denen Licht und Rauminhalt eine ebenso große Rolle spielen wie die sachlich funktionalen Möbel und die Kücheneinrichtung (oben).

L'austérité extérieure affichée se retrouve dans ces vues de l'intérieur, où la lumière et les volumes jouent un rôle aussi important que le mobilier et l'équipement de cuisine dépouillés (ci-dessus).

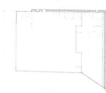

*David Adjaye plays on unexpected openings and sources of light, just as he masterfully modulates the contrast between a weighty opacity and an almost ethereal lightness.*

*David Adjaye setzt spielerisch unerwartete Öffnungen und Lichtquellen ein und moduliert meisterhaft den Kontrast zwischen massiger Opazität und einer fast ätherischen Helligkeit.*

*David Adjaye joue de sources de lumière et d'ouvertures inattendues, de même qu'il module magistralement le contraste entre une opacité pesante et une légèreté presque éthérée.*

# WERNER AISSLINGER

Studio Aisslinger
Oranienplatz 4
10999 Berlin
Germany

Tel: +49 30 315 05 400
Fax: +49 30 315 05 401
e-mail: studio@aisslinger.de
Web: www.aisslinger.de

*Loftcube*

Werner Aisslinger was born in Nördlingen, Germany in 1964. He studied design at the University of Arts (Hochschule der Künste,1987–1991), Berlin. From 1989 to 1992, he freelanced with the offices of Jasper Morrison and Ron Arad in London, and at the Studio de Lucchi in Milan. He founded Studio Aisslinger in Berlin, focusing on product design, design concepts and brand architecture, in 1993. Since 1998, he has been a Design Professor at Design College (Hochschule für Gestaltung), Karlsruhe (Department of Product Design). He created the "Juli Chair" in 1996 for Cappellini, a soft seat shell made of polyurethane integral foam – a material more frequently used in the automobile industry – which was selected as the first German chair-design since 1964 for the permanent collection of the Museum of Modern Art in New York; the "Endless Shelf" (Porro 1994/1998, Italy), a modular shelf with aluminum joints and boards made of wood or translucent plastic that won the German Design Prize in 1997 and was selected for the Museum Pinakothek der Moderne in Munich; a "Case" (Interlübke, 2002, Germany) which is a 100% modular container-trolley-system in an aluminum structure with matt plastic walls; and the "soft Gel chaise longue" (Zanotta, Italy), using gel-upholstery produced with the latest technologies.

Werner Aisslinger, 1964 in Nördlingen geboren, studierte von 1987 bis 1991 Design an der Hochschule der Künste in Berlin. Daneben war er von 1989 bis 1992 freiberuflich für die Büros von Jasper Morrison und Ron Arad in London und das Studio de Lucchi in Mailand tätig. Im Jahr 1993 gründete er in Berlin das Studio Aisslinger, das sich auf Produktdesign, Designkonzepte und Markenarchitektur spezialisierte. Seit 1998 ist er Professor an der Fakultät für Produktdesign der Hochschule für Gestaltung in Karlsruhe. 1996 entwarf er den „Juli Stuhl" für Cappellini, eine weiche Sitzschale aus Polyurethan-Integralschaum – einem Material, das in der Automobilindustrie verwendet wird. Dieses Sitzmöbel war das erste, das das New Yorker Museum of Modern Art seit 1964 für seine permanente Sammlung angekauft hat. Zu seinen weiteren Projekten zählen: „The Endless Shelf" für die italienische Firma Porro (1994/1998), ein bausteinartig erweiterbares Regalsystem mit Einlegeböden aus Holz oder durchscheinendem Kunststoff und Verbindungsteilen aus Aluminium, das 1997 mit dem Deutschen Designpreis ausgezeichnet und für die Einrichtung der Münchner Pinakothek der Moderne ausgewählt wurde; ferner „Case" für Interlübke (2002), eine modulare Kombination aus Behälter und Rollkarren aus Aluminium mit Seitenwänden aus mattiertem Kunststoff sowie die „Soft Gel Chaiselongue" für das italienische Unternehmen Zanotta, bei der eine mit neuester Technologien produzierte Gelpolsterung eingesetzt wurde.

Werner Aisslinger, né en 1964 à Nördlingen, en Allemagne, étudie le design à la Hochschule der Künste à Berlin (1987–1991). De 1989 à 1992, il travaille en indépendant pour les agences de Jasper Morrison et de Ron Arad à Londres et le Studio de Lucchi, à Milan. Il fonde en 1993 le Studio Aisslinger à Berlin, spécialisé dans le design produit, le design-concept et l'architecture commerciale. Depuis 1998, il est professeur de design à la Hochschule für Gestaltung de Karlsruhe (Département du design produit). Il crée le siège « Juli » en 1996 pour Cappellini, coque de siège molle en mousse intégrale de polyuréthane, matériau plus fréquemment utilisé dans l'industrie automobile, premier siège allemand sélectionné depuis 1964 par le Museum of Modern Art de New York ; la « Endless Shelf » (Porro, 1994–1998, Italie), étagère modulaire à portants d'aluminium, rayonnages en bois ou pastique translucide qui a remporté le Prix allemand du design en 1997 et a été sélectionnée par le Museum Pinakothek der Moderne à Munich ; « Case » (Interlübke, 2002, Allemagne), conteneur roulant 100% modulaire à structure d'aluminium, parois de plastic mat, et la « Soft Gel chaise longue » (Zanotta, Italie), à rembourrage en gel, technique issue de technologies de pointe.

# LOFTCUBE

*Berlin, Germany, 2003*

*Prototype Studio Aisslinger. Floor area: 36 m². Costs: € 55 000.*

Although the idea of mobile homes, even structures that can be carried and placed by helicopter, is far from new, Werner Aisslinger has taken the concept one step further by imagining his "Loftcubes" being located in large numbers on urban rooftops. Describing these locations as "a treasure of sunny sites in prime urban spaces," "what could a minimal home unit look like," he asks, "a temporary retreat, where urban nomads in big cities and dense urban zones could find privacy?" A first experiment with these units was carried out at Berlin's first design festival, "DesignMai" Berlin (May 3 to 18, 2003), where two "Loftcube" prototypes (a "living" version and a "home office" version, featuring real-life equipment, without connections to utilities.) were put in place. These prototypes were designed with honeycomb wooden modules with plastic laminate suitable for dismantling. 6.6 meters in width and length, the cubes are three meters high, and include 36 square meters of interior space. Made largely with material provided by DuPont, the Loftcubes in Berlin included furniture designed by Aisslinger.

Auch wenn die Idee mobiler Wohnformen, sogar Bauten, die mit dem Hubschrauber transportiert und aufgestellt werden können, alles andere als neu ist, hat Werner Aisslinger dieses Konzept einen Schritt weiter geführt, indem er „Loftcubes" in großer Zahl auf die Dächer von Stadthäusern setzen will. Aisslinger beschreibt diese Standorte als „einen Schatz sonniger Plätze" im urbanen Raum und fragt: „Wie könnte die Minimalform einer solchen Wohneinheit aussehen, als temporärer Zufluchtsort, in dem urbane Nomaden in großen und dicht besiedelten Städten Abgeschiedenheit finden können?" Ein erstes Experiment mit den Loftcubes wurde vom 3. bis 18. Mai 2003 auf dem Designfestival in Berlin, dem DesignMai durchgeführt, wo zwei Prototypen – eine Wohn- und eine Home-Office-Version mit authentischer Ausstattung, aber ohne Anschluss ans öffentliche Netz – präsentiert wurden. Diese Prototypen waren in Wabenbauweise aus Holzmodulen mit Kunststoffbeschichtung gefertigt, eine Konstruktion, die sich leicht auf- und abbauen lässt. Die Einheiten sind jeweils 6,6 m lang und breit, 3 m hoch und enthalten einen Innenraum von 36 m². Während das Baumaterial hauptsächlich von DuPont stammte, waren die Loftcubes in Berlin mit Möbeln ausgestattet, die Aisslinger selbst entworfen hatte.

Si l'idée de maisons mobiles, ou même de constructions importantes, transportées et mises en place par hélicoptère n'est pas nouvelle, Werner Aisslinger lui a fait franchir une nouvelle étape en imaginant ces «Loftcubes» que l'on pourrait imaginer déposés en grand nombre sur des toits d'immeubles urbains. Il parle de ces sites comme d'«un trésor méconnu de sites ensoleillés au cœur d'espaces urbains de qualité… une retraite temporaire où les nomades urbains des grandes cités et des zones urbaines denses pourraient retrouver l'intimité.» Une première expérimentation a été présentée au premier festival de design de Berlin «DesignMai» Berlin (3–18 mai 2003), où deux prototypes de Loftcube (une version «à vivre» et une autre de «bureau à la maison» équipée d'appareils réels mais sans connexion aux réseaux) ont été installés. Ces prototypes utilisaient des modules de bois en nid d'abeille à plastique lamifié permettant un démontage aisé. De 6,6 m de côté, ces «cubes» mesurent 3 m de haut et offrent 36 m² de surface utile. Réalisés en grande partie à partir de matériaux fournis par DuPont, le mobilier a été dessiné par Aisslinger.

*Though he is much more a designer than an architect, Werner Aisslinger seems to have imagined a new way of living – in a bright open space sitting on just about any urban rooftop.*

*Auch wenn er viel mehr Designer als Architekt ist, scheint Werner Aisslinger eine neue Form des Wohnens erfunden zu haben – in einem hellen, offenen Baukörper, der sich auf jedes Dach eines Stadthauses setzen lässt.*

*Bien qu'il soit davantage un designer qu'un architecte, Aisslinger semble avoir imaginé un nouveau style de vie dans ce volume largement ouvert qui pourrait être posé sur n'importe quelle toiture d'immeuble urbain.*

Despite its restricted dimensions, the Loftcube appears to be very spacious. This is also due to its open volumes.

*Trotz seiner geringen Ausmaße wirkt der Loftcube sehr geräumig, was nicht zuletzt an seiner offenen Bauform liegt.*

*Malgré ses dimensions réduites, le Loftcube paraît très spacieux, ce qui est également dû à l'ouverture de ses volumes.*

A bathroom or bedroom or kitchen blend into each other almost seamlessly, setting aside the traditional hierarchical division of home spaces.

*Badezimmer, Schlafzimmer oder Küche gehen fast nahtlos ineinander über und lassen die traditionell hierarchische Aufteilung von Wohnräumen hinter sich.*

*Salle-de-bains, chambre ou cuisine se fondent l'une dans l'autre presque sans barrière, rejetant la division hiérarchique traditionnelle de l'espace domestique.*

*Carlos Miele Flagship Store*

# ASYMPTOTE

Asymptote Architecture
561 Broadway, #5A
New York, NY 10012
USA

Tel: +1 212 343 7333
Fax: +1 212 343 7099
e-mail: info@asymptote.net
Web: www.asymptote.net

Lise Ann Couture was born in Montreal in 1959. She received her Bachelor of Architecture degree from Carlton University, Canada, and her Master of Architecture degree from Yale. Couture currently holds the Davenport Chair at Yale University School of Architecture. Hani Rashid received his degree as Master of Architecture from the Cranbrook Academy of Art, Bloomfield Hills, Michigan. He is presently a Professor of Architecture at Columbia University in New York and at the Swiss Federal Institute of Technology (ETH) in Zurich. They created Asymptote in 1987. Projects include their 1988 prize-winning commission for the Los Angeles West Coast Gateway, 1989; a commissioned housing project for Brig, Switzerland; and their participation in the 1993 competition for an Art Center in Tours, France (1993). Other work by Asymptote includes a theater festival structure built in Denmark in 1997, a virtual trading floor for the New York Stock Exchange, and the Guggenheim Virtual Museum, an ongoing multimedia project aiming to create an on-line museum. In 2001, Asymptote participated in competitions for the Daimler-Chrysler and Mercedes-Benz Museums in Stuttgart, an expansion of the Queen's Museum, and the Eyebeam Center in New York. Most recently Asymptote completed the construction of HydraPier in the Netherlands, a public building housing technology and art located near Schipol Airport. Asymptote was involved in the design of the 2004 Venice Biennale of Architecture, Metamorph and a new theater for the Hans Christian Andersen festival in Odense, Denmark. Asymptote is also completing a Crematorium and Memorial Chapel in Rotterdam.

Lise Ann Couture, geboren 1959 in Montreal, erwarb ihren Bachelor of Architecture an der Carlton University in Kanada und ihren Master of Architecture an der Yale University. Derzeit hat sie den Davenport Lehrstuhl an der Yale University School of Architecture inne. Hani Rashid machte seinen Master of Architecture an der Cranbrook Academy of Art in Bloomfield Hills, Michigan. Gegenwärtig ist er als Professor für Architektur an der Columbia University in New York und der Eidgenössischen Technischen Hochschule (ETH) in Zürich tätig. Zusammen gründeten sie 1987 das Architekturbüro Asymptote. Zu ihren Projekten gehören der preisgekrönte Entwurf für den Los Angeles West Coast Gateway (1989), ein Wohnhausprojekt in Brig in der Schweiz und ihr Wettbewerbsbeitrag für ein Kunstzentrum im französischen Tours (1993). Außerdem: ein Bau für ein Theaterfestival in Dänemark (1997), ein virtuelles Börsenparkett für die New Yorker Börse sowie das Guggenheim Virtual Museum, ein fortlaufendes Multimediaprojekt, das ein Online-Museum präsentiert. 2001 beteiligte sich Asymptote an den Wettbewerben für das Mercedes-Benz-Museum in Stuttgart, den Erweiterungsbau des Queen's Museum of Art und das Eyebeam Center, beide in New York. In jüngster Zeit realisierte Asymptote in den Niederlanden, nahe dem Flughafen Schiphol, das Projekt HydraPier. Außerdem ist Asymptote am Design der Architekturbiennale von 2004 in Venedig, Metamorph und eines neuen Theaters für das Hans Christian Andersen Festival im dänischen Odense beteiligt und plant ein Krematorium mit Friedhofskapelle in Rotterdam.

Lise Anne Couture, née à Montréal en 1959, est Bachelor of Architecture de la Carlton University, Canada, et Master of Architecture de Yale. Elle a été «Design Critic» du programme de maîtrise d'architecture de la Parsons School of Design, New York, et est titulaire actuellement de la chaire Davenport de la Yale University School of Architecture. Hani Rashid est Master of Architecture de Cranbrook Academy of Art, Bloomfield Hills, Michigan. Il est actuellement professeur d'architecture à Columbia University (New York) et à l'Institut fédéral suisse de technologie (ETH, Zurich). Ils créent Asymptote en 1987. Parmi leurs projets : celui primé pour la West Coast Gateway (Los Angeles, 1989), un immeuble de logements (Brig, Suisse, 1991), leur participation au concours de 1993 pour un Centre d'art à Tours, en France (1993). Parmi leurs autres réalisations : une structure pour un festival de théâtre (Århus, Danemark, 1997), une salle des marchés virtuelle pour le New York Stock Exchange et le Guggenheim Virtual Museum, projet multimédia de musée en-ligne. En 2001, Asymptote a participé aux concours pour le musée Daimler-Chrysler et Mercedes Benz à Stuttgart, l'extension du Queen's Museum et le Eyebeam Center à New York. Plus récemment, Asymptote a achevé la construction de HydraPier (Pays-Bas), situé près de l'aéroport de School, et a participé à la conception de la Biennale d'architecture de Venise 2004, de Metamorph et d'une nouvelle salle pour le festival Hans Christian Andersen à Odense (Danemark). L'équipe achève actuellement un crématorium et une chapelle du souvenir à Rotterdam.

# CARLOS MIELE FLAGSHIP STORE

*New York, New York, USA, 2002–03*

*Client: Carlos Miele, São Paulo, Brazil. Floor area: 300 m². Costs: not specified.*

Opened to the public on June 5, 2003, this fashion boutique with about 300 square meters of floor space is located on West 14th Street in Manhattan. Intended for a Brazilian clothing designer, the boutique is conceived as an open space with pale coloring meant to highlight the items that are for sale. As Asymptote's description has it, "the architectural environment is a spatial narrative, centered primarily on an abstracted reading of what constitutes Brazilian culture, landscape and architecture, while also being a contemporary Manhattan experience situated in what is now the quickly transforming meat market district of West 14th Street… The environment is a deliberate insertion and provocation of not only the worlds of fashion, art and architecture but also a trans-urban meditation that merges the cultures of New York and Sao Paulo." There is high gloss epoxy floor with embedded neon and halogen lights, while the ceiling is made of glossy stretched PVC rubber. A floor to ceiling "sculpture form," made of plywood that was cut with lasers guided by the original CAD drawings crosses through the interior space. Computer-generated drawings and digital manufacturing were used on all of the curved forms and surfaces of the shop. Finally, two Asymptote video installations developed for Dokumenta XI in Kassel and the last Venice architecture Biennale are integrated into the architecture.

Der am 5. Juni 2003 eröffnete Flagship Store hat eine Nutzfläche von circa 300 m² und liegt an der West 14th Street in Manhattan. Die für den brasilianischen Modedesigner Carlos Miele entworfene Boutique ist als offener Raum konzipiert, dessen helle Farbe die Verkaufsartikel optimal zur Geltung bringen soll. „Die Architektur", so die Beschreibung der Architektengruppe Asymptote, „stellt in räumlich narrativer Form eine Zusammenfassung dessen dar, was die brasilianische Kultur, Landschaft und Architektur ausmacht und vermittelt gleichzeitig durch ihren Standort in dem sich rasant entwickelnden Viertel um den Fleischmarkt in der West 14th Street ein authentisches Gefühl vom heutigen Manhattan. Ganz bewusst integriert und provoziert die Architektur nicht nur die Welten der Mode, der Kunst und Architektur, sondern ist auch eine trans-urbane Meditation, in der sich die Kulturen von New York und Sao Paulo vermischen." Während der Fußboden der Boutique mit hochglänzendem Epoxydharz belegt ist, in den Neon- und Halogenlampen eingelassen sind, besteht die Decke aus einer glänzenden PVC-Bespannung. Quer durch den Innenraum erstreckt sich eine vom Boden bis zur Decke reichende „sculpture form" aus Sperrholz, die durch Lasergeräte nach den CAD-Originalzeichnungen zugeschnitten wurde. Außerdem hat Asymptote Video-Installationen, die sie für die Documenta 11 in Kassel sowie die letzte Architekturbiennale in Venedig entwickelten, in ihre Gestaltung integriert.

Ouverte au public le 5 juin 2003, cette boutique de mode de 300 m² est située sur West 14th Street à Manhattan. Conçue pour un styliste brésilien, elle a été traitée en espace ouvert peint de couleurs pâles qui mettent en valeur les vêtements. Asymptote décrit ainsi son projet : « L'environnement architectural est une narration spatiale, centrée sur une lecture abstraite de ce qui constitue la culture, le paysage et l'architecture du Brésil, tout en étant implantée dans le Manhattan actuel et le quartier des bouchers de West 14th Street qui connaît une transformation rapide. L'environnement est une insertion et provocation délibérées des mondes de la mode, de l'art et de l'architecture, mais aussi une méditation transurbaine qui fusionne les cultures de New York et de Sao Paulo. » On trouve un sol verni époxy très brillant, incrusté de néons et d'halogènes et un plafond en PVS tendu tout aussi luisant. Une « forme-sculpture » en contreplaqué découpé par des lasers pilotés par commande numérique traverse l'espace. De même, ce sont des dessins et des plans techniques réalisés par ordinateur qui ont permis de tracer toutes les formes et les surfaces courbes. Deux installations vidéo d'Asymptote présentées à Documenta XI à Kassel et à la dernière Biennale d'architecture de Venise sont aussi intégrées.

*With its floating white mannequins and its continuous complex curves, the Carlos Miele Store almost seems to be carved out of a single block.*

*Mit seinen im Raum schwebenden weißen Kleiderpuppen und komplexen Kurvenlinien wirkt der Carlos Miele Store wie aus einem Guss geformt.*

*Avec ses mannequins suspendus et le flux de ses courbes complexes, la Carlos Miele Store semble avoir été sculptée dans un bloc de matière.*

Despite the overall whiteness of the shop, variations in light levels serve to define the space and to highlight its multiple curves. The white walls and floors serve to accentuate the dresses.

Trotz der durchgehend weißen Farbgebung des Interieurs gibt es Abstufungen in den Helligkeitsgraden, die den Raum definieren und seine geschwungenen Linien akzentuieren. Die weißen Wände und Böden wiederum heben die Kleidungsstücke hervor.

Si la boutique est entièrement blanche, les variations de niveau de l'éclairage définissent l'espace et font ressortir ses multiples courbes. Les murs et les sols blancs mettent en valeur les vêtements.

*Glass Shutter House*

# SHIGERU BAN

*Shigeru Ban Architects*
*5-2-4 Matubara Ban Bldg. 1Fl*
*Setagaya-ku, Tokyo 156-0043*
*Japan*

*Tel: +81 3 3324 6760*
*Fax: +81 3 3324 6789*
*e-mail: SBA@tokyo.email.ne.jp*
*Web: www.shigeruban.com*

Born in 1957 in Tokyo, Shigeru Ban studied at the Southern California Institute of Architecture (SCI-Arc) from 1977 to 1980. He attended the Cooper Union School of Architecture, where he studied under John Hejduk (1980–1982). He worked in the office of Arata Isozaki (1982–83) before founding his own firm in Tokyo in 1985. His work includes numerous exhibition designs (Alvar Aalto show at the Axis Gallery, Tokyo, 1986). His buildings include the Paper Church (Takatori, Hyogo, 1995), the Naked House (Kawagoe, Saitama, 2000), the Paper Art Museum (Mishima, Shizuoka, 2002), and the Picture Window House (Izu, Shizuoka, 2002). He has also designed ephemeral structures such as his Paper Refugee Shelter made with plastic sheets and paper tubes for the United Nations High Commissioner for Refugees (UNHCR). He designed the Japanese Pavilion at Expo 2000 in Hanover. Current work includes a small museum of Canal History in Pouilly-en-Auxois, France; Forest Park Pavilion – Bamboo Gridshell-02 (St. Louis, Missouri); Mul(ti)houses (Mulhouse, France); Sagaponac House/Furniture House-05 (Long Island, New York); Seikei University Library (Kichijoji, Tokyo); and the Centre Pompidou in Metz, France.

Shigeru Ban, 1957 in Tokio geboren, studierte von 1977 bis 1980 am Southern California Institute of Architecture (SCI-Arc) und von 1980 bis 1982 bei John Hejduk an der Cooper Union School of Architecture in New York. Von 1982 bis 1983 arbeitete er im Büro von Arata Isozaki und gründete 1985 seine eigene Firma in Tokio. Shigeru Ban gestaltete zahlreiche Ausstellungen, so die 1986 in der Galerie Axis in Tokio gezeigte Alvar-Aalto-Schau. Zu seinen Bauten gehören die Paper Church in Takatori, Hyogo (1995), das Naked House in Kawagoe, Saitama (2000), das Paper Art Museum in Mishima, Shizuoka (2002) sowie das Picture Window House in Izu, Shizuoka (2002). Ban hat auch Behelfsbauten entworfen wie sein für den Hohen Flüchtlingskommissar der Vereinten Nationen (UNHCR) aus Plastikfolie und Pappröhren gebauter Paper Refugee Shelter. Für die Expo 2000 in Hannover plante er den Japanischen Pavillon. Zu seinen jüngsten Projekten zählen ein kleines Museum für die Geschichte des Kanalbaus im französischen Pouilly-en-Auxois, der Forest Park Pavilion – Bamboo Gridshell-02 in St. Louis, Missouri, die Mul(ti)houses im französischen Mulhouse, das Haus Sagaponac/Furniture House-05 in Long Island, New York, sowie die Bibliothek der Seikei Universität in Kichijoji, Tokio, und das Centre Pompidou in Metz, Frankreich.

Né en 1957 à Tokyo, Shigeru Ban étudie au Southern California Institute of Architecture (SCI-Arc) de 1977 à 1980, puis à la Cooper Union School of Architecture, où il suit l'enseignement de John Hejduk (1980–1982). Il travaille pour Arata Isozaki (1982–83), avant de fonder son agence à Tokyo en 1985. Il a conçu de nombreuses expositions (dont celle d'Alvar Aalto, Axis Gallery, Tokyo, 1986). Ses réalisations comprennent l'Église de papier (Takatori, Hyogo, 1995), la maison nue (Kawagoe, Saitama, 2000), le Musée de l'art du papier (Mishima, Shizuoka, 2002) et le Maison-cadre (Izu, Shizuoka, 2002). Il conçoit également des structures éphémères comme un abri pour réfugiés en feuilles de plastique et tubes de papier, pour le Haut Commissariat aux Réfugiés (HCRNU). Il a signé le pavillon japonais à Expo 2000 de Hanovre. Parmi ses réalisations en cours figurent un petit musée sur l'Histoire du canal (Pouilly-en-Auxois, France) ; le Forest Park Pavilion – Bamboo Gridshell –02 (St Louis, Missouri) ; Mul(ti)houses (Mulhouse, France) ; Sagaponac House, Furniture House-05 (Long Island, New York) et la bibliothèque de l'Université Seikei (Kichijoji, Tokyo) et le centre Pompidou (Metz, France).

# GLASS SHUTTER HOUSE

*Meguro-ku, Tokyo, Japan, 2001–2003*

Client: Yashiharu Doi. Building area: 73.67 m², total floor area: 151.79 m². Costs: not specified.

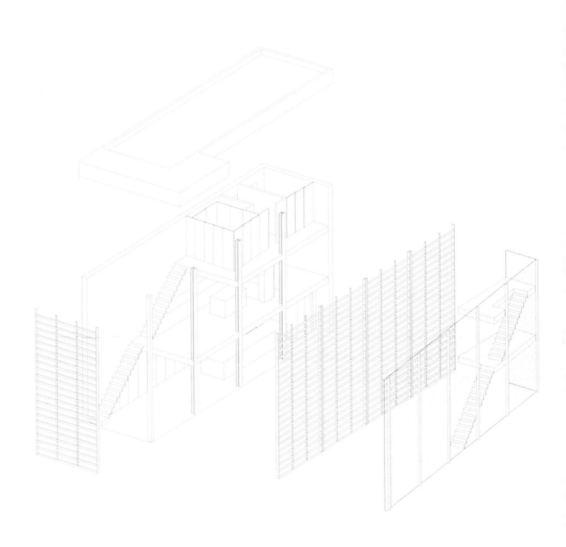

An exploded axonometric drawing shows the very simple volume and the shutters. The living spaces are above the restaurant, seen with its shutters closed to the right.

Die in Einzelteile aufgelöste axonometrische Darstellung zeigt den äußerst schlichten Baukörper mit den Jalousiewänden. Die Wohnräume liegen über dem Restaurant (rechts).

Une vue axonométrique éclatée montre le volume très simple et les volets roulants géants. Les espaces de vie se trouvent au-dessus du restaurant, ici volets fermés (à droite).

Located in the Meguro area of Tokyo, this combined residence and restaurant is located on a small, 139-square-meter site. It was built for a chef well known for his television appearances and his cooking school, also located in the new structure. The building area is just 73 square meters and total floor area is 151 square meters. The three-story 4 x 16 meter steel-frame house is remarkable because two of its façades open entirely from street level to roof. Rolling glass shutters disappear into the roof allowing an outside patio with a bamboo wall to become an integral part of the restaurant in warm weather. Local regulations normally permitted only two stories on this site, but as Shigeru Ban says, "the three-story volume which has only two floors is legally considered to be two-storied. The stairs connecting to the second level legally mean a floor dividing the first and the second floor. The whole volume is equivalent to three ordinary stories. The completed building has a restaurant on the ground floor, a kitchen studio on the second and housing on the third floor. Each area vertically conveys a sense of unity and the borderline, workplace or housing, is intentionally unclear." Ban concludes, "I have tried to connect inner space to the outside by using consecutive outward-opening doors in a series of housing projects. The shutters can be fully opened or be set at the height of each floor, which enables inner space to connect to outside in various ways and to be barrier free. Also, the fence made of bamboo defines the border to the neighboring site and secures its privacy." Because of its refined support design, the Glass Shutter House is extremely light and airy, giving new meaning to the typically Japanese idea of "in-between space."

Das im Tokioter Wohnviertel Meguro auf einem nur 139 m² großen Grundstück gelegene Gebäude ist eine Kombination aus Wohnhaus und Restaurant. Es wurde für einen Koch entworfen, der für seine Kochsendung im Fernsehen und seine – ebenfalls im Haus untergebrachte – Kochschule bekannt ist. Als besonderes Merkmal der dreigeschossigen, 4 x 16 m messenden Stahlrahmenkonstruktion lassen sich zwei seiner Fassaden vom Erdgeschoss bis zum Dach vollkommen öffnen, indem man die Glasjalousien ins Dach hochziehen kann, wodurch der offene Hof zu einem Teil des Restaurants wird. Zwar erlauben die lokalen Bauvorschriften an diesem Standort nur zwei Stockwerke, doch gilt das eigentlich dreigeschossige Haus durch die Treppe, die den ersten mit dem zweiten Stock verbindet, rechtlich als zweistöckig. Im Erdgeschoss befindet sich das Restaurant, während im ersten Stock eine Studioküche und auf den oberen Ebenen die Wohnräume liegen. Die vertikale Anordnung dieser Bereiche vermittelt einen zusammenhängenden Eindruck, wobei zwischen Arbeiten und Wohnen bewusst nicht klar getrennt wurde. Auch in anderer Hinsicht wurden Grenzen offen gelassen, wie Shigeru Ban erläutert: „Ich habe bereits zuvor bei einer Reihe von Wohnhäusern versucht, Innen und Außen durch Türen zu verbinden. Hier sind es die Jalousien, die ganz oder einzeln geöffnet werden können, wodurch sich die Innenräume auf verschiedene Weise und nahtlos mit der äußeren Umgebung verbinden lassen. Ansonsten wird durch den Bambuszaun die Grenze zum Nachbargrundstück definiert und damit die Privatsphäre gewahrt." Aufgrund seines ausgeklügelten Tragwerks ist das Glas Shutter House äußerst leicht und luftig gebaut, was dem typisch japanischen Gedanken vom „Zwischen-Raum" eine neue Bedeutung gibt.

Située à Tokyo, dans le quartier de Meguro, cette maison qui associe un restaurant et un logement, occupe un petit terrain de 139 m². Elle a été construite à l'intention d'un cuisinier connu pour ses émissions de télévision et son école de cuisine, installée à la même adresse. L'emprise au sol n'est que de 73 m² et la surface utile de 151 m². Cette construction de trois niveaux, à ossature d'acier et mesurant x 16 m, étonne par ses deux façades qui s'ouvrent entièrement, du niveau de la rue jusqu'au toit. D'énormes volets roulants de verre disparaissent dans la couverture ce qui permet à un patio extérieur à clôture de bambou de venir agrandir le restaurant à la belle saison. La réglementation locale n'autorisait que deux niveaux, mais comme l'explique Shigeru Ban : « Le volume sur trois niveaux mais avec deux planchers intérieurs est légalement considéré comme une maison à un seul étage. Il équivaut à deux étages ordinaires. La structure comprend le restaurant au rez-de-chaussée, l'école au premier et le logement au deuxième étage. Verticalement chaque zone exprime une impression d'unité et la limite entre logement et travail reste volontairement floue. » Il conclut : « J'avais déjà essayé de relier l'espace intérieur et extérieur par différents types de portes ouvrant sur l'extérieur dans de précédents projets. Les volets roulants peuvent s'ouvrir en grand ou seulement à la hauteur de chaque niveau, ce qui offre au volume intérieur des connexion variées avec l'extérieur, sans barrière. La clôture de bambou définit la frontière avec le terrain voisin et assure l'intimité. » Grâce à son dessin raffiné, cette maison extrêmement légère et aérée donne un sens nouveau au concept japonais traditionnel d'espace « entre-deux ».

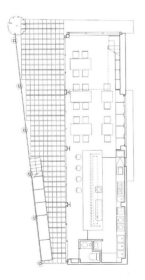

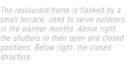

*The restaurant/home is flanked by a small terrace, used to serve outdoors in the warmer months. Above right, the shutters in their open and closed positions. Below right, the closed structure.*

*Das Restaurant wird von einer kleinen Terrasse flankiert, auf der im Sommer im Freien serviert wird. Oben rechts: die Jalousien im geöffneten und geschlossen Zustand. Unten rechts: das komplett geschlossene Gebäude.*

*Le restaurant-appartement est flanqué d'une petite terrasse utilisée pour le service pendant les mois d'été. En haut à droite: les volets fermés et ouverts. En bas à droite: la structure entièrement fermée.*

On a small site and with limited floor space, the Glass Shutter House is a very unusual mixture of restaurant and living area.

Das auf einem kleinen Grundstück errichtete Glass Shutter House bildet eine sehr ungewöhnliche Mischung aus Restaurant und Wohnhaus.

Sur un petit terrain et pour une surface réduite, la Glass Shutter House est une association assez rare de restaurant et de logement.

# BEHNISCH, BEHNISCH & PARTNER

*Behnisch, Behnisch & Partner*
*Günter Behnisch, Stefan Behnisch, Günther Schaller*
*Christophstr. 6*
*70178 Stuttgart*
*Germany*

*Tel: +49 711 607 720*
*Fax: +49 711 607 7299*
*e-mail: buero@behnisch.com*
*Web: www.behnisch.com*

Born in 1922 in Dresden, Gunter Behnisch grew up in Dresden and in Chemnitz. He studied architecture from 1947 to 1951 at the Technical University of Stuttgart (Dipl. Ing.) before setting up his own office in 1952. In 1966 he founded the firm of Behnisch & Partner, and from 1967 to 1987 he was a Professor of Design, Industrial Buildings and Planning, and Director of the Institute for Building Standardization at the Technical University, Darmstadt. In 1989, he established a city office in Stuttgart, which has today become Behnisch, Behnisch & Partner. Stefan Behnisch was born in 1957 in Stuttgart. He studied philosophy at the Philosophische Hochschule der Jesuiten, Munich (1976–1979), economics at the Ludwig Maximilians University, Munich, and architecture at the University of Karlruhe (1979–1987). He worked at Stephen Woolley & Associates (Venice, CA, 1984–85), and has been a Principal Partner at Behnisch, Behnisch & Partner since 1989. He has been involved in numerous workshops and conferences on sustainable and green buildings since 1997. Born 1959 in Neuhausen, Günther Schaller studied architecture at the Technical College of Stuttgart (Dipl. Ing. FH) and the University of Stuttgart (Dipl. Ing.) from 1982 to 1991, when he joined the offices of Behnisch & Partner. Project architect and project partner for the New Administration Building of the Landesgirokasse in Stuttgart, he has been a Partner in Behnisch, Behnisch & Partner since 1997.

Günter Behnisch, geboren 1922 in Dresden, wuchs in Dresden und Chemnitz auf. Von 1947 bis 1951 studierte er Architektur an der Technischen Universität in Stuttgart, wo er sein Ingenieurdiplom erwarb, und machte sich 1952 mit einem eigenen Architekturbüro selbstständig. 1966 gründete er die Firma Behnisch & Partner. Von 1967 bis 1987 war er Professor für Entwerfen, Industriebauten und Baugestaltung sowie Direktor des Instituts für Baunormung an der TH Darmstadt. 1989 eröffnete Günter Behnisch ein Büro in der Stuttgarter Innenstadt, das heutige Behnisch, Behnisch & Partner. Stefan Behnisch wurde 1957 in Stuttgart geboren. Er studierte Philosophie an der Philosophischen Hochschule der Jesuiten in München (1976–1979), Wirtschaftswissenschaft an der Ludwig Maximilians Universität in München und Architektur an der Universität Karlruhe (1979–1987). Von 1984 bis 1985 arbeitete er bei Stephen Woolley & Associates in Venice, Kalifornien, und ist seit 1989 in leitender Funktion bei Behnisch, Behnisch & Partner. Seit 1997 führte er durch zahlreiche Workshops und Konferenzen zum Thema nachhaltiges und ökologisches Bauen. Günther Schaller, 1959 in Neuhausen geboren, studierte von 1982 bis 1991 Architektur an der Fachhochschule für Technik (Diplom 1987) und an der Technischen Universität in Stuttgart (Diplom 1991). Anschließend trat er in das Büro Behnisch & Partner ein. Er war Projektarchitekt und Projektpartner für das neue Verwaltungsgebäude der Landesgirokasse in Stuttgart und ist seit 1997 Partner im Büro Behnisch, Behnisch & Partner.

Né en 1922 à Dresde, Gunter Behnish a grandi dans cette ville et à Chemnitz. Il étudie l'architecture de 1947 à 1951 à l'Université technique de Stuttgart (Dipl. Ing.), et crée son agence en 1952. En 1966, il fonde Behnisch & Partner et, de 1967 à 1987, est professeur de design de bâtiments industriels et de programmation ainsi que directeur de l'Institut de standardisation de la construction à l'Université technique de Darmstadt. En 1989, il ouvre une agence à Stuttgart, devenue Behnisch, Behnisch & Partner. Stefan Behnisch est né en 1957 à Stuttgart. Il étudie la philosophie à l'École supérieure de philosophie des Jésuites (Munich, 1976–1979), l'économie à l'Université Ludwig Maximilian (Munich) et l'architecture à l'Université de Karlsruhe (1979–1987). Il a travaillé chez Stephen Woolley & Associates (Venice, Californie, 1984–85) et dirige depuis 1989 l'agence créée par son père. Il a participé à de nombreux colloques et conférences sur les immeubles écologiques durables depuis 1997. Né en 1959 à Neuhausen, Günther Schaller a étudié l'architecture au Collège Technique de Stuttgart (Dipl. Ing. FH) et à l'Université de Stuttgart (Dipl. Ing.) de 1982 à 1991, date de son arrivée chez Behnisch & Partner. Architecte de projet et responsable de celui du nouvel immeuble administratif de la Landesgirokasse à Stuttgart, il est associé de l'agence depuis 1997.

# NORDDEUTSCHE LANDESBANK

*Friedrichswall, Hanover, Germany 2000–2002*

*Client: Norddeutsche Landesbank Hannover. Building area: 14 000 m², gross floor area: 75 000 m². Costs: not specified.*

This large structure (40 000 square meters of floor area; space for 1 500 workers) is located at the intersection of the city itself to the north and the residential districts of southern Hanover. With the varying heights of its different components, the building is intended to integrate itself gently into the existing town pattern. An open and easily accessible ground-floor area, which remains a part of the town, serves to underline the pivotal role of the complex in the urban pattern. The offices do not have any air conditioning. During the day, concrete ceilings serve as storage mass, while a soil heat exchanger provides cooling. Air conditioning is limited to the kitchen and restaurant. The actual bank facilities begin one level above the ground floor. They are reached via a generous freestanding stairway. Transparent tubular passageways that can be opened during the summer link the different building parts. The high-rise part of the complex detaches itself from the formal order of the blocks addressing the street, rising to 70 meters and making connections with the wider context of the city. The high-rise area accommodates special elements such as a lounge and executive rooms. The office façades respond to the different requirements of the surroundings. The sides where there is heavier traffic (Friedrichswall, Willy-Brandt-Allee) have noise- and heat-absorbing double façades. The sides of the building exposed to the sun have external shading devices, while less exposed sides have high-quality sun protection glazing. Due to the optimisation of daylight in the offices the use of artificial lighting can be considerably reduced. The performance of the shading installations and glazing have been determined on the basis of computer-assisted studies. All rooms can be ventilated naturally by opening the windows, a means of exploiting the outdoor air which exceeds 22°C during less than five per cent of the year. Although the Chief Executive Officer of the Bank, Manfred Bodin, has admitted that "for us as bankers, it was not always easy to follow the highly creative approach of the architects," the result is a spectacular, ecologically and economically responsible building.

Das Großprojekt mit 40 000 m² Nutzfläche und Raum für 1 500 Angestellte grenzt im Norden an die Innenstadt und im Süden an die Wohnbezirke von Hannover. Mit der unterschiedlichen Höhe seiner einzelnen Bauteile soll sich das Gebäude natürlich in seine Umgebung einfügen. Durch den offenen, leicht zugänglichen Bereich im Erdgeschoss, der Teil des urbanen Raums bleibt, wird die zentrale Rolle, die der Bau innerhalb des Stadtgefüges einnimmt, noch unterstrichen. Da nur die Küche und das Restaurant mit Klimaanlage ausgestattet sind, dienen die Betondecken in den Büros als Wärmespeicher, während eine Wärmeaustauschanlage für Kühlung sorgt. Die eigentlichen Bankräume beginnen im ersten Stock, in den man über einen breiten, freistehenden Treppenaufgang gelangt. Die einzelnen Bauteile des Komplexes sind durch transparente, röhrenförmige Gänge, die im Sommer geöffnet werden können, miteinander verbunden. Der mit 70 m höchste der Baukörper, der unter anderem eine Lounge und Sitzungsräume beherbergt, ist durch seine Ausrichtung zur Straße aus der Anordnung der anderen Blocks herausgelöst und stellt die Verbindung zum städtischen Umfeld her. Ansonsten entsprechen die Fassaden des Bürogebäudes den unterschiedlichen Erfordernissen des jeweiligen Umfelds. So sind die zu den verkehrsreicheren Straßen wie Friedrichswall oder Willy-Brandt-Allee gehenden Seiten mit lärm- und hitzeabsorbierenden Doppelwänden ausgestattet. Die am stärksten dem Sonnenlicht ausgesetzten Fassaden verfügen über externe Sonnenschutzvorrichtungen, während die weniger sonnenbeschienenen Wände mit einer hochwertigen Sonnenschutzverglasung versehen sind. Dabei wurden sowohl Sonnenblenden als auch Verglasungen auf der Basis von computergenerierten Raumstudien konzipiert. Aufgrund der optimalen Nutzung des Tageslichts konnte der Einsatz von künstlichem Licht auf ein Minimum reduziert werden. Sämtliche Räume lassen sich durch Öffnen der Fenster natürlich belüften. Obwohl Manfred Bodin, CEO der Norddeutschen Landesbank, zugibt, dass es „für uns als Banker nicht immer leicht war, den äußerst kreativen Zugang der Architekten nachzuvollziehen", ist das Resultat ein großartiges, ökologisch und ökonomisch verantwortungsvolles Gebäude.

Cette importante construction (40 000 m² de surface utile, prévue pour 1 500 employés), se trouve à la limite de la ville et des quartiers résidentiels du sud de Hanovre. Par la variété de ses hauteurs, l'ensemble cherche à s'intégrer à la trame urbaine existante. Le rez-de-chaussée, ouvert et aisément accessible, fait encore partie de la ville et souligne le rôle charnière du complexe dans son contexte urbain. Les bureaux ne sont pas climatisés. De jour, les plafonds en béton servent de masse de stockage, tandis qu'un échangeur de chaleur au sol rafraîchit l'atmosphère. La climatisation est limitée à la cuisine et au restaurant. Les bureaux de la banque commencent au premier étage et sont accessibles par un escalier autoporteur de généreuses dimensions. Des passages tubulaires transparents, ouvrables en été, relient les différentes parties du bâtiment. La tour de 70 m de haut se détache de la composition des blocs longeant la rue et crée une connexion avec le contexte plus vaste de la ville. Elle accueille des installations particulières comme un salon et les bureaux de la direction. Les façades des bureaux répondent aux différentes exigences de l'environnement. Les façades latérales, devant lesquelles la circulation est plus dense (Friedrichswall, Willy-Brandt-Allee), possèdent une double peau absorbant le bruit et la chaleur. Celles orientées au soleil sont équipées de screens externes, tandis que les autres, moins exposées, sont équipées de verre de protection solaire de haute qualité. L'optimisation de la lumière du jour dans les bureaux permet de réduire considérablement le recours à l'éclairage artificiel. Les performances en matière de protection solaire ont été déterminées par des études informatiques. Toutes les pièces peuvent être naturellement ventilées par l'ouverture des fenêtres, ce qui permet de bénéficier d'un air frais extérieur dont la température ne dépasse 22° C que cinq pourcent du temps chaque année. Bien que le président de la banque, Manfred Bodin, ait déclaré que « pour nous, en tant que banquiers, il n'est pas toujours facile de suivre l'approche hautement créative des architectes », le résultat est un immeuble de haute qualité écologique et de maintenance économique.

The rotated volumes of the main tower sit atop a base that recalls the scale of an older building seen to the right (above).

Die ausschwenkenden Baukörper des Hauptturms ruhen auf einem Unterbau, der die Struktur eines älteren, im Bild rechts sichtbaren Gebäudes aufnimmt (oben).

Les volumes pivotés de la tour principale sont posés sur une base qui rappelle l'échelle de l'ancien immeuble que l'on aperçoit à droite (en haut).

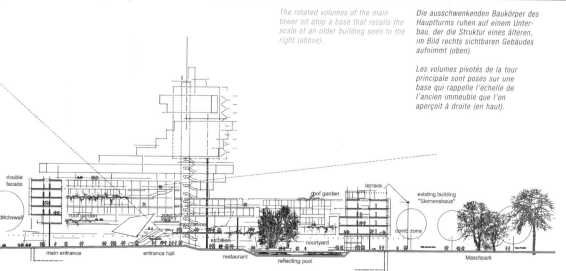

Glass-tube walkways link elements of the complex structure and allow users to view the rest of the building as they move through it.

Gläserne Röhrengänge verbinden die einzelnen Bauteile miteinander und gewähren ihren Benutzern Ausblicke auf den übrigen Gebäudekomplex.

Des passerelles tubulaires en verre relient les éléments du complexe et permettent à ceux qui les empruntent de voir le reste de l'immeuble en se déplaçant.

Transparency and a technologically oriented lightness make the building agreeable to be in, even as it responds to high standards of ecological awareness and office efficiency.

Transparenz und eine gewisse technologisch geprägte Helligkeit sorgen für ein angenehmes Raumgefühl, wobei das Gebäude hohen ökologischen und bürotechnischen Standards entspricht.

La transparence et une certaine légèreté d'esprit technologique rendent agréable à vivre cet immeuble qui obéit à des standards élevés de respect de l'environnement et d'efficacité fonctionnelle.

Gardens and reflecting pools to some extent obviate or counteract the harshness of some surfaces of this rather complicated series of volumes.

Wintergärten und Wasserbecken bilden ein Gegengewicht zur kantigen Strenge, die einige der komplexen Baukörper ausstrahlen.

Les jardins et les bassins adoucissent la rudesse de certaines surfaces de cet ensemble de volumes assez complexe.

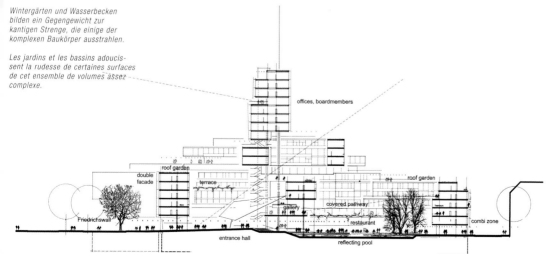

section b-b

Rather than the closed facades that
many modern office buildings present
in urban areas, the Norddeutsche
Landesbank appears to move and
breathe with its surroundings.

Im Unterschied zu den geschlossenen
Fassaden, die viele moderne Bürogebäude in urbanen Zonen präsentieren,
scheint die Norddeutsche Landesbank
mit ihrer Umgebung mitzuschwingen.

À la différence des façades fermées
de nombreux immeubles de bureaux
en ville, la Norddeutsche Landesbank
semble bouger et respirer avec son
environnement.

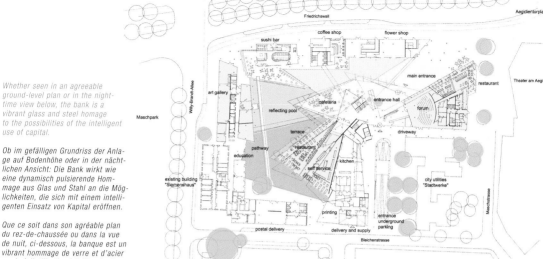

*Whether seen in an agreeable
ground-level plan or in the night-
time view below, the bank is a
vibrant glass and steel homage
to the possibilities of the intelligent
use of capital.*

*Ob im gefälligen Grundriss der Anla-
ge auf Bodenhöhe oder in der nächtlichen Ansicht: Die Bank wirkt wie
eine dynamisch pulsierende Hommage aus Glas und Stahl an die Mög-
lichkeiten, die sich mit einem intelli-
genten Einsatz von Kapital eröffnen.*

*Que ce soit dans son agréable plan
du rez-de-chaussée ou dans la vue
de nuit, ci-dessous, la banque est un
vibrant hommage de verre et d'acier
rendu à l'utilisation intelligente du
capital.*

Ysios Winery

# SANTIAGO CALATRAVA

*Santiago Calatrava SA*
*Parkring 11*
*8002 Zürich*
*Switzerland*

*Tel: +41 1 204 50 00*
*Fax: +41 1 204 50 01*
*e-mail: zurich-admin@scsa-mail.com*
*Web: www.calatrava.com*

Born in Valencia in 1951, Santiago Calatrava studied art and architecture at the Escuela Técnica Superior de Arquitectura in Valencia (1968–1973) and engineering at the ETH in Zurich (doctorate in Technical Science, 1981). He opened his own architecture and civil engineering office the same year. His built work includes Gallery and Heritage Square, BCE Place (Toronto, 1987), the Bach de Roda Bridge (Barcelona, 1985–1987), the Torre de Montjuic (Barcelona, 1989–1992), the Kuwait Pavilion at Expo '92 in Seville, and the Alamillo Bridge for the same exhibition, as well as the TGV Station Lyon-Saint-Exupéry (1989–1994). He completed the Oriente Station in Lisbon in 1998. He was a finalist in the competition for the Reichstag in Berlin, and he recently completed the Valencia City of Science and Planetarium, (Valencia, Spain, 1996–2000); the Sondica Airport (Bilbao, Spain, 1990–2000); and a bridge in Orléans (1996–2000). Other current work includes: Blackhall Place Bridge (Dublin, Ireland, 2003); Tenerife Auditorium (Santa Cruz, Canary Islands, 2003); Petach Tikvah Bridge, (Tel Aviv, Israel, 2003); Quatro Ponte sul Canal Grande (Venice, 2004); Turtle Bay Bridge (Redding, California, 2004); the Athens Olympic Sports Complex (summer 2004); and the Valencia Opera House (2004), the last major building in his City of Arts and Sciences. Calatrava has also been selected to design Christ the Light Cathedral for the Roman Catholic Diocese of Oakland, California; the expansion of the Museo dell'Opera del Duomo in Florence, Italy; and the Symphony Center for the Atlanta Symphony Orchestra in Atlanta, Georgia.

Santiago Calatrava, geboren 1951 in Valencia, studierte von 1968 bis 1973 an der dortigen Escuela Técnica Superior de Arquitectura Kunst und Architektur sowie Ingenieurbau an der Eidgenössischen Technischen Hochschule (ETH) in Zürich, wo er 1981 promovierte. Im selben Jahr gründete er sein eigenes Architektur- und Ingenieurbüro. Zu Calatravas Bauten gehören der Gallery and Heritage Square, BCE Place, in Toronto (1987), die Bach-de-Roda-Brücke (1985–1987) und die Torre de Montjuic (1989–1992), beide in Barcelona, der Kuwait-Pavillon und die Alamillo-Brücke für die Expo '92 in Sevilla sowie der TGV-Bahnhof Lyon-Saint-Exupéry (1989–1994). 1998 realisierte er den Bahnhof Oriente in Lissabon. Calatravas Entwurf für den Reichstag in Berlin kam in die Endauswahl. Zwischen 1996 und 2000 wurden das Wissenschaftsmuseum und Planetarium in Valencia, der Flughafen Sondica in Bilbao und eine Brücke in Orléans fertig gestellt. Zu seinen jüngsten Arbeiten gehören: die Blackhall-Place-Brücke in Dublin (2003), das Tenerife Auditorium in Santa Cruz auf den Kanarischen Inseln (2003), die Petach-Tikvah-Brücke in Tel Aviv (2003), die Quatro Ponte über den Canal Grande in Venedig (2004), die Turtle-Bay-Brücke im kalifornischen Redding (2004), eine Sportanlage für die Olympischen Spiele in Athen (2004) sowie, als letztes Hauptgebäude seiner Stadt der Künste und Wissenschaften, die Oper in Valencia (2004). Außerdem erhielt Calatrava die Aufträge für die Kathedrale Christ the Light für die römisch-katholische Diözese im kalifornischen Oakland, den Erweiterungsbau des Museo dell'Opera del Duomo in Florenz und das Symphony Center for the Atlanta Symphony Orchestra in Atlanta, Georgia.

Né à Valence en 1951, Santiago Calatrava étudie l'art et l'architecture à la Escuela Técnica Superior de Arquitectura de Valence (1968–1973) et l'ingénierie à l'ETH de Zurich. Docteur en science des techniques en 1981, il ouvre sa propre agence d'architecture et d'ingénierie civile la même année. Parmi ses réalisations : Gallery and Heritage Square, BCE Place, (Toronto, Canada, 1987) ; le pont Bach de Roda (Barcelone, 1985–1987) ; la Torre de Montjuic (Barcelone, 1989–1992) ; le Pavillon du Koweït à l'Expo '92 et le pont de l'Alamillo (Séville) ; la gare de TGV de l'aéroport Lyon-Saint-Exupéry (1989–1994) ; la gare de l'Orient (Lisbonne, 1998). Il a été finaliste du concours du Reichstag à Berlin, et a récemment achevé la Cité des Sciences et le Planetarium de Valence (Valence, Espagne, 1996–2000) ; l'aéroport de Sondica (Bilbao, Espagne, 1990–2000) ; le pont de l'Europe à Orléans (1996–2000). Parmi ses chantiers actuels : pont de Blackhall Place (Dublin, Irlande, 2003) ; auditorium de Ténérife (Santa Cruz, Îles Canaries, 2003) ; pont Petach Tikvah (Tel Aviv, Israël, 2003) ; Quatro Ponte sur le Grand Canal (Venise, Italie, 2004) ; pont de Turtle Bay (Redding, Californie, 2004) ; complexe pour les Jeux Olympiques d'Athènes (été 2004), et l'opéra de Valence, dernier grand élément de sa Cité des arts et des sciences. Calatrava a également été sélectionné pour concevoir la Cathédrale de lumière pour le diocèse catholique d'Oakland (Californie) ; l'extension du Museo dell'Opera del Duomo (Florence, Italie) et le Symphony Center pour l'Atlanta Symphony Orchestra d'Atlanta (Géorgie, USA).

# YSIOS WINERY

*Laguardia, Álava, Spain, 1998–2001*

*Client: Bodegas & Bebidas SA. Building area: 8 000 m². Costs: not specified.*

The Bodegas & Bebidas group wanted a building that would be an icon for its prestigious new Rioja Alavesa wine. They called on architect Santiago Calatrava to design an 8 000-square-meter winery complex, a building that had to be designed to make, store and sell wine. Half of the uneven, rectangular site is occupied by vineyards. The linear program for the wine-making process dictated that the structure should be rectangular and it was set along an east-west axis. Two longitudinal concrete load-bearing walls, separated from each other by 26 meters, trace a 196-meter-long sinusoidal shape in plan and elevation. These walls are covered with wooden planks, which are mirrored in a reflecting pool and "evoke the image of a row of wine barrels." The roof, composed of a series of laminated wood beams, is designed as a continuation of the façades. The result is a "ruled surface wave," which combines concave and convex surfaces as it evolves along the longitudinal axis. The roof is clad in aluminum, creating a contrast with the warmth of the wooden façades.

Die Bodegas & Bebidas Gruppe wollte ein Gebäude, das ihren berühmten Rioja Alavesa Wein symbolisieren soll, und beauftragte Santiago Calatrava, eine 8 000 m² große Weinkellerei zu gestalten. Die Anlage sollte so konzipiert sein, dass dort Wein hergestellt, gelagert und verkauft werden kann. Das dafür vorgesehene Grundstück wird zur Hälfte von Weingärten eingenommen. Der linear verlaufende Herstellungsprozess schrieb eine rechteckige Anlage vor, deren Mittelachse in ost-west-licher Richtung verläuft. Die zwei längs gerichteten, im Abstand von 26 m aufgestellten tragenden Außenwände des Gebäudes beschreiben in Grundriss und Erhebung eine 196 m lange Sinuslinie. Sie sind mit Holzplanken verkleidet, die sich in einem Teich spiegeln, und evozieren das Bild aneinander gereihter Weinfässer. Die Fassadengestaltung setzt sich in dem aus Schichtholzbalken konstruierten Dach fort. Hierdurch ergibt sich eine „linierte Oberflächenwelle", die in ihrem längs gerichteten Verlauf konkave und konvexe Elemente kombiniert. Das Dach ist zudem mit Aluminium verkleidet, was einen reizvollen Kontrast zum warmen Charakter der Holzwände ergibt.

Le groupe Bodegas & Bebidas souhaitait édifier un immeuble symbolique pour son prestigieux vin de Rioja, Alavesa. C'est la raison du choix de Santiago Calatrava pour ce nouveau chais de 8 000 m², destiné à l'élaboration, la conservation et la vente du vin. La moitié du terrain rectangulaire de niveau irrégulier est occupée par la vigne. Le déroulement linéaire du processus vinicole impliquait une construction rectangulaire, orientée selon un axe est-ouest. Deux murs porteurs en béton, séparés de 26 m l'un de l'autre, déterminent un volume de 196 m de long, sinusoïdal en plan comme en élévation. Ces deux parois sont bardées de planches qui se reflètent dans un bassin et « évoquent l'image d'un alignement de tonneaux ». Le toit, soutenu par des poutres en bois lamellé-collé, vient dans la continuation des façades, d'où un effet de « vague de surface régulière » qui combine des plans concaves et convexes le long de l'axe longitudinal. La toiture est en aluminium, matériau qui contraste avec la chaleur des façades de bois.

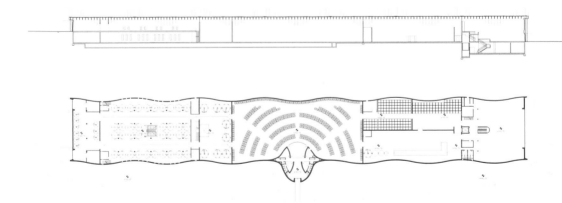

*Laid out as a long rectangle for functional reasons, the winery's most distinctive feature is its undulating roof.*

*Auffallendstes Merkmal der aus funktionalen Gründen als langgestrecktes Rechteck angelegten Weinkellerei ist ihr wellenförmig gestaltetes Dach.*

*Le composant le plus caractéristique de ce chais en forme de rectangle allongé, pour des raisons fonctionnelles, est la vigoureuse ondulation de son toit.*

The stepped, undulating roof cul-
minates in a surprising canopy over
the main entrance that juts forward.

Das Dach schwingt sich in Stufen bis
zu einem über den Haupteingang her-
ausragenden Vordach auf.

Le point culminant de la toiture
en vague est l'étonnant auvent qui
se projette au-dessus de l'entrée
principale.

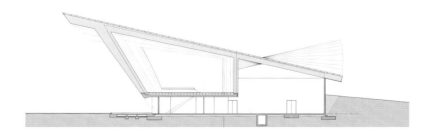

The entrance canopy covers the space visible to the left, with a broad view onto the surrounding landscape.

*Das Vordach überdeckt den links abgebildeten Raum mit einem weiten Ausblick auf die Landschaft.*

*L'auvent de l'entrée abrite le volume visible à gauche, d'où l'on bénéficie d'une ample vue sur le paysage.*

# COOK/FOURNIER

Peter Cook, Colin Fournier
The Bartlett School of Architecture, UCL University College London
22 Gordon Street, London WC1H OQB, UK

Tel: +44 20 7679 -4830 / -4861,
Fax: +44 20 7679 4831
e-mail: peter.cook@ucl.ac.uk, c.fournier@ucl.ac.uk

*Kunsthaus Gra*

Peter Cook was born in 1936 in Southend-on-Sea, England. He studied architecture at the Bournemouth College of Art (1953–1958) and then at the Architectural Association in London. He created the magazine *Architecture + Gram* in 1961, and with Warren Chalk, Dennis Crompton, David Green, Ron Herron and Michael Webb the Archigram group set out to do nothing less than "revolutionize" architecture beginning in 1963. This group of young London-based architects began and sustained a campaign of "environmental revolution." They created images based on mechanical invention and pop culture. Archigram explored the continuities of change and choice using the opportunities offered by new technologies. "Plug-in City," "Living Pod," "Instant City" and "Ad Hoc" design were Archigram inventions that became part of the vocabulary of modern art and architecture. More recently, together with Christine Hawley, Peter Cook has built the social housing scheme of Lützowplatz in Berlin and the cantine of the Staedelschule in Frankfurt. He is currently Chairman of the Bartlett School of Architecture, University College, London (UCL). Together with the other founding members of Archigram, he won the RIBA Gold Medal in 2002. Colin Fournier was born in 1944 in London and is a Professor of Architecture and Urbanism at the Bartlett School (UCL). He was the partner of Bernard Tschumi for the overall planning and design of the Parc de la Villette in Paris, and developed the Master Plan for the city of Yanbu, Saudi Arabia. He is a joint founding partner with Peter Cook of the firm SpaceLab Cook-Fournier GmbH which was created in Graz for the Kunsthaus project.

Peter Cook, 1936 im englischen Southend-on-Sea geboren, studierte von 1953 bis 1958 am Bournemouth College of Art und anschließend an der Architectural Association in London. 1961 gründete er die Zeitschrift *Architecture + Gram*. Zusammen mit Warren Chalk, Dennis Crompton, David Green, Ron Herron und Michael Webb bildete er die Gruppe Archigram, die kein geringeres Ziel hatte, als die Architektur zu „revolutionieren". Ab 1963 führte diese Gruppe junger Londoner Architekten eine Kampagne durch, die sich „Umwelt-Revolution" nannte. Dabei schufen sie Bilder, die auf mechanischen Erfindungen und Popkultur basierten, und erforschten die Kontinuität von Veränderung und Wahl unter Einsatz neuer Technologien. „Plug-in City", „Living Pod", „Instant City" und „Ad Hoc Design" waren Erfindungen von Archigram, die in den Sprachschatz moderner Kunst und Architektur eingingen. In jüngerer Zeit hat Peter Cook zusammen mit Christine Hawley den Sozialwohnungsbau am Lützowplatz in Berlin und die Kantine der Städelschule in Frankfurt am Main realisiert. Derzeit ist Cook Präsident der Bartlett School of Architecture am University College London (UCL). Im Jahr 2002 gewann er zusammen mit den anderen Gründungsmitgliedern von Archigram die RIBA Goldmedaille. Colin Fournier, 1944 in London geboren, ist Professor für Architektur und Stadtplanung an der Bartlett School of Architecture. Als Partner von Bernard Tschumi erarbeitete er den Generalplan und das Gestaltungskonzept des Parc de la Villette in Paris und entwickelte den Masterplan für die Stadt Yanbu in Saudi-Arabien. Im Rahmen des Kunsthaus-Projekts gründete er zusammen mit Peter Cook die Firma SpaceLab Cook-Fournier GmbH in Graz.

Peter Cook est né en 1936 à Southend-on-Sea, en Grande-Bretagne. Il étudie l'architecture au Bournemouth College of Art (1953–1958) et à l'Architectural Association de Londres. Il crée le magazine *Architecture + Gram* en 1961 et fonde en 1963, avec Warren Chalk, Dennis Crompton, David Green, Ron Herron et Michael Webb, le groupe Archigram qui ne propose rien de moins que de «révolutionner» l'architecture. Ce groupe de jeunes architectes londoniens lance une campagne de «révolution environnementale», crée des images inspirées de la culture pop et de la mécanique, explore les problématiques du changement et du choix à travers les opportunités offertes par les technologies nouvelles. «Plug in City», «Living Pod», «Instant City» et «Ad hoc» sont des inventions d'Archigram qui finissent par faire partie du vocabulaire de l'architecture et de l'art modernes. Plus récemment, avec Christine Hawley, Peter Cook a réalisé un projet de logements sociaux à Lützowplatz à Berlin et la cantine de la Staedelschule à Francfort. Il est actuellement président de la Bartlett School of Architecture, University College, à Londres. Avec les autres membres fondateurs d'Archigram, il a remporté la médaille d'or du RIBA en 2002. Colin Fournier, né en 1944 à Londres, est professeur d'architecture et d'urbanisme à la Bartlett School (UCL). Il a été associé à Bernard Tschumi pour le plan d'ensemble et la conception du Parc de la Villette à Paris et a développé le plan directeur de la ville de Yanbu en Arabie saoudite. Avec Peter Cook, il est cofondateur et associé de SpaceLab Cook-Fournier GmbH créer à Graz pour le projet de la Kunsthaus.

# KUNSTHAUS GRAZ

*Graz, Austria, 2002–03*

*Client: Town of Graz, Kunsthaus Graz AG. Gross floor area: 13 100 m². Costs: € 40 000 000.*

Described as a "friendly alien" by its creators, the Kunsthaus Graz is located on the bank of the Mur river, at the corner of Südtiroler Platz and Lendkai. The bluish skin of the structure appears to float above the glass-walled ground floor. The biomorphic upper section of the building contains two large exhibition decks. Sixteen nozzle-like north oriented openings project upward from the skin of the building to admit daylight. In the upper levels, bridges link the 23-meter-high new structure with the "Eisernes Haus" whose cast-iron construction – which is the oldest of its kind in Europe and listed as an historical monument – was renovated as part of the construction work on the Kunsthaus. As Fournier has written, "the genealogy of the project's biomorphic form lies in its designers' fascination with the animal presence of architecture and in the checkered history of the competition for the Kunsthaus, which was originally intended to inhabit a large cavity within the Schlossberg, the hill standing in the center of the city. The part adopted by the authors at the time was to line this rocky cavity with an organically shaped membrane filling its complex and rough internal contours and to allow this membrane to protrude out of the mountain and into the city, like the tail or tongue of a dragon. When the location of the museum was changed to its current site, the dragon skin found its way across the river, flowed into the irregular geometric boundary of the new site and wrapped itself around the two elevated decks of the museum, forming an environmental enclosure that resembles neither roofs nor walls nor floors but a seamless morphing of the three."

Das von seinen Gestaltern als „friendly alien" bezeichnete Kunsthaus Graz liegt am Ufer der Mur, an der Ecke von Südtiroler Platz und Lendkai. Die bläuliche Ummantelung des biomorphen Baukörpers, der zwei große Ausstellungsplattformen beherbergt, scheint über den Glaswänden des Unterbaus zu schweben. Das Tageslicht kommt über 16 tentakelartige Öffnungen, die über die Außenhaut verteilt sind. In den oberen Etagen ist das 23 m hohe Gebäude durch Brücken mit dem „Eisernen Haus" verbunden. Dessen Gusseisenkonstruktion ist die älteste ihrer Art in Europa und wurde im Zuge der Arbeiten am Kunsthaus renoviert. Wie Fournier schreibt: „Die Genealogie der biomorphen Form dieses Entwurfs liegt in der Faszination seiner Gestalter für die animalische Seite der Architektur und in der wechselvollen Geschichte des Wettbewerbs um das Kunsthaus, das ursprünglich in einer großen Höhle im Schlossberg untergebracht werden sollte. Die Planer hatten die Absicht, diese Felsenhöhle mit einer organisch geformten Membran auszukleiden, deren Spitze sich wie der Schweif oder die Zunge eines Drachens aus dem im Stadtzentrum liegenden Berg herausstrecken sollte. Als dann der Standort des Museums verlegt wurde, fand die Drachenhaut ihren Weg über den Fluss, glitt in das geometrisch unregelmäßig eingehegte neue Grundstück und legte sich schließlich um die beiden erhöhten Plattformen des Museums, was ein Gebilde ergab, das weder Dach noch Wand oder Boden ist, sondern ein nahtloses Ineinanderverschmelzen aller drei Elemente."

Décrite comme « un aimable extra-terrestre » par ses créateurs, la Kunsthaus de Graz est située sur la rive de la Mur, à l'angle de la Südtiroler Platz et du Lendkai. Sa peau bleuâtre semble flotter au-dessus de son rez-de-chaussée paré de verre. Sa partie supérieure biomorphique contient deux grands plateaux d'exposition. Seize ouvertures en forme de lances d'arrosage, orientées vers le nord, se projettent vers le ciel pour attirer la lumière. Aux niveaux supérieurs, des passerelles relient le nouveau bâtiment de 23 m de haut à l'Eisernes Haus dont le bâtiment en fonte – le plus ancien de ce type en Europe, classé monument historique – a été rénové à l'occasion du chantier de la Kunsthaus. Comme l'a écrit Fournier : « La généalogie de la forme biomorphique du projet tient à la fascination de ses concepteurs pour la présence animale de l'architecture et pour l'histoire même du concours de la Kunsthaus, qui devait au départ occuper une énorme cavité dans le Schlossberg, la colline qui se dresse au milieu de la ville. Le parti adopté à l'époque était de doubler cette cavité rocheuse par une membrane organique remplissant ses contours complexes et laissés bruts et de permettre à celle-ci de se projeter de la montagne vers la ville, comme la queue ou la langue d'un dragon. Lorsque la localisation du musée a été modifiée au profit du site actuel, la peau de dragon a suivi, s'est infiltrée dans les limites géométriques irrégulières du nouveau terrain et s'est enveloppée autour des deux plates-formes du musée pour former un enclos environnemental qui ne ressemble ni à un toit, ni à des murs, ni à des sols, mais est une mise en forme (morphing) lissée de ces trois éléments. »

*Overhanging a pre-existing building and imposing its very surprising shape on the otherwise quite traditional city, the Kunsthaus is a new focal point for Graz.*

*Ein älteres Gebäude überragend und das eher traditionelle Stadtbild mit seiner ungewöhnlichen Form prägend, ist das Kunsthaus zu einem neuen Brennpunkt für Graz geworden.*

*Superposée à un bâtiment ancien et imposant sa forme étonnante dans une cité assez traditionnelle, la Kunsthaus est le nouveau centre d'attraction de Graz.*

In the section below and the image above, the bulbous upper volume stands out in contrast to the base and neighboring structures.

*Dans la coupe ci-dessous et l'image ci-dessus, le volume bulbeux contraste fortement avec son soubassement et les constructions voisines.*

Wie in unterem Querschnitt und der Abbildung oben sichtbar, steht der kugelige Baukörper in starkem Kontrast zu seinem Unterbau und den Nachbargebäuden.

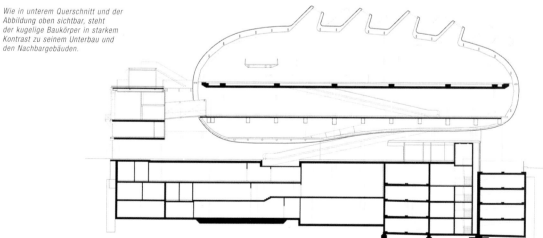

Seen from within, the low display
walls sit under the dark ceiling and
its halo lights. Below, a plan demon-
strates the correspondence between
the bulb-like exterior and interior
spaces.

Im Innern stehen niedrige Ausstel-
lungswände unter der dunklen Decke
mit ihren Halogenlampen. Unten: Der
Grundriss demonstriert die Übereinstimmung zwischen dem kugelförmi-
gen Äußeren und den Innenräumen.

Vu de l'intérieur, les murs de
cimaises blancs et bas sous un
plafond sombre et haut équipé de
luminaires circulaires. Ci-dessous,
plan montrant l'implantation des
volumes intérieurs par rapport à la
façade bulbeuse.

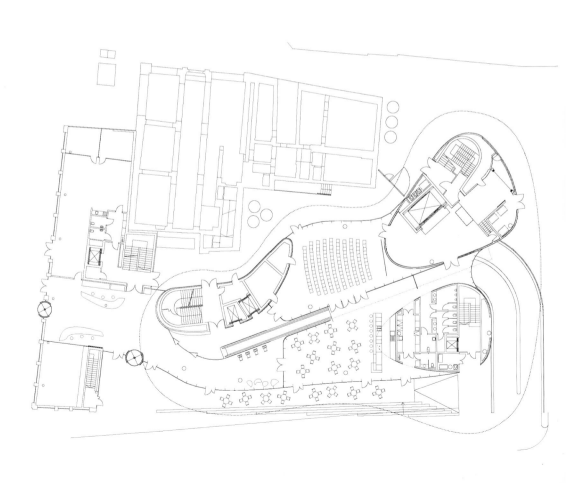

Glowing like a space-ship that has
landed in the midst of the city, the
building's skylights jut out in a
tentacle arrangement (right).

Wie bei einem gleißenden Raum-
schiff, das mitten in der Stadt gelan-
det ist, stehen die Skylights des
Gebäudes in einer tentakelartigen
Anordnung hervor (rechts).

La Kunsthaus irradie de lumière, telle
un vaisseau spatial qui aurait atterri
au milieu de la ville. Sur le toit, les
lanterneaux évoquent des départs de
tentacules (à droite).

# CHARLES DEATON

*Praxis Design LLC, Nicholas Antonopoulos*
*Mariko Arts, Charlee Deaton*
*1035 South Gaylord Street*
*Denver, CO 80209*
*USA*

*Tel: +1 303 282 1100*
*Fax: +1 303 733 1688*
*e-mail: praxarc@yahoo.com*

Born in Clayton, New Mexico in 1921, Charles Deaton and his family lived in a tent on the Oklahoma plains for two years until they were able to afford building a one-room house. By the age of 16, he was supporting himself as a commercial artist. He studied structural engineering, industrial design and architecture on his own, and earned certification. Deaton eventually became the designer of several buildings, including a two-stadium sports complex in Kansas City, Missouri known as the Truman Sports Complex or Arrowhead Stadium. An inventor and holder of over thirty US Patents, industrial designer, and creator of some 100 products in manufacture, Deaton died in 1996. Born in Centralia, Illinois in 1950, Charlee Deaton grew up in Colorado. She studied fine art, interior design, and graphic design at the Kansas City Art Institute, the Maryland Art Institute, and the Art Institute of Colorado. Her formal training was complemented by an apprenticeship with her father, Charles Deaton. In addition to her interior design practice, Charlee has worked as an artist, art educator and gallery owner and curator. She is principal and head designer of Mariko Arts. Nicholas Antonopoulos was born in Athens, Greece in 1955. He emigrated to the United States at an early age. As Principal and head designer of Praxis Design LLC, Nicholas Antonopoulos' professional background spans back to the offices of I. M. Pei and Partners in New York, where he received his architectural training. He apprenticed with architect Charles Deaton after receiving his Masters in architecture at the University of Colorado at Denver.

Charles Deaton, geboren 1921 in Clayton, New Mexico, lebte mit seiner Familie zwei Jahre lang in einem Zelt in der Prärie von Oklahoma, bevor sie es sich leisten konnte, ein Haus zu bauen, das aus einem Raum bestand. Im Alter von 16 Jahren verdiente er sich seinen Lebensunterhalt als Werbegrafiker. Nach einem Selbststudium in Bauingenieurwesen, Industriedesign und Architektur erwarb er eine amtliche Beglaubigung und plante im Anschluss mehrere Gebäude, darunter eine Sportanlage mit zwei Stadien in Kansas City, Missouri, die als Truman Sports Complex oder Arrowhead Stadium bekannt wurde. Deaton, der außerdem als Erfinder tätig war, über 30 US-Patente besaß und etwa 100 Industrieerzeugnisse gestaltet hatte, starb 1996. Seine Tochter, Charlee Deaton, wurde 1950 in Centralia, Illinois, geboren und wuchs in Colorado auf. Sie studierte Kunst, Innenarchitektur und Grafikdesign am Kansas City Art Institute, am Maryland Art Institute und am Art Institute of Colorado. Ihre akademische Ausbildung ergänzte sie durch eine Lehre bei ihrem Vater, Charles Deaton. Zusätzlich zu ihrer Arbeit als Innenarchitektin war Charlee Deaton als freie Künstlerin, Kunsterzieherin, Galeriebesitzerin und Kuratorin tätig. Heute ist sie Direktorin und leitende Designerin von Mariko Arts. Nicholas Antonopoulos, 1955 in Athen geboren, wanderte in jungen Jahren in die Vereinigten Staaten aus. Nicholas Antonopoulos, heute als Direktor und leitender Designer von Praxis Design LLC tätig, begann seine Laufbahn in den Büros von I. M. Pei and Partners in New York, wo er seine Ausbildung als Architekt erhielt. Nachdem er seinen Master of Architecture an der University of Colorado in Denver erworben hatte, absolvierte er eine Lehre bei Charles Deaton.

Charles Deaton, né à Clayton (Nouveau-Mexique) en 1921, et sa famille vivent sous une tente dans les plaines de l'Oklahoma pendant deux ans avant de pouvoir se construire une maison d'une pièce. À l'âge de 16 ans, il gagne déjà sa vie comme illustrateur. Il étudie l'ingénierie structurelle, le design industriel et l'architecture de lui-même et obtient les diplômes d'exercice de sa profession. Il conçoit plusieurs réalisations dont un complexe sportif de deux stades à Kansas City, Missouri, le Truman Sports Complex ou Arrowhead Stadium. Inventeur et dépositaire de plus de trente brevets, designer industriel et créateur de quelques 100 produits fabriqués, il disparaît en 1996. Née à Centralia, dans l'Illinois, en 1950, Charlee Deaton a grandi au Colorado. Elle étudie les beaux-arts, l'architecture intérieure et le graphisme au Kansas City Art Institute, au Maryland Art Institute et à l'Art Institute du Colorado. Sa formation est complétée par un apprentissage chez son père, Charles Deaton. En dehors de ses interventions d'architecte d'intérieur, elle exerce des activités d'artiste, d'enseignante, de galeriste et de conservatrice de musée. Elle dirige Mariko Arts. Nicholas Antonopoulos est né à Athènes, en Grèce, en 1955. Il émigre très tôt aux USA. Directeur et principal designer de Paxis Design LLC, son curriculum comprend un long passage dans l'agence de I. M. Pei and Partners à New York, où il se forme à l'architecture. Il fait son apprentissage auprès de Charles Deaton après avoir obtenu son Master of Architecture de l'Université du Colorado à Denver.

# CHARLES DEATON SCULPTURE HOUSE

*Genesee Mountain, Golden, Colorado, USA 1963–1965/2000*

*Client: Charles Deaton/John Huggins. Floor area: 250/500 m². Costs: $ 2 000 000 (year 2000 addition).*

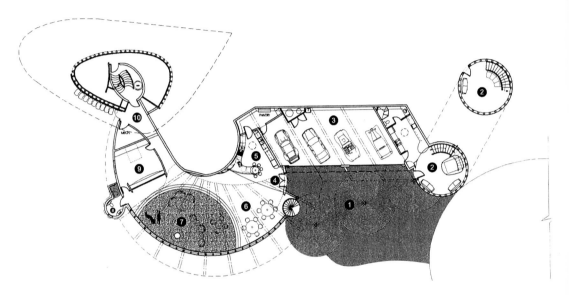

*Conceived as a sculpture, the Deaton House was carefully restored and extended by the architect's daughter Charlee and Nicholas Antonopuolos.*

*Das als Skulptur entworfene Haus wurde von der Tochter des Architekten Charlee und von Nicholas Antonopuolos restauriert und erweitert.*

*Conçue comme une sculpture, la maison a été restaurée et agrandie par la fille de l'architecte, Charlee Deaton, et Nicholas Antonopoulos.*

Charles Deaton, a self-taught architect, designed this house in 1963 as a "sculpture you could live in." Set on the north slope of Genesee Ridge outside of Denver at an altitude of over 2 000 meters, the house was built between 1963 and 1965, but its interior was not completed when the architect died in 1996. The house, described as a "clamshell" or "flying saucer," was a 250-square-meter shell. Praxis Design completed a new 500-square-meter addition in 2000. Charlee Deaton of Mariko Arts, the architect's daughter, designed the interior of the original house and the addition. As Charles Deaton described the original house, "I felt, first of all, the shape should be strong and simple enough to stand in a gallery as a work of art. On being enlarged to the size of the dwelling, it could be subdivided into living quarters. I knew, of course, when I started the sculpture that it would develop into a house. There was, however, no attempt to simply wrap a shell around a floor plan. In fact, no scale was set until the sculpture was done. The floor plan followed the modeling and contouring at a respectable distance."

Der Autodidakt Charles Deaton entwarf das Haus 1963 als eine „Skulptur, in der man leben kann". Es wurde zwischen 1963 und 1965 in der Nähe von Denver in einer Höhe von über 2 000 m errichtet, doch die Innenausstattung war noch nicht fertig, als der Architekt 1996 starb. Der als „Muschelschale" und „fliegende Untertasse" bezeichnete Bau hatte ursprünglich eine Nutzfläche von 250 m². Im Jahr 2000 realisierten die Planer von Praxis Design einen 500 m² umfassenden Anbau. Charlee Deaton von Mariko Arts, die Tochter des Architekten, gestaltete die Innenräume sowohl des ursprünglichen Hauses als auch des Erweiterungsbaus. Ihr Vater über seinen Entwurf: „Ich hatte das Gefühl, in erster Linie sollte die Form stark und einfach genug sein, um in einer Galerie als Kunstwerk zu bestehen. Wenn man dieses zu einem Haus vergrößerte, sollte es in einzelne Wohnbereiche unterteilt werden. Ich wusste natürlich von Anfang an, dass sich diese Skulptur zu einem Haus entwickeln würde, es war aber nie beabsichtigt, daraus einfach eine Hülle für einen Grundriss zu machen. Tatsächlich wurde kein Maßstab festgesetzt, bis die Skulptur fertig war."

C'est en 1963 que Charles Deaton, architecte autodidacte a conçu cette maison, qui est une « sculpture à vivre ». Édifiée entre 1963 et 1965 à 2 000 m d'altitude sur le flanc nord de la Genesee Ridge, près de Denver, son aménagement intérieur n'était pas encore achevé à la mort de l'architecte en 1996. Coque de 250 m², la maison est tantôt décrite comme une « palourde » tantôt comme une « soucoupe volante ». Praxis Design lui a ajouté une extension de 500 m² en 2000. Charlee Deaton, de Mariko Arts, fille de l'architecte, a conçu l'intérieur de la maison et son extension. Charles Deaton a décrit ainsi son projet : « Au départ, j'ai senti que la forme devait être suffisamment puissante et simple pour être installée dans un musée, comme une œuvre d'art. Agrandie à la taille d'une maison, elle pouvait se subdiviser en zones à vivre. Je savais, bien sûr, en commençant qu'elle serait par la suite développée en maison. Ce n'était cependant pas une simple tentative d'envelopper un plan au sol dans une coquille. En fait, son échelle n'a pas été déterminée avant que la sculpture ne soit achevée. Le plan suit le modelé et les contours à distance respectable. »

Looking like a self-contained viewing
deck, the house boasts a view over
more than 180° of the neighboring
mountain landscape.

Das wie eine Aussichtsplattform
wirkende Bauwerk bietet einen
Rundblick von mehr als 180° auf
die umliegende Berglandschaft.

Telle un belvédère, la maison bénéficie d'une vue à 180° sur le paysage
et les montagnes.

Despite its essentially abstract form, and its artistic origins, the house shows a modernist propensity for functional efficiency, even where the viewing platform (above) is concerned.

Trotz seiner im Wesentlichen abstrakten Form und seines künstlerischen Ursprungs zeigt das Haus einen modernistisch anmutenden Hang zu funktionaler Effizienz, was auch für die Aussichtsterrasse gilt (oben).

Bien qu'elle soit de forme essentiellement abstraite et issue d'une réflexion artistique, la maison n'en a pas moins opté pour l'efficacité fonctionnelle, y compris dans ses aspects de plate-forme d'observation.

The curved, sleek forms of the house do recall its origins in the early 1960's, but the renovation allows the viewer to appreciate how little many shapes of modernity have evolved despite the rise of computer-driven technologies, for example.

Wenn auch die geschwungenen, glatten Linien des Gebäudes an seine Entstehungszeit in den frühen 1960er Jahren erinnern, lässt die Renovierung den Betrachter dankbar erkennen, dass sich viele Formen der Moderne trotz des Aufkommens computergesteuerter Gestaltungstechniken seither kaum verändert haben.

Les formes lisse et incurvées de la maison rappellent ses origines du début des années 1960, mais sa rénovation permet au visiteur d'apprécier à quel point de nombreux aspects formels de la modernité ont faiblement évolué, malgré l'arrivée, par exemple, des technologies de CAO.

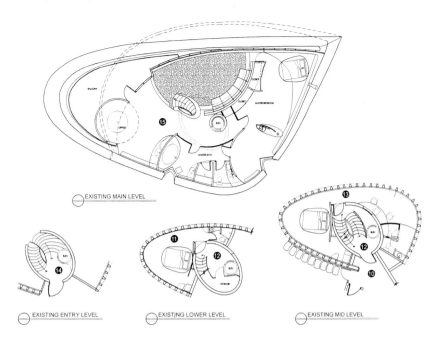

EXISTING MAIN LEVEL

EXISTING ENTRY LEVEL

EXISTING LOWER LEVEL

EXISTING MID LEVEL

This spiraling staircase is in perfect harmony with the curving exterior shapes of the house. An emphasis on sculptural shapes pervades the entire design.

Die Wendeltreppe befindet sich in vollkommener Harmonie mit den gewölbten Außenwänden des Hauses. Diese Vorliebe für skulpturale Formen durchzieht die gesamte Gestaltung.

L'escalier en spirale est en parfaite harmonie avec les formes extérieures de la maison. L'accent mis sur la qualité sculpturale des formes est omniprésent.

*The entrance door to the rear of the house expresses its "flying-saucer" esthetic, and is surprisingly closed vis-à-vis the openness of the interior.*

*Die Hinterseite des Hauses mit der Eingangstür hat etwas von der Ästhetik einer fliegenden Untertasse. Im Gegensatz zur Offenheit des Interieurs überwiegt hier eine geschlossene Gestaltung.*

*La porte d'entrée, à l'arrière de la maison exprime une esthétique de « soucoupe volante. » Elle s'oppose à l'impression d'ouverture donnée par l'intérieur.*

*Whiteness, rounded shapes and an alternation of opaque and translucent surfaces characterize the interior of the restored house.*

*Weiße Wände, gerundete Formen und der Wechsel von opaken und transluzenten Oberflächen kennzeichnen das Innere des restaurierten Hauses.*

*La maison restaurée se caractérise par des formes blanches et arrondies et l'alternance de surfaces opaques et transparentes.*

Finishes, bathroom design and windows confirm the concept of the house where every aspect seems conceived to emphasize continuity and modernity.

Oberflächen, Badezimmerdesign und Fenster folgen einem Gestaltungskonzept, in dem jedes Element Kontinuität und Modernität ausdrückt.

Les finitions comme la conception de la salle-de-bains et des fenêtres confirment le concept de la maison : tout semble conçu pour mettre en valeur la continuité et la modernité.

A couch offers a rare touch of bright color to the otherwise almost entirely white and beige interior.

Die Couch bringt einen fröhlichen Farbtupfer in das ansonsten fast ausschließlich weiße und beige Interieur.

Un canapé apporte une des rares touches de couleur dans un intérieur par ailleurs presque entièrement blanc et beige.

A flat-screen computer monitor seems very much in tune with the furniture and with the structural simplicity of the house at the level of the viewing platform.

Der Computer-Flachbildschirm auf der Ebene der Aussichtsplattform passt sehr gut zu den Möbeln und der strukturellen Schlichtheit des Hauses.

L'écran plat de l'ordinateur est en accord avec le mobilier et la simplicité de structure de la maison au niveau de la plate-forme d'observation.

# DECOI ARCHITECTS

*Mark Goulthorpe*
*Room 10-461*
*Massachusetts Institute of Technology*
*77 Massachusetts Avenue*
*Cambridge, MA 02139*
*USA*

*Tel: +1 617 452 3061*
*e-mail: mg_decoi@mit.edu*

dECOi is a small architectural/design practice that seeks to open the boundaries of conventional practice by a fresh and exploratory approach to design. In 1991 Mark Goulthorpe established dECOi to undertake a series of architectural competitions, often with a theoretical base. dECOi's work ranges from pure design and artwork through interior design to architecture and urbanism. Projects include: Bankside Paramorph (addition of a penthouse to the top of a tower, South Bank, London, 2004); Glaphyros House (Paris, France, 2002); Dietrich House (London, 2000); Swiss Re Headquarters (technical/design studies for Foster & Partners, London, 1998); Missoni Showroom (Paris, France, 1996); and the Chan (Origin) House (Kuala Lumpur, 1995). Art and research works include: Excideuil Folly (parametric 3D glyphting, Excideuil, France, 2001); Aegis Hyposurface (dynamically reconfigurable interactive architectural surface, Birmingham, 2000); and in 1993, "In the Shadow of Ledoux" (an "application/implication" exhibition, Le Magasin, Grenoble). Born in Kent, educated in Liverpool and Oregon, Mark Goulthorpe established dECOi in 1991 after having worked for four years in the office of Richard Meier in New York. He was a Unit Master Intermediate, Unit 2 at the Architectural Association (London, 1995–96); and is currently teaching Advanced Digital Design at MiT in Cambridge, Massachusetts.

dECOi ist ein kleines Architektur- und Designbüro, das sich zum Ziel gesetzt hat, die Grenzen der konventionellen Gestaltungspraxis durch einen frischen und experimentellen Zugang aufzubrechen. 1991 gründete Mark Goulthorpe das dECOi Atelier, um seine Beiträge für eine Reihe von Architekturwettbewerben einreichen zu können. dECOi's Arbeiten schließen Design und Grafik, Innenraumgestaltung sowie Architektur und Stadtentwicklung ein. Zu ihren Projekten zählen: das Haus Chan (Origin) in Kuala Lumpur (1995), der Missoni Showroom in Paris (1996), die Zentrale von Swiss Re – Technik- und Designstudien für Foster & Partners, London (1998), das Haus Dietrich in London (2000), das Haus Glaphyros in Paris (2002) und das Wohnprojekt Bankside Paramorph – die Erweiterung eines Penthouses auf einem Hochhausturm an der South Bank in London (2004). Zu seinen Kunst- und Forschungsprojekten gehören: 1993 eine „Applikation/Implikation"-Ausstellung im Le Magasin, Grenoble, mit dem Titel „In the Shadow of Ledoux", Aegis Hyposurface, eine dynamisch konfigurierbare und interaktive Architekturoberfläche in Birmingham (2000) und Excideuil Folly, eine parametrische 3D-Glyphographie im französischen Excideuil (2001). Bevor der in Kent geborene, in Liverpool und Oregon ausgebildete Mark Goulthorpe dECOi gründete, hatte er vier Jahre im Büro von Richard Meier in New York gearbeitet. Von 1995 bis 1996 war er Unit Master Intermediate der Unit 2 an der Architectural Association in London und lehrt gegenwärtig das Fach Advanced Digital Design am MIT in Cambridge, Massachusetts.

dECOi est une petite agence d'architecture et de design qui se propose de bousculer les frontières conventionnelles par une approche exploratoire nouvelle de la conception. En 1991, Mark Goulthorpe fonde dECOi-atelier pour participer à une série de concours d'architecture, souvent à partir d'une réflexion théorique. Les interventions de dECOi vont du design et de la création artistique purs à l'architecture et l'urbanisme en passant par l'architecture intérieure. Parmi ses réalisations : Bankside Paramorph (extension d'une penthouse au sommet d'une tour, South Bank, Londres, 2004) ; Glaphyros House (Paris, France, 2002) ; Dietrich House (Londres, 2000) ; siège de Swiss Re (études de design et techniques pour Foster & Partners, Londres, 1998) ; showroom Missoni (Paris, France, 1996) et Chan House (Kuala Lumpur, Malaisie, 1995). Parmi les travaux artistiques et de recherche : Excideuil Folly (glyphage paramétrique en 3D, Excideuil, France, 2001) ; Hyposurface Aegis (surface architecturale interactive à reconfiguration dynamique, Birmingham, 2000) ; « À l'ombre de Ledoux » (exposition « d'application/implication », Le Magasin, Grenoble, France, 1993). Né dans le Kent, après des études à Liverpool et en Oregon, Mark Goulthorpe fonde dECOi en 1991 après avoir travaillé quatre ans chez Richard Meier à New York. Il a été Unit Master Intermediate, Unit 2, de l'Architectural Association de Londres (1995–96) et enseigne actuellement la conception avancée par ordinateur au MIT.

# BANKSIDE PARAMORPH

*London, UK, 2003–04*

*Client: private. Floor area: 320 m². Costs: not specified.*

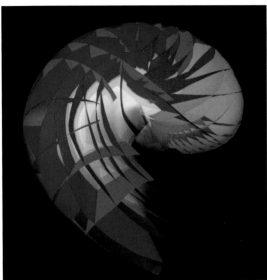

*Despite its apparent complexity, the Bankside Paramorph is designed to be manufactured and assembled within the budgets of "normal" construction methods.*

*Trotz seiner offensichtlichen Komplexität ist das Bankside Paramorph so konzipiert, dass es im Rahmen des Budgets „normaler" Konstruktionsmethoden umgesetzt werden kann.*

*Malgré sa complexité apparente, le Bankside Paramorph est conçu pour être fabriqué et assemblé pour le coût de méthodes de construction « normales. »*

This project includes the remodeling of an existing 320-square-meter flat and, above all, the rooftop addition of a 130 square-meter-aluminum honeycomb structure. Taken from airline or space technology, the aluminum honeycomb skin has sufficient strength to replace traditional structural elements and the addition is to cost no more than an ordinary space (about £500,000 in this instance). With half the weight of "normal" construction, the new elements are to be delivered in six sections and bolted together on top of this apartment building located near the Tate Modern in the Southwark area of London. Working with the engineers Arup, dECOi feels that their method of parametric modeling and their ability, with the use of new materials, to "make the skin the structure" is nothing short of revolutionary. Shaped something like a seashell, the addition is described by architect Mark Goulthorpe as an "accelerating curve," and he says he is not surprised that the mathematically derived shape approaches some of those found in nature.

Das Projekt beinhaltet den Umbau einer 320 m² großen Wohnung und einen 130 m² umfassenden Dachausbau in aluminiumverkleideter Wabenbauweise. Die aus der Raumfahrt entlehnte Aluminiumaußenhaut verfügt über genügend Formfestigkeit, um traditionelle Konstruktionsmaterialien zu ersetzen, und die Kosten für den Dachausbau liegen mit 500 000 Pfund auch nicht höher als bei weniger ausgefallenen Methoden. Der halb so viel wie „normale" Konstruktionen wiegende Aluminiumkörper wurde in sechs Abschnitten geliefert und auf dem Dach des nahe der Tate Modern liegenden Wohnblocks zusammengeschraubt. Die Architekten von dECOi, die bei diesem Projekt mit der Ingenieurfirma Arup zusammengearbeitet haben, sind davon überzeugt, dass ihre Methode des parametrischen Modellierens zusammen mit dem Einsatz neuer Materialien durchaus revolutionär ist. Der wie eine Muschel geformte Aufbau wird von dem Planer Mark Goulthorpe als eine „sich beschleunigende Kurve" beschrieben. Es habe ihn zudem nicht überrascht, dass die mathematisch entwickelte Form Ähnlichkeit mit Gebilden hat, die man in der Natur findet.

Ce projet porte sur le réaménagement d'un appartement de 320 m² non loin de la Tate Modern (Southwark, Londres) et surtout sur l'addition en toiture d'une structure en nid d'abeille d'aluminium de 130 m². Empruntée à la technologie spatiale ou aéronautique, la peau d'aluminium en nid d'abeille offre une résistance suffisante pour remplacer les éléments structurels traditionnels et cette extension ne devrait pas coûter au total plus cher qu'une construction classique (environ 500 000 de livres sterling). Pesant moitié moins qu'une solution « normale », ces nouveaux éléments ont été livrés en six parties et boulonnés ensemble sur place. Collaborant avec les ingénieurs d'Arup, dECOi pense que cette méthode de modélisation paramétrique et le recours à des matériaux nouveaux pour « faire de la peau la structure » est quasiment révolutionnaire. Pour Mark Goulthorpe, il n'est pas étonnant que cette forme issue de calculs mathématiques se rapproche de celles de la nature. Pour lui, ce volume qui évoque un coquillage fait penser à « une courbe en accélération ».

The Bankside Paramorph is conceptually related to an earlier dECOi design, the Excideuil Folly (parametric 3D glyphting, Excideuil, France, 2001).

Das Bankside Paramorph ist konzeptionell mit einem früheren dECOi Entwurf verwandt, dem 2001 entstandenen Projekt Excideuil Folly, einer parametrischen 3D-Glyphograpie in Excideuil, Frankreich.

Conceptuellement, le Bankside Paramorph est voisin d'un précédant projet de dECOi, l'Excideuil Folly (Paramétric 3D Glyphting, Excideuil, France, 2001).

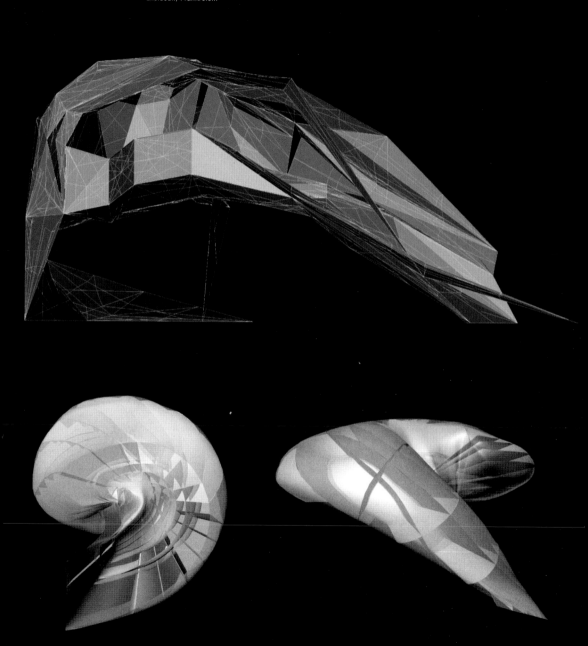

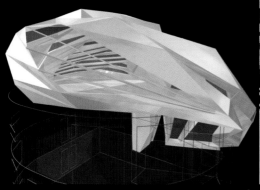

Intended for computer-driven manufacture, the addition to the roof of a
building located just next to the Tate
Modern is seen in the photo-montage
below.

Die Fotomontage (unten) zeigt den
für eine computergesteuerte Produktion entworfenen Dachausbau auf
einem Gebäude direkt neben der Tate
Modern.

Dans le photomontage ci-dessus, une
extension en toiture d'un immeuble
tout proche de la Tate Moderne,
prévue pour être réalisée selon des
processus de production pilotés par
informatique.

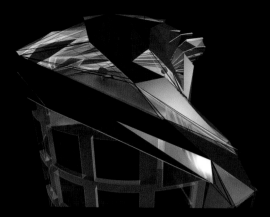

In the picture below, the edge of Tate Modern can be seen on the left. The Thames is just to the right of the field of this image.

Am linken Rand der unteren Abbildung ist eine Außenwand der Tate Modern zu erkennen. Die Themse befindet sich rechts von dem im Bild dargestellten Ausschnitt.

Dans l'image ci-dessous, un angle de la Tate Modern, à gauche. La Tamise est à droite, hors champ.

# NEIL M. DENARI

*Neil M. Denari Architects Inc.*
*12615 Washington Boulevard*
*Los Angeles, CA 90066*
*USA*

*Tel: +1 310 390 3033*
*Fax: +1 310 390 9810*
*e-mail: info@nmda-inc.com*
*Web: www.nmda-inc.com*

Neil M. Denari received a Bachelor of Architecture in 1980 from the University of Houston, and a Master of Architecture degree from Harvard in 1982, where he also studied art theory and the philosophy of science. He then spent six months working as an intern for Aerospatiale, the French aviation and space company. Neil Denari worked in New York from 1983 to 1988 as a senior designer at James Stewart Polshek & Partners before teaching at Columbia's Graduate School of Architecture and Planning. Denari moved to Los Angeles in 1988 and taught at the Southern California Institute of Architecture (SCI-Arc). In 1997, he was named the third Director of SCI-Arc. In 1996, he completed the construction of a small, experimental space at Gallery Ma in Tokyo. His other work, though highly influential, has often remained in its rather seductive virtual form. Recent projects and proposals include: L. A. Eyeworks, Showroom/Store (Los Angeles, 2001–02); Concept Design for SUN Microsystems Trade Show Structure and Office/Work Environment; Concept Design for QWEST Communications Broadband Kiosk; Concept design for SONY Qualia brand hotel and retail store; 15-story Loft Building, Union Square (New York), Feasibility study/envelope design; Water Center (Nashville, TN); D/J House, house renovation and addition (Mt. Washington, LA); NCAP Master Plan, a 16.5-acre plan for housing, park space, lease space, commissioned by the Nashville Cultural Arts Project; and Endeavor Talent and Literary Agency Offices and Theater (Beverly Hills, CA).

Neil M. Denari erwarb 1980 den Bachelor of Architecture an der University of Houston und 1982 den Master of Architecture in Harvard, wo er außerdem Kunsttheorie und Wissenschaftsphilosophie studierte. Anschließend arbeitete er ein halbes Jahr als Praktikant bei dem französischen Flugzeug- und Raumfahrtunternehmen Aerospatiale. Von 1983 bis 1988 war Denari als Planungsleiter bei James Stewart Polshek & Partners in New York tätig und lehrte an der Graduate School of Architecture and Planning der Columbia University. 1988 zog er nach Los Angeles und lehrte am Southern California Institute of Architecture (SCI-Arc). 1996 führte er die Konstruktion eines kleinen, experimentellen Raums in der Galerie Ma in Tokio aus. Obgleich sehr einflussreich, blieben viele seiner Arbeiten virtuelle Konstrukte. Zu seinen jüngsten Projekten und Entwürfen gehören: der Laden/Showroom von L. A. Eyeworks in Los Angeles (2001–02), die Designkonzepte für Messestand und Büro/Workstation von SUN Microsystems, für den Verkaufspavillon von QWEST Communications Broadband und für das Qualia Hotel mit Ladenlokal von SONY, die Machbarkeitsstudie und das Umhüllungsdesign für ein 15-stöckiges Loftgebäude am Union Square in New York, das Water Center in Nashville, Tennessee, Renovierung und Anbau für das D/J House in Mt. Washington, Los Angeles, der Masterplan für NCAP, der vom Nashville Cultural Arts Project in Auftrag gegebene Bebauungsplan für ein 16,5 ha großes Gelände mit Wohnanlage, Geschäften und Parkplatz sowie Büro und Theater für die Endeavor Talent and Literary Agency im kalifornischen Beverly Hills.

Neil M. Denari est Bachelor of Architecture de l'Université de Houston (1980) et Master of Architecture de Harvard (1982), où il a également étudié la théorie de l'art et la philosophie des sciences. Il travaille ensuite pendant six mois chez le constructeur aéronautique Aérospatiale, en France. Il est senior designer chez James Stewart Polshek & Partners à New York (1983–1988) avant d'enseigner à la Graduate School of Architecture and Planning de la Columbia University. Il s'installe à Los Angeles en 1988 et enseigne au Southern California Institute of Architecture (SCI-Arc) dont il sera le troisième directeur en 1997. En 1996, il achève la construction d'un petit espace expérimental pour la Galerie Ma à Tokyo. Ses autres travaux, bien que très influents, restent souvent sous une forme virtuelle séduisante. Parmi ses projets et propositions récents : le showroom-magasin d'Eyeworks (Los Angeles, 2001–02) ; le concept structurel de salle des marchés et d'environnement de bureaux de SUN Microsystems ; le concept de kiosque de communications ADSL de QWEST ; le concept d'hôtel et de magasin SONY Qualia ; l'immeuble de lofts de 15 niveaux, Union Square (New York, étude de faisabilité/conception de l'enveloppe) ; Water Center (Nashville, Tennessee) ; D/J House, rénovation et extension d'une maison (Mount Washington, Los Angeles) ; le plan directeur de la NCAP, plan pour logements, parc, locaux à louer, commande du Nashville Cultural Arts Project ; les bureaux et théâtre de l'agence littéraire Endeavor (Beverly Hills, Californie).

# TOMIHIRO HOSHINO MUSEUM

*Azuma-Mura, Gunma, Japan, 2001*

*Client: Tomihiro Museum of Shi-Ga, Azuma-Mura. Floor area: 3 000 m². Costs: not specified.*

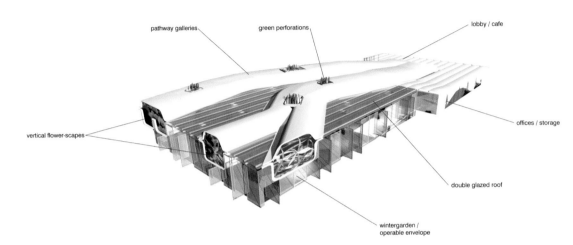

pathway galleries · green perforations · lobby / cafe · offices / storage · vertical flower-scapes · double glazed roof · wintergarden / operable envelope

Like many small, isolated Japanese villages, the community of Azuma-Mura in the mountains of Gunma prefecture decided that certain government credits would be well spent on a new museum. They organized a competition for a 3 000-square-meter facility to be dedicated to the work of a locally famous painter, Tomihiro Hoshino. Severely injured in a 1972 gymnastics accident, the artist began painting with pencil or brush held in his mouth. He calls his work "shi-ga" – watercolors of flowers and poetry. As the architect puts it, "his poetic images are an expression of his search for the essence of life, its simplicity and gentleness as reflected in the form of flowers." Of some 300 works painted by Tomihiro Hoshino in the past 30 years, 120 are to be exhibited in this museum at any one time. Offices, a gift shop, café, temporary exhibition space and a learning center were also part of the program requirements. As Neil Denari has written, "the scheme has a formal relation to the artist's brush and to the flower itself, but more importantly it articulates the Tomihiro galleries as pathways intended to generate a feeling of movement, of a search for essences. The entrance area is located 1.5 meters below grade with a winter garden level at 3.0 meters below grade. The galleries float above this level." There were 1 250 entries in this open international competition for which Toyo Ito chaired a jury that included Kengo Kuma, Rikken Yamamoto and Wiel Arets. Neil Denari was in the final 60, but did not win the competition.

Wie viele kleine und abgelegene Gemeinden Japans entschied sich auch die Verwaltung des in den Bergen der Präfektur Gunma gelegenen Dorfes Azuma-Mura, die von der Landesregierung bereitgestellten Gelder für ein neues Museum auszugeben. Der Wettbewerb zur Gestaltung der 3 000 m² umfassenden Anlage war dem regional berühmten Maler Tomihiro Hoshino gewidmet. Nach einer schweren Verletzung, die sich der Künstler 1972 bei einem Sportunfall zugezogen hatte, begann er zu malen, indem er Bleistift oder Pinsel mit dem Mund führt. Er nennt seine Bilder „shi-ga" – Aquarelle der Blumen und Poesie. „Hoshinos poetische Bilder", so Neil Denari, der Planer des hier vorgestellten Entwurfs, „sind Ausdruck seiner Suche nach der Essenz des Lebens, seiner Schlichtheit und Sanftheit, wie sie sich in der Gestalt der Blumen spiegelt." Von den 300 Bildern, die der Künstler im Lauf der letzten 30 Jahre gemalt hat, sollen 120 in einer Dauerausstellung zu sehen sein. Darüber hinaus sollte das Projekt Büros, einen Museumsshop, ein Café sowie Räume für Sonderausstellungen und für ein Lernzentrum umfassen. Sein Entwurf, so Denari, stellt einen formalen Bezug zu dem Pinsel des Künstlers und zu einer Blume her. In erster Linie wird hier jedoch die Anordnung der Ausstellungsräume als Weg inszeniert, der dem Besucher ein Gefühl von Bewegung und der Suche nach dem Wesentlichen hervorruft. Der Eingangsbereich wurde 1,5 m und der Wintergarten 3 m unter die Grasnarbe versenkt, während sich die Ausstellungsräume auf der darüber liegenden Ebene befinden. Für den offenen, internationalen Wettbewerb, bei dem Toyo Ito einer Jury vorsaß, zu der unter anderem Kengo Kuma, Rikken Yamamoto und Wiel Arets gehörten, wurden 1 250 Beiträge eingereicht. Neil Denaris Vorschlag kam zwar in die aus 60 Entwürfen bestehende Endauswahl, ging aber nicht als Sieger aus dem Wettbewerb hervor.

Comme plusieurs petits bourgs japonais isolés, la commune d'Azuma-Mura dans les montagnes de la préfecture de Gunma a décidé de consacrer certains crédits publics à un nouveau musée. Elle a donc lancé un concours pour un bâtiment de 3 000 m² consacré à l'œuvre d'un célèbre peintre de la région, Tomihiro Hoshino. Gravement blessé en 1972 en faisant de la gymnastique, l'artiste peint en tenant ses instruments dans sa bouche. Il qualifie ses œuvres de *shi-ga*, d'aquarelles de fleurs et de poésie. Pour Neil Denari : « Ses images poétiques sont une expression de sa quête de l'essence de la vie… sa simplicité et sa gentillesse se retrouvent dans les formes de ses fleurs. » 120 des 300 œuvres réalisées par le peintre au cours de ces 30 dernières années sont exposées en permanence. Des bureaux, une boutique, un café, un lieu d'expositions temporaires et un centre d'éducation figuraient également au programme. « Le projet évoque une relation formelle avec la brosse utilisée par l'artiste et les fleurs elles-mêmes, mais surtout articule les galeries selon des itinéraires qui génèrent un sentiment de mouvement à la recherche de l'essentiel. L'entrée est située à 1,5 m au-dessous du niveau du sol et le jardin d'hiver à 3 m. Les galeries semblent flotter au-dessus. » 1 250 participations ont été adressées au jury du concours présidé par Toyo Ito, qui comprenait Kengo Kuma, Rikken Yamamoto et Wiel Arets. Neil Denari, retenu lors de la première sélection de 60 projets, n'a pas remporté ce concours.

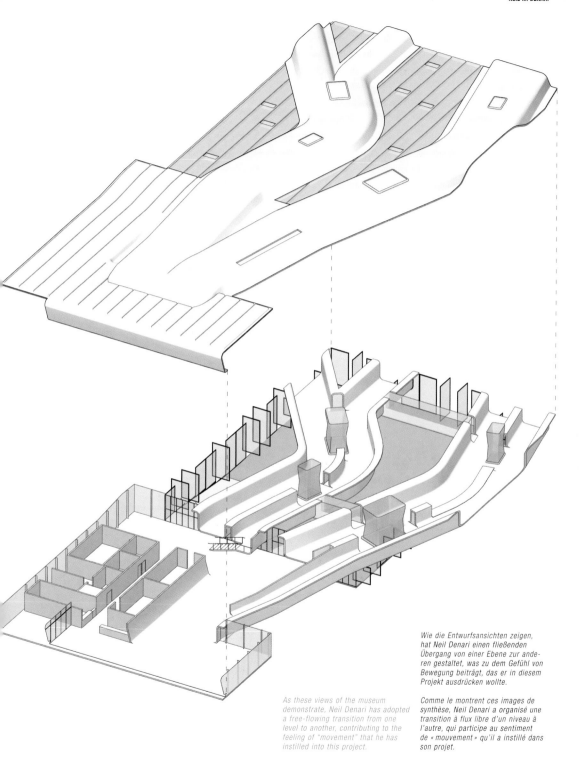

Wie die Entwurfsansichten zeigen,
hat Neil Denari einen fließenden
Übergang von einer Ebene zur ande-
ren gestaltet, was zu dem Gefühl von
Bewegung beiträgt, das er in diesem
Projekt ausdrücken wollte.

As these views of the museum
demonstrate, Neil Denari has adopted
a free-flowing transition from one
level to another, contributing to the
feeling of "movement" that he has
instilled into this project.

Comme le montrent ces images de
synthèse, Neil Denari a organisé une
transition à flux libre d'un niveau à
l'autre, qui participe au sentiment
de « mouvement » qu'il a instillé dans
son projet.

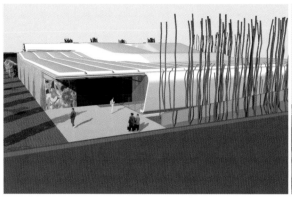

Faithful to the seamless, unified surfaces that he favors, Denari redefines such essential features as the museum entrance and its glazing.

Den von ihm bevorzugten, nahtlos ineinanderübergehenden Oberflächen treu bleibend, bietet Denari eine Neudefinition so wesentlicher Merkmale wie des Museumseingangs mit seiner Verglasung.

Fidèle aux type de surfaces fluides et unies qu'il apprécie, Denari a redéfini des éléments essentiels comme l'entrée du musée et son vitrage.

Wrap-around surfaces and a generally light-toned color scheme used for these interior views emphasize the continuity of the architecture from inside to outside.

Umlaufende Wandoberflächen und eine durchgehend helle Farbgebung für die Innenräume unterstreichen das architektonische Kontinuum von Innen und Außen.

Des surfaces enveloppantes et une palette chromatique de tons généralement légers soulignent la continuité architecturale entre extérieur et intérieur.

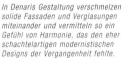

In Denari's hands, solid facades and glazing blend into one another giving a feeling of unity that escaped more box-like modernist designs of the past.

In Denaris Gestaltung verschmelzen solide Fassaden und Verglasungen miteinander und vermitteln so ein Gefühl von Harmonie, das den eher schachtelartigen modernistischen Designs der Vergangenheit fehlte.

Les façades pleines et les parois vitrées fusionnent pour donner un sentiment d'unité différent des précédents projets de l'architecte, davantage orientés vers des formes de boîtes modernistes.

The presence of natural forms, but also a flowing openness in the design, seem well adapted to the artist's paintings of flowers.

Die Präsenz natürlicher Formen und eine fließende Offenheit in der Gestaltung bilden einen passenden Hintergrund für die Blumenbilder des Malers Hoshino.

La présence de formes naturelles, mais aussi l'ouverture et la fluidité, semblent bien adaptée aux peintures de fleurs de l'artiste.

# DILLER + SCOFIDIO

*Diller + Scofidio*
*36 Cooper Sq 5F*
*New York, NY 10003*
*USA*

*Tel: +1 212 260 7971*
*Fax: +1 212 260 7924*
*e-mail: disco@dillerscofidio.com*
*Web: www.dillerscofidio.com*

Elizabeth Diller is Professor of Architecture at Princeton University and Ricardo Scofidio is Professor of Architecture at The Cooper Union in New York. According to their own description, "Diller + Scofidio is a collaborative, interdisciplinary studio involved in architecture, the visual arts and the performing arts. The team is primarily involved in thematically-driven experimental works that take the form of architectural commissions, temporary installations and permanent site-specific installations, multi-media theater, electronic media, and print." Their work includes "Slither," 100 units of social housing in Gifu, Japan, and "Moving Target," a collaborative dance work with Charleroi/Danse Belgium. Installations by Diller + Scofidio have been seen at the Cartier Foundation in Paris (Master/Slave, 1999); the Museum of Modern Art in New York, and the Musée de la Mode in Paris. Recently, they completed The Brasserie Restaurant (Seagram Building, New York, 1998–99) and the Blur Building, (Expo.02, Yverdon-les-Bains, Switzerland, 2000–2002). They were selected as architects for the Institute of Contemporary Art in Boston, the Eyebeam Institute in the Chelsea area of Manhattan, and Lincoln Center (New York).

Elizabeth Diller ist als Professorin für Architektur an der Princeton University und Ricardo Scofidio als Professor für Architektur an der Cooper Union School of Architecture in New York tätig. Ihrer eigenen Beschreibung zufolge ist „Diller + Scofidio ein interdisziplinäres Gemeinschaftsprojekt, das sich mit Architektur, bildender und darstellender Kunst beschäftigt. Das Team führt hauptsächlich experimentelle Arbeiten durch, die sich auf der Grundlage von Architektur, Installation, Multimedia-präsentation, elektronischen Medien und Druckgrafik mit bestimmten Themen auseinandersetzen." Zu ihren Projekten zählen: „Slither", 100 Sozialwohnungen in Gifu, Japan, und „Moving Target", eine Tanztheaterproduktion in Zusammenarbeit mit der Tanzformation Charleroi/Danse Belgium. Installationen von Diller + Scofidio wurden in der Fondation Cartier in Paris (Master/Slave, 1999), im Museum of Modern Art in New York und im Musée de la Mode in Paris gezeigt. Zu ihren neueren Architektur-arbeiten gehören das Restaurant The Brasserie im Seagram Building in New York (1998–99) und das Blur Building für die Expo.02 im schweizerischen Yverdon-les-Bains (2000–2002). Außerdem erhielten sie die Aufträge für das Institute of Contemporary Art in Boston, das Eyebeam Institute im Manhattener Stadtteil Chelsea sowie das Lincoln Center in New York.

Elizabeth Diller est professeur associé à Princeton et Ricardo Scofidio professeur d'architecture à The Cooper Union, New York. Selon leur présentation: «Diller + Scofidio est une agence interdisciplinaire coopérative qui se consacre à l'architecture, aux arts plastiques et aux arts du spectacle. L'équipe travaille essentiellement sur des recherches thématiques expérimentales qui prennent la forme de commandes architecturales, d'installations temporaires, d'installations permanentes adaptées au site, théâtre multimédia, médias électroniques et édition.» Parmi leurs projets récents: Slither, 100 logements sociaux (Gifu, Japon), Moving Target, œuvre chorégraphique en collaboration avec Charleroi/Danse (Belgique). Les installations de Diller + Scofidio ont été présentées à la Fondation Cartier à Paris (Master/Slave, 1999) au Museum of Modern Art de New York et au Musée de la mode à Paris. Plus récemment, ils ont achevé le Brasserie Restaurant (Seagram Building, New York, 1998–99); le Blur Building (Expo.02, Yverdon-les-Bains, Suisse, 2000–2002) et ont été sélectionnés pour la construction de l'Institute of Contemporary Art à Boston, l'Eyebeam Institute à Manhattan (Chelsea) et le Lincoln Center (New York).

# BLUR BUILDING, EXPO.02

*Yverdon-les-Bains, Switzerland, 2000–2002*

*Client: Swiss Expo.02. Dimensions: 100 x 60 x 12 m (fog structure). Costs: $ 7 500 000.*

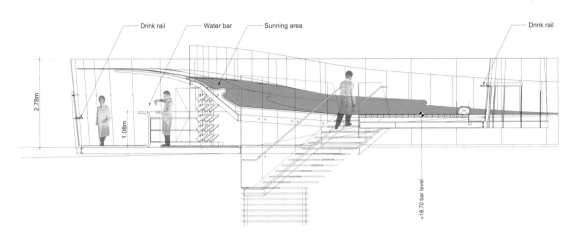

Drink rail · Water bar · Sunning area · Drink rail

2.78m

1.08m

+18.70 bar level

Like other structures intended for the Swiss Expo.02, the Blur Building was conceived as an ephemeral building anchored in the lake. Here the tube-like structure with the water-mist emitting nozzles is visible. Below, the mist begins to emerge around the frame.

Wie andere Beiträge für die Schweizer Expo.02 wurde auch das Blur Building als eine vorübergehend im See verankerte Architektur konzipiert. Hier ist die röhrenförmige Anlage mit den Nebel-Düsen sichtbar. Unten: Der Nebel beginnt, sich um die Rahmenkonstruktion auszubreiten.

Comme d'autres projets réalisés pour l'Expo nationale suisse de 2002, le Blur Building est un pavillon éphémère au-dessus du lac. Ici, on aperçoit la structure en forme de tube et la brume émise par les buses. Ci-dessous, la brume commençant à se développer autour de la structure.

Flat exit ramp of prefabricated FVK sections
Flache Ausgangsrampe aus vorfabriziertem FVK-Material

Sloped entrance ramp of prefabricated FVK sections
Aufsteigende Eingangsrampe aus vorfabriziertem FVK-Material

FVK landing

FVK landing

boardwalk(opt.)

boardwalk(o

This structure was intended to resemble nothing so much as a cloud hovering over Lake Neuchatel. 100 m wide by 60 m deep and 25 m high, rising above the water, the "cloud" effect was obtained through the use of filtered lake water "shot as a fine mist through a dense array of 31 500 high-pressure water nozzles integrated into a large cantilevered tensegrity structure." The first fog building was made by the Japanese artist Fujiko Nakaya for the 1970 Osaka World's Fair. Hers was a fog layer surfacing a geodesic dome. Nakaya was an advisor to the architects in Yverdon on technical and esthetic matters. A ramp led visitors into the cloud where they were enveloped by a sort of sensory deprivation due to the "white-out" accompanied by "white noise" related to the mist projectors. "Unlike entering a space, entering Blur," say Diller and Scofidio, "is like stepping into a habitable medium, one that is formless, featureless, depthless, scaleless, massless, surfaceless, and dimensionless." As the architects further explained, "Blur is a reaction to the over-saturation of visual media in recent national and world expositions that, more and more, have become competition grounds for state-of-the-art immersion technologies and simulation extravaganzas. These large-scale exhibitions feed our insatiable appetite for visual stimulation with ever-greater digital virtuosity. In concert with consumer culture, satisfaction is measured in pixels per inch. High definition has become the new orthodoxy. By contrast, Blur is decidedly low-definition." In somewhat more poetic terms, the English newsweekly *The Economist* published an article on the Blur Building under the title "Heaven's Gate" (August 24, 2002). They wrote: "To enter this sublime building perched in the landscape of the Swiss Alps feels like walking into a poem – it is part of nature but removed from reality."

Das Blur Building, eine 100 m lange und 60 m breite Konstruktion, die sich 25 m über dem Wasserspiegel erhob, sollte aussehen wie eine über dem Neuburger See schwebende Wolke. Dieser Wolken-Effekt wurde durch gefiltertes Seewasser erzielt, das als feiner Nebel aus 31 500 Hochdruck-Wasserdüsen versprüht wurde, die in eine große, freitragende Seilnetz-Konstruktion eingebaut waren. Das erste „Nebelgebäude" stammte von der japanischen Künstlerin Fujiko Nakaya, das 1970 für die Weltausstellung in Osaka entworfen wurde. Nakaya fungierte bei der Realisierung des Blur Building als Beraterin für technische und ästhetische Fragen. In Yverdon gelangten die Besucher über eine Rampe ins Innere der Wolke, wo sie aufgrund eines optischen „weißen Nichts", begleitet vom „weißen Rauschen" der Nebelapparate, eine Art sensorischen Entzug erlebten. „Im Gegensatz zum Betreten eines Raums", so Diller und Scofidio, „ist das Betreten des Blur, als schritte man in ein bewohnbares Medium, aber eines ohne Form, ohne besondere Merkmale, ohne Tiefe, ohne Volumen, ohne Gewicht, ohne Oberfläche und ohne Dimension. Blur ist eine Reaktion auf die Übersättigung durch visuelle Medien, wie sie in letzter Zeit auf nationalen und internationalen Ausstellungen üblich geworden ist. Diese Großereignisse sind mehr und mehr zum Austragungsort von Wettbewerben der neuesten und ausgefallensten Technologien und Simulationen geworden und bedienen unseren unstillbaren Appetit nach visuellen Reizen mit immer größerer digitaler Virtuosität. In Übereinstimmung mit unserer Konsumkultur wird die Qualität nur mehr in Pixelauflösung gemessen, und ‚high definition' ist zur neuen Religion geworden. Blur dagegen ist entschieden ‚low-definition'." In etwas poetischeren Worten wird das Blur Building in einem Artikel der englischen Wochenzeitung *The Economist* beschrieben, der am 24. August 2002 unter der Überschrift „Heaven's Gate" erschien: „Wenn man dieses grandiose, in der Landschaft der Schweizer Alpen gelandete Bauwerk betritt, kommt es einem vor, als betrete man ein Gedicht – es ist Teil der Natur, aber weit entfernt von der Realität."

Cette réalisation avait pour ambition de créer un nuage au-dessus du lac de Neuchâtel. De 100 m de large, 60 de profondeur et 25 de haut, « flottant » au-dessus de l'eau, elle obtenait l'effet recherché grâce à la projection d'eau du lac « en une fine brume générée par un réseau de 31 500 buses haute-pression intégrées à une grande ossature en porte-à-faux et tenségrité ». La première construction de ce genre, vue à l'Exposition universelle d'Osaka en 1970, était signée de l'artiste japonais Fujiko Nakaya. Il avait recréé un brouillard à la surface d'un dôme géodésique, et a d'ailleurs conseillé les architectes d'Yverdon aussi bien sur le plan technique qu'esthétique. En Suisse, une rampe menait les visiteurs à l'intérieur du nuage, où ils se trouvaient plongés dans une atmosphère de privation sensorielle due à l'effet de trop-plein produit par la projection d'eau et le bruit écrasant. « À la différence de la sensation de pénétrer dans un volume », expliquent Diller et Scofidio, « c'était comme accéder à un médium habitable, mais sans forme, sans caractéristique quelconque, sans profondeur, sans échelle, sans masse, sans surface et sans dimension… Blur est une réaction à la sursaturation des médias visuels dans les expositions internationales récentes qui deviennent de plus en plus un lieu de compétition pour technologies d'avant-garde et jeux sur la stimulation des sens. Ces grandes expositions nourrissent notre appétit insatiable pour la stimulation visuelle et une virtuosité numérique sans cesse croissante. De concert avec la culture de consommation, la satisfaction se mesure maintenant en pixels au cm². La haute définition est devenue la nouvelle orthodoxie. Par contraste, Blur, est résolument basse-définition. » En termes presque poétiques, l'hebdomadaire britannique *The Economist* a publié un article sur ce projet sous le titre de « La Porte du ciel » (24 août 2002), écrivant : « Entrer dans ce bâtiment sublime perché dans les Alpes suisse est comme entrer dans un poème, c'est un morceau de nature mais détaché du réel. »

*In good weather and wind conditions, the Blur Building was a remarkable success, almost appearing to be a cloud floating on the lake. Visitors within the structure saw only shadow-like forms of each other.*

*Bei guten Wetter- und Windverhältnissen war das Blur Building ein großer Erfolg und sah fast aus, wie eine über dem See schwebende Wolke. Die Besucher im Innern waren nur schemenhaft zu erkennen.*

*Par beau temps et lorsque le vent était favorable, le Blur Building, nuage au-dessus du lac, s'est révélé une remarquable réussite. Les visiteurs ne voyaient d'eux-mêmes que des formes fantomatiques.*

*The Weather Proje*

# OLAFUR ELIASSON

*Tanya Bonakdar Gallery*
*521 West 21st Street*
*New York, NY 10011*
*USA*

*Tel: +1 212 414 4144*
*Fax: +1 212 414 1535*
*e-mail: mail@tanyabonakdargallery.com*
*Web: www.olafureliasson.net*

Olafur Eliasson was born in 1967 in Copenhagen, Denmark of Icelandic parents. He attended the Royal Academy of Arts in Copenhagen (1989-95). He has participated in numerous exhibitions and his work is included in collections ranging from the Solomon R Guggenheim Museum, New York, the Museum of Contemporary Art, Los Angeles and the Deste Foundation, Athens to the Tate Modern, London. Recently he has had solo exhibitions at Kunsthaus Bregenz, the Musée d'Art Moderne de la Ville de Paris and the ZKM in Karlsruhe and represented Denmark in the 2003 Venice Biennale. He lives and works in Berlin. His installations feature elements appropriated from nature – billowing steam evoking a water geyser, rainbows or fog-filled rooms. By introducing "natural" phenomena, such as water, mist or light, into an artificial setting, be it a city street or an art gallery, the artist encourages the viewer to reflect on their own perception of the physical world. This moment of perception, when the viewer pauses to consider what they are experiencing, has been described by Eliasson as "seeing yourself sensing." For "The Mediated Motion" at the Kunsthaus Bregenz (2001), Eliasson created a sequence of spaces filled with natural materials including water, fog, earth, wood, fungus and duckweed. During their visit to the exhibition, visitors were exposed to a variety of sights, smells, and textures – which had been precisely selected by the artist. Eliasson also modified the orthogonal nature of the building by inserting a slanting floor, which made visitors more conscious of the act of movement through the gallery space.

Olafur Eliasson, 1967 als Kind isländischer Eltern in Kopenhagen geboren, studierte von 1989 bis 1995 an der Königlichen Kunstakademie in Kopenhagen. Er war bereits auf zahlreichen Ausstellungen vertreten und seine Arbeiten befinden sich in den Sammlungen von Museen wie dem Solomon R. Guggenheim Museum in New York, dem Museum of Contemporary Art in Los Angeles, der Stiftung Deste in Athen sowie der Tate Modern in London. In jüngster Zeit waren ihm Einzelausstellungen im Kunsthaus Bregenz, dem Musée d'Art Moderne de la Ville de Paris und dem Zentrum für Kunst und Medientechnologie (ZKM) in Karlsruhe gewidmet. Außerdem vertrat er Dänemark auf der Biennale 2003 in Venedig. Derzeit lebt und arbeitet er in Berlin. Seine Installationen enthalten häufig Elemente aus der Natur – wogende Dampfschwaden, die an Geysire denken lassen, Regenbogen oder nebelgefüllte Räume. Indem er „natürliche" Phänomene wie Wasser, Nebel oder Licht in ein künstliches Umfeld integriert, sei es eine Innenstadtstraße oder eine Kunstgalerie, lädt er die Betrachter dazu ein, über ihre Wahrnehmung der physischen Welt zu reflektieren. Dieser Moment der Bewusstwerdung, in dem der Betrachter innehält, um darüber nachzudenken, was er oder sie gerade erlebt, wurde von Eliasson als „seeing yourself sensing" beschrieben, als ein Sich-dabei-zusehen, wie man empfindet. Für die Ausstellung „The Mediated Motion", die 2001 im Kunsthaus Bregenz gezeigt wurde, schuf Eliasson eine Abfolge von Innenräumen, die mit natürlichen Materialien wie Wasser, Nebel, Erde, Holz, Schwämmen und Wasserpflanzen gefüllt waren. Während die Besucher durch die Ausstellung gingen, wurden sie mit einer Vielzahl von Anblicken, Gerüchen und Oberflächen konfrontiert – Sinneseindrücken, die der Künstler genau kalkuliert hatte. Darüber hinaus verlegte Eliasson in den Ausstellungsräumen einen geneigten Fußboden, durch den sich die Besucher ihrer Bewegungen bewusster wurden.

Olafur Eliasson est né à Copenhague en 1967 de parents islandais. Il étudie à l'Académie royale des arts de Copenhague (1989–1995). Il a participé à de nombreuses expositions et ses travaux sont présents dans des collections comme le Solomon R. Guggenheim Museum, New York, le Museum of Contemporary Art, Los Angeles, la Deste Foundation, Athènes ou la Tate Modern de Londres. Il a tenu des expositions personnelles à la Kunsthaus de Bregenz (Suisse), au Musée d'art moderne de la ville de Paris, au ZKM à Karlsruhe (Allemagne) et a représenté le Danemark à la Biennale de Venise (2003). Il vit et travaille à Berlin. Ses installations utilisent des éléments pris dans la nature : geyser d'eau tourbillonnante et fumante, arc-en-ciel, pièces remplies de brouillard. En introduisant des phénomènes « naturels » comme l'eau, la brume ou la lumière dans un cadre artificiel que ce soit dans une rue ou une galerie, il encourage le spectateur à réfléchir sur sa perception du monde physique. Ce moment de perception est décrit par Eliasson comme « se voir soi-même en train de ressentir ». Pour « Le mouvement médiatisé » à la Kunsthaus Bregenz (2001), il a créé une séquence d'espaces remplis de matériaux naturels : eau, brouillard, terre, bois, champignons et duvet de canard. Au cours de leur visite, les spectateurs sont exposés à diverses visions, odeurs et textures, choisies par l'artiste. Il a également modifié le caractère orthogonal du bâtiment en insérant un sol incliné.

# THE WEATHER PROJECT

*Turbine Hall, Tate Modern, London, UK, October 16, 2003–March 21, 2004*

*Client: Tate Modern/Unilever. Size: 3 250 m² (mirrored surface). Costs: £ 250 000.*

In The Weather Project, the fourth in the annual Unilever Series of commissions for the Turbine Hall, Olafur Eliasson takes the ubiquitous subject of the weather as the basis for exploring ideas about experience, mediation and representation. The earlier participants in the series, Louise Bourgeois, Juan Munoz, and Anish Kapoor, saw the expanse of the Turbine Hall as a location of sculptures or environments on the scale of une space. Eliasson has occupied it just as surely, but in a much less intrusive way. Representations of the sun and sky dominate the expanse of the Hall. The entire ceiling is covered by a mirror, giving visitors the rare opportunity to see themselves "from above." At the end of the Hall a giant semi-circular form made up of hundreds of mono-frequency lamps is reflected in the mirrors, giving the impression of a full, setting sun. Often used in street lighting, mono-frequency lamps emit light at a narrow frequency making colors other than yellow and black invisible, transforming the area around the "sun" into "a vast duotone landscape." A fine mist permeates the space, as though visitors had suddenly been transported to an unnamed outdoor location. Throughout the day, the mist accumulates into faint, cloud-like formations, before dissipating across the space. Although photographs do capture something of the magic of this installation, the surprise of actually seeing it in the space is unequalled. The industrial volume of the Turbine Hall has less to do with architects Herzog & de Meuron than it does with the initial design of the Bankside Power Station. More than the architects themselves, this artist, Olafur Eliasson, has transformed the space with little more than smoke and mirrors – an act of architectural magic.

In „The Weather Project", dem vierten Teil der alljährlich von Unilever veranstalteten Auftragsserie für die Turbinenhalle in der Tate Modern, setzt sich Olafur Eliasson ausgehend vom Thema Wetter mit Ideen über Erfahrung, Vermittlung und Repräsentation auseinander. Während die früheren Teilnehmer, Louise Bourgeois, Juan Muñoz und Anish Kapoor, den ausgedehnten Raum für Skulpturen oder Environments nutzten, die in ihren Ausmaßen dem Standort entsprachen, hat Eliasson den Raum zwar ebenso selbstbewusst, aber wesentlich weniger invasiv in Besitz genommen. In seiner Installation mit Darstellungen der Sonne und des Himmels wird der gesamte Deckenbereich von einer Spiegelfläche eingenommen. Am hinteren Ende der Halle sieht man eine riesige, kreisrunde Form, die aus Hunderten Monofrequenzlampen besteht, und wie eine untergehende Sonne wirkt. Die häufig bei Straßenbeleuchtungen verwendeten Monofrequenzlampen verströmen ihr Licht als schmales Strahlenbündel, wodurch alle Farben außer Gelb und Schwarz ausgeblendet werden. In Eliassons Installation führt dieser Effekt dazu, dass sich der Bereich um die „Sonne" in eine weite Zweifarbenlandschaft verwandelt. Außerdem liegt ein feiner Nebel über der Szenerie, was das Ganze noch unwirklicher macht. Im Lauf des Tages verdichtet sich der Nebel regelmäßig in zarte, wolkenähnliche Gebilde, die sich im ganzen Raum verteilen und wieder auflösen. Obwohl auch auf Fotografien etwas von der Magie dieser Installation einfangen lässt, ist das Raumerlebnis in Natura unvergleichlich. Der industrielle Charakter der Turbinenhalle wurde von den Architekten Herzog & de Meuron unverändert gelassen und erinnert damit an ihren ursprünglichen Zweck im ehemaligen Kraftwerk. Und so hat Olafur Eliasson mehr als die Architekten der Tate Modern selbst den Raum mit wenig mehr als Nebel und Spiegeln transformiert – ein Akt architektonischer Magie.

Dans The Weather Project, quatrième des commandes Unilever pour le Turbine Hall de la Tate Modern, Olafur Eliasson s'est emparé du sujet du temps pour explorer l'expérimentation, la médiation et la représentation. Les précédents participants, Louise Bourgeois, Juan Muñoz et Anish Kapoor avaient créé des sculptures ou des environnements à l'échelle de ce hall gigantesque. Eliasson l'a occupé tout aussi efficacement, mais d'une façon beaucoup moins intrusive. Ses représentations du soleil et du ciel dominent le volume du hall. Le plafond tout entier est recouvert d'un miroir qui permet aux visiteurs de se voir « du dessus ». À l'extrémité du hall, une forme géante semi-circulaire composée de centaines de lampes monofréquence se reflète dans les miroirs donnant l'impression d'un soleil couchant. Souvent utilisées en éclairage public, ces ampoules émettent une lumière de fréquence réduite qui rend les couleurs autres que le noir et le jaune invisibles, et transforment la zone autour du « soleil » en un « vaste paysage en bichromie ». Une brume très fine envahit le volume comme si les spectateurs étaient subitement transportés dans un lieu extérieur et inconnu. Tout au long de la journée, la brume s'accumule en petites formations nuageuses, avant de se dissiper dans l'espace. Si les photographies captent une partie de la magie de cette installation, la surprise provoquée par la réalité reste extraordinaire. Plus encore qu'Herzog & de Meuron, Olafur Eliasson a su transformer cet immense espace avec juste un peu de fumée et quelques miroirs : un tour de magie architecturale.

*Using a simple combination of mono-frequency lamps, mirrors on the ceiling and mist, Eliasson succeeded in transforming the cavernous volume of Tate Modern's Turbine Hall into a remarkable, sun-lit, interior space.*

*Mit einer einfachen Kombination aus Monofrequenzlampen, Deckenspiegeln und Nebel gelang es Eliasson, die höhlenartige Turbinenhalle in einen ungewöhnlichen, sonnenbeleuchteten Innenraum zu verwandeln.*

*A partir d'une combinaison de lampes monofréquence, de miroirs au plafond et de projections de brume, Eliasson a réussi à transformer le caverneux volume du Hall de la turbine en un surprenant espace ensoleillé.*

Though it could be described as
nothing more than "smoke and mirrors" the Olafur Eliasson installation
at Tate Modern came as close to a
magical effect as imaginable in the
vast industrial space of the former
power plant.

Obwohl sie im Grunde aus nichts weiter als „Nebel und Spiegel" bestand,
kam Olafur Eliassons Installation in
der Tate Modern einer magischen
Raumwirkung so nahe, wie es in dem
riesigen Raum des ehemaligen Kraft-
werks nur denkbar ist.

Bien qu'elle ne soit rien de plus que
« un peu de fumée et des miroirs »
l'installation d'Olafur Eliasson a
réussi à créer un effet aussi magique
que possible dans le vaste volume
industriel d'une ancienne centrale
thermique.

# MASAKI ENDOH
# AND MASAHIRO IKEDA

*Masaki Endoh*
*EDH Endoh Design House*
*2-13-8, Honnmachi, Shibuya-ku, Tokyo, 151-0071 Japan*
*Tel: +81 3 3377 6293, Fax: +81 3 3377 6293*
*e-mail edh-endoh@mvi.biglobe.ne.jp, Web: www.edh-web.com*

*Masahiro Ikeda*
*MIAS Masahiro Ikeda Architecture Studio*
*202 Silhouette-Ohyamacho 1-20 Ohyama-cho, Shibuya-ku, Tokyo, 151-0065 Japan*
*Tel: +81 3 5738 5564, Fax: +81 3 5738 5565*
*e-mail: info@miascoltd.net*

Masaki Endoh was born in Tokyo, Japan in 1963. He graduated from the Science University of Tokyo in 1987 and completed the Master Course of Architecture in 1989, at the same University. He worked the KAI-Workshop (1989–1994) and established his firm EDH Endoh Design House in 1994. He is currently a lecturer at the Science University of Tokyo. He was awarded the Tokyo House Prize for "Natural Shelter" in 2000, the Yoshioka Award for "Natural Shelter" in 2000, and the JIA "Rookie of the Year 2003" for "Natural Ellipse" in 2003. His works include "Natural Shelter" (Tokyo, 1999); "Natural Illuminance" (Tokyo, 2001); "Natural Slats" (Tokyo, 2002); "Natural Ellipse" (Tokyo, 2002); "Natural Wedge" (Tokyo, 2003); and "Natural Strata" (Kawasaki, 2003). Masahiro Ikeda was born in Shizuoka, Japan in 1964. He graduated from the Nagoya University in 1987 and completed the School of Engineering at Nagoya University in 1989. He worked with Kimura Structural Engineers (1989–1991) and Sasaki Structural Consultants (1991–1994) before establishing his firm MIAS (Masahiro Ikeda Architecture Studio) in 1994. Masahiro Ikeda has acted as the architect and structural designer for these houses. As Masaki Endoh says, however, Masahiro Ikeda has played such a significant role in these projects that he too should be considered as one of the architects.

Masaki Endoh, geboren 1963 in Tokio, schloss 1987 sein Studium an der Wissenschaftsuniversität in Tokio ab und erwarb 1987 dort auch seinen Master of Architecture. Von 1989 bis 1994 arbeitete er im KAI-Workshop und gründete 1994 seine eigene Firma EDH Endoh Design House. Derzeit ist er Dozent an der Tokioter Wissenschaftsuniversität. Im Jahr 2000 wurde ihm der Tokyo House Prize und der Yoshioka Award, beide für Natural Shelter verliehen, und 2003 erhielt er den vom japanischen Architekturinstitut verliehenen Preis Rookie of the Year 2003 für Natural Ellipse. Zu seinen Projekten zählen: Natural Shelter (1999), Natural Illuminance (2001), Natural Slats (2002), Natural Ellipse (2002), Natural Wedge (2003), alle in Tokio, sowie Natural Strata in Kawasaki (2003). Masahiro Ikeda, geboren 1964 in Shizuoka, Japan, schloss 1987 sein Architekturstudium und 1989 sein Ingenieurstudium an der Universität in Nagoya ab. Von 1989 bis 1991 arbeitete er bei Kimura Structural Engineers und von 1991 bis 1994 bei Sasaki Structural Consultants, bevor er 1994 seine eigene Firma MIAS (Masahiro Ikeda Architecture Studio) gründete. Masahiro Ikeda war als Architekt und Bauzeichner für Endohs Architekturprojekte tätig. Wie Masaki Endoh jedoch betont, hat Masahiro Ikeda eine so bedeutende Rolle bei diesen Projekten gespielt, dass auch er als einer der Architekten zu betrachten ist.

Masaki Endoh est né à Tokyo en 1963. Diplômé de l'Université des Sciences de Tokyo en 1987, il est Master of Architecture de la même université en 1989. Il a travaillé pour KAI-Workshop (1989–1994) et a créé son agence EDH Endoh Design House, en 1994. Il est actuellement assistant à l'Université des Sciences de Tokyo. Il a reçu le Prix de la maison de Tokyo et le Prix Yoshioka pour son «Abri naturel» en 2000 ainsi que le «Rookie de l'année 2003» JIA pour «Ellipse naturelle». Parmi ses travaux: «Abri naturel» (Tokyo, 1999); «Illumination naturelle» (Tokyo, 2001); «Ardoises naturelles» (Tokyo, 2002); «Ellipse naturelle» (Tokyo, 2002); «Coin naturel» (Tokyo, 2003) et «Strates naturelles» (Kawasaki, 2003). Masahiro Ikeda est né à Shizuoka, Japon, en 1964. Il est diplômé de l'Université de Nagoya en 1987 et a étudié à l'École d'ingéniérie de l'Université de Nagoya en 1989. Il a collaboré avec Kimura Structural Engineers (1989–1991) et Sasaki Structural Consultants (1991–1994), avant de créer son agence MIAS (Masahiro Ikeda Architecture Studio) en 1994. Il est l'architecte et l'ingénieur structurel des maisons présentées ici. Pour Masaki Endoh cependant: «Masahiro Ikeda a joué un tel rôle dans ces projets qu'il devrait en être considéré comme l'un des architectes.»

# NATURAL ELLIPSE

*Tokyo, Japan 2001–02*

*Client: private. Building area: 31.20 m², total floor area: 131.74 m². Costs: not specified.*

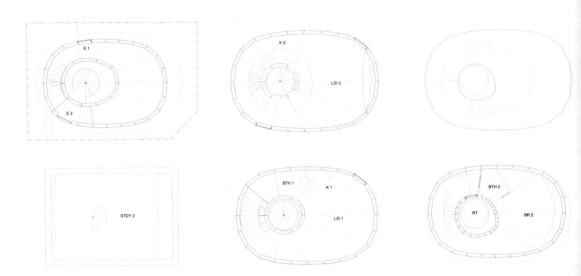

This unusual house with a floor area of 132 square meters is set on just 31 square meters of a tiny 53-square-meter site located at the edge of the Shibuya shopping and entertainment district. The architect chose to compose the house out of 24 elliptical steel rings. As Masaki Endoh says, "the ellipse makes it possible to adjust the form according to the external requirements, or to modify the allocation of space by varying the ratio between its major and minor axes. Also, its double focus deprives this figure of centrality, making it possible to erase the hierarchy of details such as the pillar or the beam, and to create a continuity from the outside toward the interior. The plan consists of a cylindrical central block composed of these rings and zones for natural lighting and longitudinal flow lines that continue from the exterior, radiating outward. FRP (Fiber-Reinforced Polymer) is employed for the external finish, as a material capable of joining the rings and expressing such continuity. It has the merit of being waterproof, and can be molded and applied at will, to realize a seamless exterior."

Das ungewöhnliche Haus mit einer Nutzfläche von 132 m² und einer Grundfläche von nur 31 m² liegt auf einem winzigen, 53 m² großen Grundstück am Rand des Tokioter Einkaufs- und Vergnügungsviertels Shibuya. Der Architekt Masaki Endoh zu seiner Konstruktion, die aus 24 elliptischen Stahlringen besteht: „Die Ellipse ermöglicht es, die Form des Hauses an die äußeren Anforderungen anzupassen oder die Raumeinteilung zu modifizieren, indem man das Verhältnis zwischen Haupt- und Nebenachse der Ellipse variiert. Außerdem wird diese Figur durch den Doppelfokus ihrer Zentralität beraubt, wodurch sich unter Umgehung der Hierarchie solcher Einzelteile wie Säule oder Balken ein Raumkontinuum von außen nach innen herstellen lässt. Der Grundriss besteht aus einem zylindrischen Kern, der sich aus Ringen und Zonen für natürliche Belichtung und aus Längslinien, die nach außen strahlen, zusammensetzt. Für die Fassaden wurde eine Beschichtung aus faserverstärktem Polymer (FRP) gewählt, da sich mit diesem Material die einzelnen Ringe fugenlos miteinander verbinden lassen. Darüber hinaus hat es den Vorteil, wasserfest zu sein und dass man es nach Belieben formen und auftragen kann."

Cette curieuse maison de 132 m² de surface totale occupe 31 m² d'une petite parcelle de 53 m² en bordure du quartier commercial et de nuit de Shibuya, à Tokyo. L'architecte a réalisé ce projet à l'aide de 24 anneaux elliptiques en acier : « Les ellipses ont permis d'ajuster la forme aux contraintes externes et de modifier l'allocation de l'espace en variant le rapport entre le grand et le petit axe. La double ellipse supprime tout point central, ce qui permet d'éliminer la hiérarchie d'éléments comme les piliers ou les poutres, et de créer une continuité de l'extérieur vers l'intérieur. Le plan consiste en un bloc central cylindrique composé des anneaux et de zones naturellement éclairées qui s'orientent vers l'extérieur à l'horizontale. La couverture est en FRP (polymère renforcé de fibres), matériau capable de maintenir ensemble les anneaux et d'exprimer la continuité recherchée. De plus, il est étanche et peut être plié ou appliqué comme on veut, afin d'obtenir une couverture lisse, sans interruption. »

*The drawings for the Natural Ellipse resemble mathematical constructions almost more than they do architecture. The elliptical shape of the house makes this digital logic possible, while creating a truly unexpected residence.*

*Die Entwurfszeichnungen für das Natural Ellipse Haus gleichen eher mathematischen Konstruktionen als Architektur. Die elliptische Form des Gebäudes macht diese digitale Logik möglich. Daraus resultiert ein wahrhaftig ungewöhnliches Wohnhaus.*

*Les dessins préparatoires à la Natural Ellipse font davantage penser à des constructions mathématiques qu'à de l'architecture. La forme elliptique de la maison permet cette logique numérique, tout en créant une maison totalement inattendue.*

MASAKI ENDOH
AND MASAHIRO IKEDA

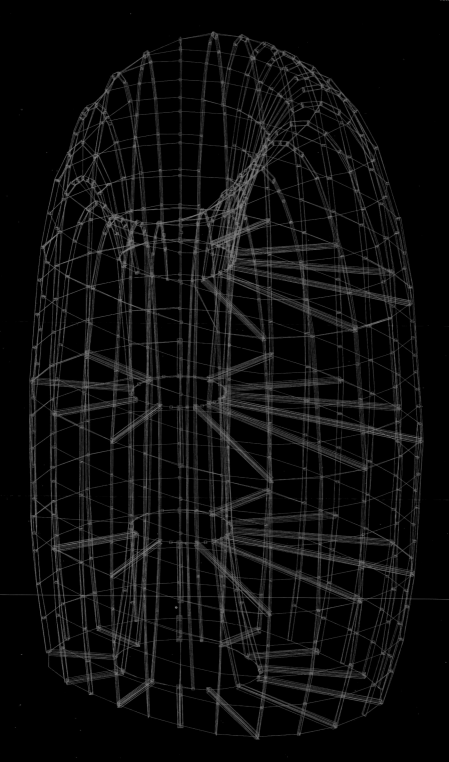

*A spiral staircase links the different levels of the house, as can be seen in the drawing to the right and the image to the left.*

*Eine Wendeltreppe bildet die Verbindung zwischen den verschiedenen Ebenen des Hauses, wie in der Zeichnung rechts und der Abbildung links erkennbar.*

*Un escalier en spirale réunit les différents niveaux de la maison, comme le montrent les dessins, à droite, et l'image de gauche.*

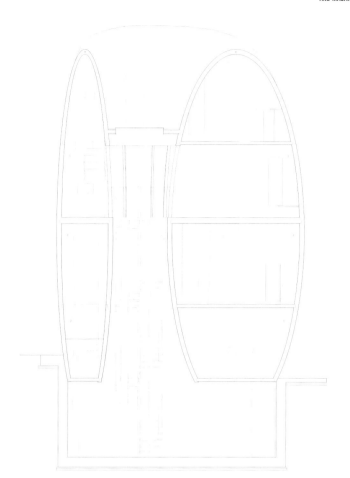

*Light enters the top of the structure and filters down the staircase.*

*Das von oben einfallende Licht wird durch das Treppenhaus gefiltert.*

*La lumière pénètre par le haut de la structure et suit la cage de l'escalier en spirale.*

# NATURAL ILLUMINANCE

*Tokyo, Japan, 2001*

*Client: private. Building area: 34.46 m², total floor area: 65.56 m². Costs: not specified.*

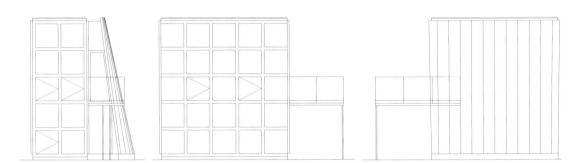

Also located in a densely populated residential area of Tokyo, Natural Illuminance is even smaller than the Natural Ellipse house. It has a total floor area of 65 square meters and a narrow site measuring just 80 square meters. The built area on this site is precisely 34.46 square meters. Preoccupied, as are many Japanese architects, with the ideas of boundaries and the presence of "nature" in a highly urbanized environment, Endoh placed the emphasis here on natural light. As he says "my proposition consists specifically of a masonry construction composed of 1200mm-square wall units made of insulated steel. Natural light is introduced through the gaps between the units along the four sides… As a result, the numerical values of illumination are uniform at every point of this space. There is a lack of hierarchy because of the absence of a feeling of being surrounded, and the fact that the edges of the materials are all imperceptible. This turns out to be effective in relieving the feeling of spatial narrowness in the house."

Das ebenfalls in einer dichtbesiedelten Wohngegend von Tokio gelegene Haus Natural Illuminance ist sogar noch kleiner als das Haus Natural Ellipse. Es hat eine Nutzfläche von 65 m² und nimmt auf dem schmalen, 80 m² großen Grundstück exakt 34,46 m² ein. Endoh, der sich wie viele japanische Architekten intensiv mit den baulichen Aspekten von Grenzen und der Präsenz von Natur in einem hoch urbanisierten Umfeld auseinandersetzt, legte den Schwerpunkt im vorliegenden Entwurf auf das natürliche Licht. „Meine Konstruktion", so Endoh, „besteht in der Hauptsache aus einem Mauerwerk, das sich aus 1,2 m² großen Platten aus Isolierstahl zusammensetzt. An den vier Außenwänden wird das natürliche Licht durch die Spalten zwischen den einzelnen Tafeln nach innen geführt. Daraus folgt, dass die numerischen Lichtwerte an jeder Stelle des Innenraums einheitlich sind. Außerdem entsteht keine Hierarchie, weil sämtliche Materialränder unsichtbar bleiben. Das hat sich als wirksam erwiesen, um in diesem kleinen Haus kein Gefühl von räumlicher Enge aufkommen zu lassen."

Également située dans un quartier résidentiel de Tokyo très peuplé, cette maison est encore plus petite que la Natural Ellipse House. Sur un étroit terrain de 80 m², elle offre 65 m² de surface utile, pour 34,46 m² d'emprise au sol. Préoccupé, comme beaucoup d'architectes japonais, par les notions de limites et la présence de la « nature » dans un environnement hautement urbanisé, Endoh a mis l'accent sur l'éclairage naturel : « Ma proposition consiste en une construction en maçonnerie habillée de plaques d'acier isolant carrées de 1 200 m² de côté. L'éclairage naturel pénètre par des fentes ménagées entre les quatre côtés de ces plaques… Les valeurs numériques d'illumination sont ainsi uniformes en chaque point du volume. L'absence de hiérarchie est due au fait que l'on ne se sent pas enfermé, et que les bords des matériaux sont tous imperceptibles. Ceci réduit efficacement la perception de l'étroitesse spatiale de la maison. »

*Applying the same mathematical rigor used for the Natural Ellipse, the Natural Illuminance house is based on a subdivided cube.*

*Unter Anwendung mathematischer Strenge wie bei Natural Ellipse, basiert auch Natural Illuminance auf einem gegliederten Kubus.*

*Appliquant la même rigueur mathématique que pour la Natural Ellipse, cette maison repose sur un principe de cube subdivisé.*

MASAKI ENDOH
AND MASAHIRO IKEDA

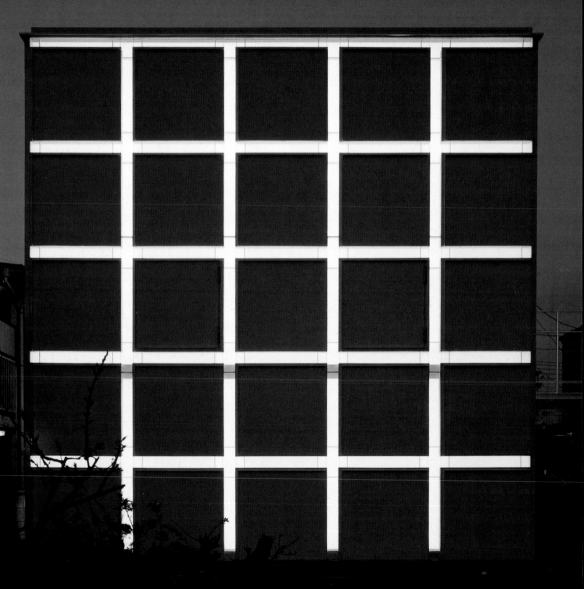

The openings visible between the grid lines of the exterior correspond to interior wall panels encircled with light during the day.

*Die zwischen den Außenplatten sichtbaren Lücken korrespondieren mit den Tafeln der Innenwände, die tagsüber von Licht umrandet sind.*

*Les ouvertures visibles dans la trame extérieure correspondent aux panneaux muraux intérieurs, encadrés de lumière pendant la journée.*

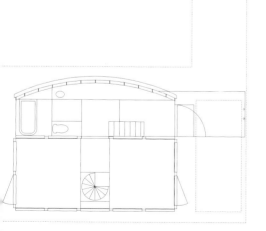

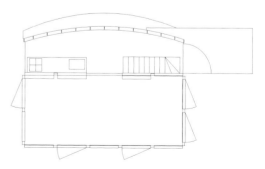

Despite its cubic appearance, plans show that the basic form of the house is rectangular with one side in the shape of an arc.

*Trotz seiner kubischen Gestalt zeigen die Grundrisse, dass die Grundform des Hauses ein Rechteck mit einer bogenförmigen Seite ist.*

*Malgré l'apparence cubique, les plans montrent que la forme de base de la maison est un rectangle dont un côté est arqué.*

# FOA

*FOA*
*55 Curtain Road*
*London EC2A 3PT*
*UK*

*Tel: +44 20 7033 9800*
*Fax: +44 20 7033 9801*
*e-mail: mail@f-o-a.net*
*Web: www.f-o-a.net/flash/*

*Yokohama International Port Term*

FOA is led by architects Farshid Moussavi and Alejandro Zaera Polo, and is "dedicated to the exploration of contemporary urban conditions, lifestyles and construction technologies." Aside from the Yokohama International Port Terminal published here, they have worked on: Barcelona South-East Coastal Park; Municipal Theater and Auditorium, Torrevieja, Spain; Publishing Headquarters, Paju, South Korea; Belgo restaurants in London, Bristol and New York; and Blue Moon Housing and Tent projects in Groningen, The Netherlands. They have also designed a central police station (La Vila Joyosa, Spain); harbor facilities for Amersfoort, The Netherlands; and a car park for Basel, Switzerland. Farshid Moussavi received her Masters in Architecture from the Harvard Graduate School of Design. She worked for the Renzo Piano Building Workshop in Genoa in 1988 and for the Office for Metropolitan Architecture (OMA) in Rotterdam (Rem Koolhaas, 1991–1993), while establishing Foreign Office Architects (FOA) in 1992. Also educated at Harvard, Alejandro Zaera Polo worked with OMA in Rotterdam at the same time as Farshid Moussavi.

FOA wird von den Architekten Farshid Moussavi und Alejandro Zaera Polo geleitet und widmet sich laut eigener Aussage der Erforschung zeitgenössischer urbaner Wohnverhältnisse, Lebensstile und Konstruktionstechnologien. Neben dem hier präsentierten Terminal für den internationalen Hafen in Yokohama zählen zu ihren Projekten: ein Park am Meer in Barcelona, ein Theater mit Auditorium im spanischen Torrevieja, ein Verlagsgebäude in Paju, Südkorea, Belgo Restaurants in London, Bristol und New York sowie das Wohnbauten und Zelte umfassende Projekt Blue Moon im niederländischen Groningen. Außerdem gestalteten Moussavi und Zaera Polo ein Polizeirevier in der Innenstadt von La Vila Joyosa, Spanien, Hafengebäude im niederländischen Amersfoort und einen Parkplatz in Basel. Farshid Moussavi erwarb ihren Master of Architecture an der Harvard Graduate School of Design. 1988 arbeitete sie im Baubüro von Renzo Piano in Genua und von 1991 bis 1993 im Office for Metropolitan Architecture (OMA) von Rem Koolhaas in Rotterdam. 1992 gründete sie die Firma Foreign Office Architects (FOA). Alejandro Zaera Polo studierte ebenfalls in Harvard und arbeitete zur selben Zeit wie Farshid Moussavi im OMA in Rotterdam.

FOA est animé par les architectes Farshid Moussavi et Alejandro Zaera Polo. L'agence se consacre à « l'exploration des conditions urbaines, des styles de vie et des technologies de construction contemporaines ». En dehors du terminal du port international de Yokohama publié ici, ils ont travaillé sur le parc côtier du sud-est de Barcelone ; le théâtre et l'auditorium municipaux de Torrevieja (Espagne) ; le siège d'une maison d'édition (Paju, Corée du Sud) ; les restaurants Belgo à Londres, Bristol et New York, et le programme de logements Blue Moon Housing and Tent à Groningue (Pays-Bas). Ils ont également conçu un poste de police central (La Villa Joyosa, Espagne) ; des installations portuaires (Amersfoort, Pays-Bas) et un parking à Bâle (Suisse). Farshid Moussavi est Master of Architecture de la Harvard Graduate School of Design. Elle a travaillé pour Renzo Piano à Gènes (1988) et pour OMA de Rem Koolhaas à Rotterdam (1991–1993), tout en créant Foreign Office Architects (FOA) en 1992. Après avoir également effectué ses études à Harvard, Alejandro Zaera Polo a travaillé chez OMA au même moment que Farshid Moussavi.

# YOKOHAMA INTERNATIONAL PORT TERMINAL

*Yokohama, Japan, 2000–2002*

*Client: The City of Yokohama Port & Harbor Bureau. Floor area: 17 000 m² (cruise terminal), 13 000 m² (citizens amenities), 18 000 m² (traffic facilities). Costs: € 220 000 000.*

*Rectangular and functional, FOA's Pier has little other resemblance to traditional facilities of its type. One layer wraps into another, like an artificial, computer generated landscape.*

*Der rechteckig funktionale Pier von FOA hat wenig Ähnlichkeit mit traditionellen Konstruktionen dieser Art. Eine Schicht legt sich hier um die andere, wie bei einer künstlichen, vom Computer erzeugten Landschaft.*

*Rectangulaire et fonctionnelle, la jetée de FOA ne ressemble cependant pas aux équipement traditionnels de ce type. Ses strates s'enroulent les unes autour des autres, tel un paysage artificiel généré par ordinateur.*

The 1995 competition organized by the Port and Harbor Authority and the City of Yokohama, Japan, marked the emergence of Foreign Office Architects as an important architectural practice. The actual construction of the project marked a significant step in the adaptation of computer-driven design techniques to the "real-world" problems of a large building. In fact, the sophisticated design has a bearing on much more than esthetics, as FOA explains: "Our proposal for the Yokohama project is generated from a circulation diagram that aspires to eliminate the linear structure characteristic of piers, and the directionality of the circulation… Rather than developing the building as an object or figure on the pier, the project is produced as an extension of the urban ground, constructed as a systematic transformation of the lines of the circulation diagram into a folded and bifurcated surface… the folded ground distributes the loads through the surfaces themselves, moving them diagonally to the ground. This structure is also especially adequate in coping with the lateral forces generated by seismic movements that affect Japan. The result is the hybridization of given types of space and program through a distinct tectonic system, in this case, a folded surface."

Mit ihrem prämierten Beitrag zu dem 1995 von der Hafen- und Stadtverwaltung von Yokohama organisierten Wettbewerb trat das Büro Foreign Office Architects erstmals als bedeutende Architektengruppe in Erscheinung. Die Konstruktion dieser Anlage war ein wichtiger Schritt in der Anwendung computergenerierter Gestaltungstechniken auf die realen Probleme bei der Fertigstellung von Großbauten. Dabei bezieht sich das ausgeklügelte Design nicht nur auf die gestalterische Ästhetik, wie einer der FOA-Architekten erläutert: „Unser Entwurf leitet sich von einem Umlaufdiagramm ab, das die für einen Pier typische lineare Anordnung sowie die übliche Zirkulationsrichtung durchbrechen soll … Statt das Gebäude als isoliertes Objekt oder als geometrische Form zu entwickeln, wurde das gesamte Yokohama-Projekt als eine Erweiterung des städtischen Raums angelegt. Es ist aus einer systematischen Transformation der Linien des Zirkulationsdiagramms in eine gabelförmig gefaltete Oberfläche entstanden … welche die Lasten auf den diagonal angeordneten Bodenflächen verteilt. Diese Konstruktionsweise ist außerdem besonders geeignet, um den Lateralkräften entgegenzuwirken, die in Japan häufig durch seismische Bewegungen verursacht werden. Das Resultat ist eine Hybridisierung eines bestehenden Raumtyps und Bauprogramms durch ein spezielles tektonisches System, in diesem Fall eine gefaltete Oberfläche."

Le concours organisé en 1995 pour ce terminal par l'Autorité du port et la ville de Yokohama est à l'origine de l'émergence internationale de Foreign Office Architects parmi les agences qui comptent. La mise en œuvre du projet a marqué une nouvelle étape dans l'application des techniques de CAO aux problèmes concrets d'un vaste bâtiment. En fait, cette conception sophistiquée a porté sur beaucoup plus que l'esthétique comme l'explique FAO : « Notre proposition pour Yokohama est issue du schéma de circulation qui veut éliminer la structure linéaire caractéristique en jetée et la directionn habituelle des circulations… Au lieu d'être un bâtiment qui ne serait qu'un objet posé sur une jetée, le projet devient une extension de la ville, dans une transformation systématique des axes du plan de circulation en une surface pliée et bifurquée… le sol replié distribue les charges à travers les plans, et les reporte en diagonale vers le sol. Cette structure est particulièrement adaptée pour résister aux forces latérales générées par les mouvements sismiques qui affectent le Japon. Le résultat final est une hybridation de types d'espaces et d'éléments du programme dans un système tectonique original, en l'occurrence, une surface pliée. »

*Surfaces on the Pier bend and fold together in ways that architecture could hardly have imagined, let alone executed before the full development of computer-assisted design.*

*Die Oberflächen des Piers biegen und falten sich in einer Weise, wie sie in der Architektur kaum vorstellbar war, geschweige denn vor der Entwicklung von CAD-Programmen.*

*Les surfaces de la jetée se plient et se replient d'une manière rarement vue en architecture, surtout dans les réalisations d'avant l'apparition de la CAO.*

Despite their attachment to nature, the Japanese are particularly accustomed to architecture and landscape design that mimics or recreates an artificial "natural" world.

Bei all ihrer Liebe zur Natur sind die Japaner besonders vertraut mit einer Architektur und Landschaftsgestaltung, die eine künstliche Form von Natur schafft oder nachahmt.

Malgré leur attachement à la nature, les Japonais sont particulièrement ouverts à une conception de l'architecture et du paysage qui imite ou recrée un monde « naturel » artificiel.

Intended for heavy use, the Yokohama Pier succeeds in reconciling an esthetically ambitious concept with a rigorous and challenging program.

Für eine hohe Beanspruchung konzipiert, vereint das Yokohama Pier ein ästhetisch ambitiöses Konzept mit einem anspruchsvollen Bauplan.

Prévu pour un usage intensif, le terminal de Yokohama réussit à concilier un concept esthétique ambitieux et un programme rigoureux et chargé.

Interior areas continue the bending, folding rhythm of the exterior, admitting daylight into spaces where pure horizontal or vertical surfaces are relatively rare.

Die Innenräume führen den äußeren Rhythmus weiter und lassen Tageslicht in Zonen, in denen es kaum eine ungebrochen horizontale oder vertikale Oberfläche gibt.

Les espaces intérieurs reprennent le rythme de pliage de l'extérieur, et admettent l'éclairage naturel dans des volumes où les plans horizontaux ou verticaux sont relativement rares.

Again, despite the playfulness of the seemingly eccentric design, it is clear that FOA have thought out the very real demands of such a facility.

Trotz des spielerischen Charakters ihres exzentrischen Entwurfs haben die Architekten von FOA die realen Anforderungen einer solchen Anlage wohl bedacht.

L'aspect ludique et légèrement excentrique du projet, ne doit pas masquer que FOA a réfléchi à toutes les contraintes d'un tel équipement.

Mimicking the surface of the earth or natural formations, on the outside the Pier gives way to this cathedral-like space within.

Der äußerlich der Erdoberfläche oder Naturformen nachgebildete Pier öffnet sich in seinem Innern zu einem kathedralenartigen Raum.

Si, vue de l'extérieur, la jetée semble imiter une formation géologique naturelle, elle n'en laisse pas moins place à l'intérieur à un volume aux dimensions de cathédrale.

# FRANK O. GEHRY

*Gehry Partners LLP*
*12541 Beatrice Street*
*Los Angeles, CA 90066*
*USA*

*Tel: +1 310 482 3000*
*Fax: +1 310 482 3006*

Born in Toronto, Canada, in 1929, Frank Gehry studied at the University of Southern California, Los Angeles (1949–1951), and at Harvard (1956–57). Principal of Gehry Partners LLP., Los Angeles, since 1962, he received the 1989 Pritzker Prize. Some of his notable projects are the Loyola Law School, Los Angeles (1981–1984); the Norton Residence, Venice, California (1983); California Aerospace Museum, Los Angeles (1982–1984); Schnabel Residence, Brentwood (1989); Festival Disney, Marne-la-Vallée, France (1989–1992); Guggenheim Museum, Bilbao, Spain (1991–1997); Experience Music Project (Seattle, Washington, 1995–2000); and the unbuilt Guggenheim Museum (New York, 1998–). Recent work includes: DG Bank Headquarters (Berlin, Germany, 2000); Fisher Center for the Performing Arts at Bard College (Annandale-on-Hudson, NY, 2003); Walt Disney Concert Hall (Los Angeles, 2003, published here); and the Massachusetts Institute of Technology Stata Complex (Cambridge, MA, 2003).

Frank O. Gehry, 1929 in Toronto geboren, studierte von 1949 bis 1951 an der University of Southern California (USC) in Los Angeles und von 1956 bis 1957 in Harvard. Seit 1962 ist er Leiter der Firma Gehry Partners LLP. in Los Angeles. 1989 erhielt er den Pritzker Prize. Zu seinen bekanntesten Bauten gehören die Loyola Law School in Los Angeles (1981–1984), das California Aerospace Museum in Los Angeles (1982–1984), die Villa Norton im kalifornischen Venice (1983), die Villa Schnabel in Brentwood (1989), das Festival Disney im französischen Marne-la-Vallée (1989–1992), das Guggenheim Museum in Bilbao (1991–1997) und das Experience Music Project in Seattle, Washington (1995–2000). Sein 1998 entworfener Bau für das Guggenheim Museum in New York blieb bislang unrealisiert. Zu seinen jüngsten Projekten zählen: die Zentrale der DG Bank in Berlin (2000), das Fisher Center for the Performing Arts am Bard College in Annandale-on-Hudson, New York (2003), die hier gezeigte Walt Disney Concert Hall in Los Angeles (2003) sowie der Stata Complex für das Massachusetts Institute of Technology in Cambridge, Massachusetts (2003).

Né à Toronto, Canada, en 1929, Frank Gehry étudie à l'University of Southern California, Los Angeles (1949–1951), puis à Harvard (1956–57). Directeur de l'agence Gehry Partners LLP., Los Angeles, depuis 1962, il reçoit en 1989 le prix Pritzker. Parmi ses projets les plus remarqués : la Loyola Law School, Los Angeles (1981–1984) ; la Norton Residence, Venice, Californie (1983) ; le California Aerospace Museum, Los Angeles (1982–1984) ; la Schnabel Residence, Brentwood (1989) ; Festival Disney, Marne-la-Vallée, France (1989–1992) ; le Guggenheim Museum, Bilbao, Espagne (1991–1997) ; Experience Music Project, Seattle, Washington (1995–2000) et le Guggenheim Museum de New York (1998–) qui reste à construire. Parmi ses chantiers récents : siège de la DG Bank (Berlin, Allemagne, 2000) ; Fisher Center for the Performing Arts at Bard College (Annandale-on-Hudson, NY, 2003) ; Walt Disney Concert Hall (Los Angeles, 2003, publié ici) et le Massachusetts Institute of Technology Stata Complex (Cambridge, Massachusetts, USA, 2003).

# WALT DISNEY CONCERT HALL

*Los Angeles, California, USA, 1999–2003*

*Client: Walt Disney Concert Hall Committee. Total floor area: 18 600 m². Costs: $ 274 000 000.*

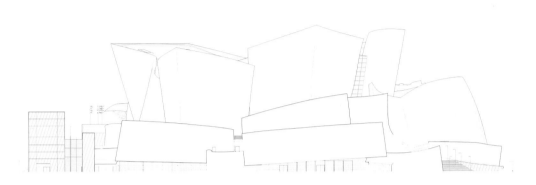

It had long been noted that, in spite of his international notoriety, Los Angeles architect Frank Gehry had not built a significant public building in his home town. With the opening of the Walt Disney Concert Hall in the fall of 2003, that failing was rectified. Located in the Bunker Hill area of downtown Los Angeles, close to Arata Isozaki's Museum of Contemporary Art, the project originated in 1987 with a $50 million gift from the late Lillian Disney. Since then, other gifts and accumulated interest bring the Disney family's total contribution to over $100 million. The County of Los Angeles agreed to provide the land and significant additional funding to finance Walt Disney Concert Hall's six-level subterranean parking garage. Total cost was $274 million for the 2 265-seat facility. Gehry was selected as the architect in 1988 and his design became public in 1991. The garage was built between 1992 and 1996 and work on the Concert Hall began in November 1999. As was the case for the Bilbao Guggenheim, Gehry used Dassault's CATIA program to design and help build the structure. Rather than titanium cladding, stainless steel was used in Los Angeles, though he did consider a combination of limestone and steel at one point. According to Terry Bell, project architect for Gehry's office, "It's an enormously complicated structure because of the curved shapes and intricate joinery. The esthetic goals with the exterior wall, all the acoustic issues, there is so much that is atypical... this is in no sense a conventional building." The architect was also closely involved in the Concert Hall interior – designing it in wood. Even the wooden pipe organ, built with Manuel Rosales, was designed by Frank Gehry.

Seit langem wurde festgestellt, dass es trotz der internationalen Berühmtheit von Frank O. Gehry kein wichtiges öffentliches Gebäude in seiner Heimatstadt gab. Mit der Eröffnung der Walt Disney Concert Hall im Herbst 2003 wurde dieser Mangel behoben. Für die Realisierung des Projekts im Bezirk Bunker Hill von Downtown Los Angeles ging man von den 50 Millionen Dollar aus, die die inzwischen verstorbene Lillian Disney 1987 gespendet hatte und die durch weitere Spenden und Zinsen auf über 100 Millionen Dollar angewachsen waren. Schließlich beschloss die Kreisverwaltung, das Grundstück und eine beträchtliche Summe öffentlicher Gelder für die Finanzierung der unterirdisch angelegten Parkgarage zur Verfügung zu stellen. Die Gesamtkosten für das mit 2 265 Sitzen ausgestattete Konzerthaus lagen letztendlich bei 274 Millionen Dollar. Gehry wurde 1988 als Architekt ernannt, 1991 wurde sein Entwurf der Öffentlichkeit präsentiert. Zwischen 1992 und 1996 entstand die Parkgarage, und im November 1999 wurde mit dem Bau des Konzerthauses begonnen. Wie beim Bilbao Guggenheim setzte Gehry für die Gestaltung das Computerprogramm CATIA der Firma Dassault ein, nur dass in Los Angeles statt Titan eine Verkleidung aus Edelstahl verwendet wurde, obwohl der Architekt ursprünglich an eine Kombination aus Kalkstein und Stahl gedacht hatte. Wie Terry Bell, Projektarchitektin in Gehrys Firma, erläutert: „Es ist eine ungeheuer komplizierte Konstruktion wegen seiner geschwungenen Formen und der ausgeklügelten Schreinerarbeiten. Der ästhetische Anspruch bei der Fassadengestaltung, all die akustischen Fragen, da ist so viel Neues und Ungewohntes dabei, dass es in keiner Hinsicht ein konventionelles Gebäude ist." Gehry war außerdem zum großen Teil verantwortlich für die Innenraumgestaltung des Konzertsaals, die er ganz in Holz ausführte. Selbst die in Zusammenarbeit mit Manuel Rosales konstruierte hölzerne Orgel ist ein Entwurf von Frank Gehry.

On savait depuis longtemps qu'en dépit de sa notoriété internationale, Frank Gehry n'avait pas construit d'édifice public important dans sa ville natale. Avec l'ouverture du Walt Disney Concert Hall à l'automne 2003, cette absence est enfin compensée. Situé en centre-ville dans le quartier de Bunker Hill, ce projet est né d'un don de 50 millions de dollars de feu Lilian Disney en 1987. Depuis, d'autres dons et le cumul des intérêts ont porté la contribution de la famille Disney à plus de 100 millions de dollars. Le comté de Los Angeles a fourni le terrain et d'importantes subventions pour financer le parking souterrain de six niveaux. Le coût total de cette salle de 2 265 places s'est élevé à 274 millions de dollars. Gehry a été choisi en 1988 et ses plans rendus publics en 1991. Le garage a été construit entre 1992 et 1996, et les travaux sur la salle ont débuté en novembre 1999. Comme pour le Guggenheim de Bilbao, Gehry a utilisé le logiciel CATIA de Dassault aussi bien en conception que pour la construction. L'acier inoxydable a été préféré à un habillage en titane, même si l'architecte a pensé à un certain moment à utiliser la pierre et l'acier. Selon Terry Bell, architecte projet pour Gehry, « c'est une structure extrêmement compliquée du fait de ses formes en courbes et de l'imbrication de ses joints. Ambitions esthétiques du mur extérieur, enjeux acoustiques : il y a tellement d'éléments atypiques que ce n'est certainement pas une construction traditionnelle. » L'architecte s'est également beaucoup impliqué dans les aménagements intérieurs, traités en bois. En collaboration avec Manuel Rosales, il a même dessiné l'orgue.

*An elevation of the building reveals something of its irregular profile.*

*Der Aufriss des Gebäudes offenbart dessen unregelmäßiges Profil.*

*L'élévation ci-dessus montre l'irrégularité marquée du profil.*

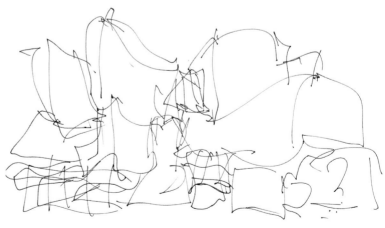

A sketch by Gehry and the nearly completed work bear an uncanny resemblance to each other, showing again that his methods are not truly those of computer-based design.

Die Skizze von Gehry und das fast vollendete Bauwerk weisen eine starke Ähnlichkeit auf, was zeigt, dass sein Vorgehen nicht wirklich dem computergenerierten Gestalten folgt.

Le croquis de Gehry et l'œuvre presque achevée se ressemblent indéniablement, ce qui montre une fois de plus que sa méthode se démarque de l'approche informatique.

Gehry's Disney Concert Hall may be his most dramatic and complete work to date. Far from the small houses he designed in nearby Santa Monica or Venice, this is a mature masterpiece.

Die Disney Concert Hall ist vielleicht das bislang dramatischste und vollkommenste von Gehrys Werken. Weit entfernt von den kleinen Häusern in Santa Monica oder Venice handelt es sich um ein reifes Meisterwerk.

Le Disney Concert Hall de Gehry est peut-être son œuvre la plus spectaculaire et la plus achevée à ce jour. Loin des petites maisons conçues pour Santa Monica ou Venice, il s'agit d'un chef-d'œuvre de sa maturité.

Sitting above a parking garage across the street from Arata Isozaki's MoCA, the Disney Concert Hall has something of a ship to it. The volume of the complex also brings to mind natural rock formations or a rocky island rising from the urban sea of conformity that afflicts all its neighbors aside from the MoCA.

Die auf der gegenüberliegenden Straßenseite von Arata Isozakis MoCA auf einer Parkgarage errichtete Konzerthalle hat etwas von einem Schiff an sich. Gleichzeitig lässt der Baukörper auch an Felsformationen oder eine Felseninsel denken, die sich aus dem urbanen Meer der Konformität erhebt.

Au-dessus d'un vaste parking et face au MoCA d'Arata Isozaki, le Disney Concert Hall rappelle des images nautiques. Le volume du complexe fait aussi penser à des formations rocheuses naturelles ou à une île de rocaille surgie de la mer urbaine du conformisme.

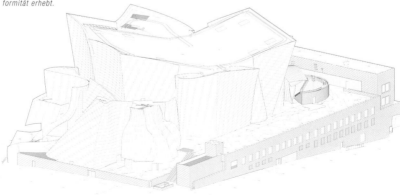

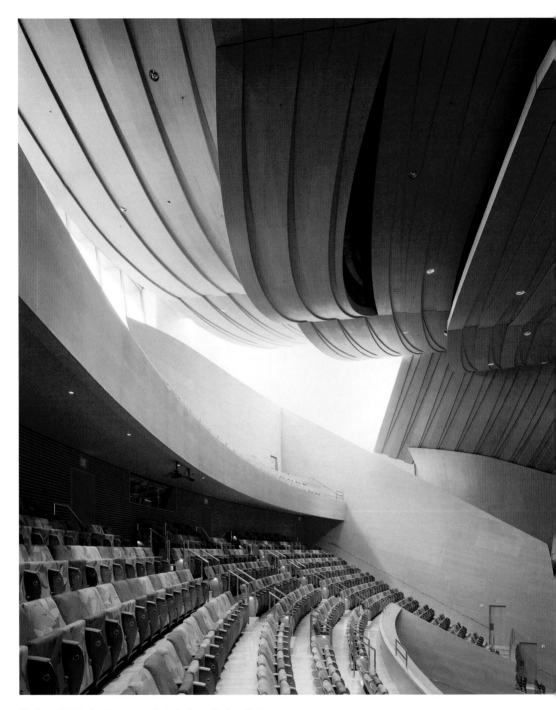

The Concert Hall itself is also very
much a work of the architect, right
down to the extravagantly "decon-
structed" organ visible on the right
page.

Auch das Innere der Konzerthalle
trägt in hohem Maß die Handschrift
des Architekten, bis hin zu der rechts
abgebildeten, phantastisch „dekonstruktivistischen" Orgel.

La salle de concert elle-même est
également typique du style de l'architecte, jusque dans son extravagant
orgue « déconstruit » (page de droite).

# GIGON/GUYER

*Annette Gigon/Mike Guyer Architekten*
*Carmenstrasse 28*
*8032 Zürich*
*Switzerland*

*Tel: +41 1 257 1111*
*Fax: +41 1 257 1110*
*e-mail: info@gigon-guyer.ch*
*Web: www.gigon-guyer.ch*

*Archeological Museum and P*

Born in 1959, Annette Gigon received her diploma from the ETH in Zurich in 1984. She worked in the office of Herzog & de Meuron in Basel (1985–1988) before setting up her own practice (1987–1989) and creating her present firm with Mike Guyer in 1989. Born in 1958, Mike Guyer also graduated from the ETH in 1984, worked with Rem Koolhaas (OMA, 1984–1987), and taught with Hans Kollhoff at the ETH (1987–88). Their built work includes the Kirchner Museum (Davos, 1990–1992); the Vinikus Restaurant (Davos, 1990–1992); and a renovation of the Oskar Reinhart Collection (Am Römerholz, Winterthur, 1997–98). Gigon/Guyer have participated in numerous international competitions such as those for the Nelson-Atkins Museum extension (Kansas, 1999), or the Santiago de Compostela "City of Culture" project (1999). Current work includes the extension of the Aviation/Space Museum in Lucerne (2000–2003); the Museum for the Albers/Honegger collection (Mouans Sartoux, France, 2003); and a housing project in Rüschlikon, Switzerland. The office currently employs a total of 18 architects.

Annette Gigon, geboren 1959, erwarb 1984 ihr Diplom an der ETH in Zürich. Von 1985 bis 1988 arbeitete sie im Büro von Herzog & de Meuron in Basel, bevor sie 1987 ein eigenes Büro und 1989 zusammen mit Mike Guyer ihre jetzige Firma gründete. Auch der 1958 geborene Mike Guyer schloss 1984 sein Studium an der ETH ab. Von 1984 bis 1987 arbeitete er im Office for Metropolitan Architecture (OMA) von Rem Koolhaas und lehrte von 1987 bis 1988 zusammen mit Hans Kollhoff an der ETH. Zu den in der Schweiz realisierten Projekten von Gigon/Guyer gehören das Kirchner-Museum in Davos (1990–1992), das Restaurant Vinikus in Davos (1990–1992) und die Renovierung der Sammlung Oskar Reinhart 'Am Römerholz' in Winterthur (1997–98). Darüber hinaus nahmen sie an zahlreichen internationalen Wettbewerben teil, so für die Erweiterung des Nelson-Atkins Museum in Kansas City (1999) oder das „City of Culture" Projekt in Santiago de Compostela (1999). Zu den jüngsten Arbeiten des Büros Gigon/Guyer, das derzeit 18 Architekten beschäftigt, zählen: der Erweiterungsbau des Museums für Flugwesen und Raumfahrt in Luzern (2000–2003), das Museumsgebäude für die Sammlung Albers/Honegger im französischen Mouans Sartoux (2003) sowie ein Wohnbauprojekt im schweizerischen Rüschlikon.

Née en 1959, Annette Gigon est diplômée de l'ETH de Zurich (1984). Elle a travaillé dans l'agence de Herzog & de Meuron à Bâle (1985–1988) avant de créer sa propre structure (1987–1989) devenue l'agence actuelle après son association avec Mike Guyer en 1989. Né en 1958, Mike Guyer, également diplômé de l'ETH en 1984, a travaillé chez Rem Koolhaas (OMA, 1984–1987) et enseigné avec Hans Kollhoff à l'ETH (1987–88). Leurs réalisations comprennent le musée Kirchner (Davos, 1990–1992) ; le restaurant Vinikus (Davos, 1990–1992) et la rénovation de la Collection Oskar Reinhart (Am Römerholz, Winterthur, 1997–98). Gigon/Guyer a participé à de nombreux concours internationaux dont ceux de l'extension du Nelson-Atkins Museum (Kansas, 1999), ou le projet de « Cité de la culture » de Saint-Jacques-de-Compostelle (1999). Ils travaillent actuellement à la présentation de la collection Albers/Honegger (Mouans-Sartoux, France, 2003) et un projet de logements à Rüschlikon (Suisse). Leur agence emploie 18 architectes.

# ARCHEOLOGICAL MUSEUM AND PARK

*Bramsche-Kalkriese, Germany, 1999–2002*

*Client: Kalkriese Archeological Museum Park GmbH, Osnabrück. Total floor area: 1 972 m² (museum).*
*Total Costs: € 14 000 000.*

This museum and its 20-hectare park are located on the site of the famous "Battle of Varus" or "Battle in the Teutoburgen Forest" fought by the Teutons against the Romans in 9 AD. Unlike more traditional archeological sites where the remains of buildings can be put into evidence, the Kalkriese project was at the outset more abstract. A flattened earthen rampart was the only tangible evidence of this ancient triumph of the Germans over Roman invaders. Large iron plates mark the probable path of the Romans, while the Teutons' positions are outlined by narrow wood chip paths. More recent agricultural paths permit visitors to move more freely between one area and the other. As the architects say, "the coexistence of the curving, so-called "Roman route," the fine branches of the so-called "Teutonic trails" and the contemporary visitor trails traced out in agrarian patterns elucidate and symbolize a superimposition of the layers of time and cultures present at this place." The location and assumed height of the former Teutonic earthen rampart is marked by a series of iron poles. Three pavilions set in the park and titled "Seeing," "Hearing," and "Questioning" "broaden and put into perspective the impressions gained outdoors." Like the pavilions, the museum is constructed with a steel skeleton and clad with large, rusting steel plates. The museum consists of a one-story volume raised up from the earth and a tower-like structure on top. The landscape and battlefield can be seen from nearly 40 meters above the ground. The actual exhibition is to be found in the "torso" of the building where artifacts discovered on the site are stored and exhibited.

Das Museum und sein 20 ha großer Park befinden sich an dem Ort, den man heute für den Schauplatz der Varusschlacht oder Schlacht im Teutoburger Wald hält, die 9 n. Chr. zwischen Cheruskern und Römern stattfand. Im Gegensatz zu anderen archäologischen Stätten gab es beim Kalkriese-Projekt keinerlei Überreste von Gebäuden, sondern lediglich einen abgeflachten Erdwall. Große Eisenplatten markieren den Weg, den die römische Truppenkolonne wahrscheinlich genommen hat, während die teutonischen Positionen durch schmale, mit Holzspänen ausgelegte Pfade kenntlich gemacht sind. Die in jüngster Zeit angelegten Feldwege erlauben den Besuchern inzwischen, sich freier von einem Bereich zum anderen zu bewegen. Die beiden Architekten erklären: „Die Koexistenz der gewundenen Römerstraße mit der feinverzweigten Spur der Teutonen und den nach dem Muster von Feldwegen angelegten neuen Besucherpfaden erhellt und symbolisiert eine Überlagerung der an diesem Ort präsenten Schichten der Zeiten und Kulturen." Lage und angenommene Höhe des teutonischen Erdwalls werden durch eine Reihe von Eisenpfosten markiert. Drei im Parkgelände verteilte und mit „Sehen", „Hören" und „Fragen" betitelte Pavillons liefern Hintergrundinformationen für die draußen gesammelten Eindrücke. Ebenso wie diese Pavillons besteht das Museumsgebäude aus einem Stahlskelett, das mit großformatigen, rostigen Stahlplatten umhüllt wurde. Sein eingeschossiger, direkt auf den Erdboden aufgesetzter Bauteil trägt an einem Ende einen turmartigen Aufbau. Von dort kann man aus einer Höhe von fast 40 m die umliegende Landschaft überblicken. Die eigentliche Ausstellung befindet sich im „Torso" des Gebäudes, wo auf dem Gelände gefundene Artefakte präsentiert und gelagert werden.

Ce musée et son parc de 20 hectares sont situés sur le site de la fameuse bataille de Varus, ou bataille de la forêt de Teutobourg, qui vit s'affronter les Germains et les Romains en l'an 9. À la différence de nombreux sites archéologiques où des vestiges peuvent être mis en évidence, ce projet reposait au départ sur des bases plus abstraites. Un rempart en terre battue était la seule preuve tangible de cette ancienne victoire des Germains. De grandes plaques de fer indiquent les mouvements probables des troupes romaines, tandis que les positions germaines sont soulignées par d'étroits chemins recouverts de copeaux de bois. Des cheminements plus récents permettent aux visiteurs de se déplacer plus librement d'une zone à l'autre. Pour les architectes : « La coexistence dans les champs de la courbe de la voie romaine, des fines ramifications des ‹pistes› germaines et des chemins pour les visiteurs actuels éclairent et symbolisent la superposition des strates du temps et des cultures en ce lieu. » La situation et la hauteur présumée de l'ancien rempart de terre germain est marquée par un alignement de poteaux de fer. Trois pavillons nommés « Voire », « Entendre » et « Questionner » mettent en perspective et précisent les impressions données par la découverte du champ de bataille. Comme les pavillons, le musée se compose d'un volume d'un seul niveau surélevé par rapport au sol, et surmonté d'une sorte de tour. Le paysage et le champ de bataille peuvent être ainsi observés de ce belvédère de 40 m de haut. Une exposition est aménagée dans le « torse » du bâtiment où des objets découverts sur place sont conservés et présentés.

*The forms can be described as mini-*
*mal or harsh. Despite their modernity,*
*they have a weathered appearance*
*related to the age of the site.*

*Die Formen lassen sich als reduziert*
*oder sogar abweisend beschreiben.*
*Trotz ihrer Modernität wirken sie mit*
*Bezug auf den Standort verwittert.*

*Les formes peuvent être décrites*
*comme minimalistes voire même bru-*
*tales. Malgré leur modernité, elles*
*présentent un aspect patiné.*

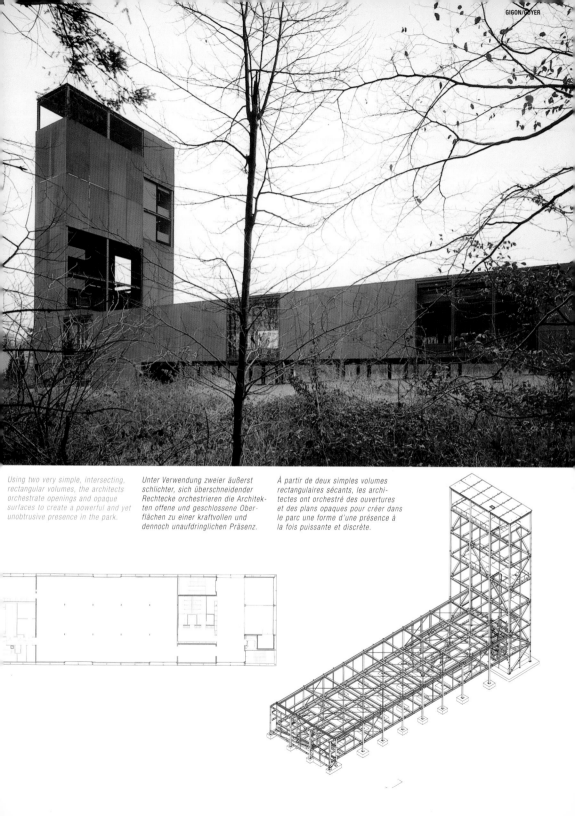

Using two very simple, intersecting, rectangular volumes, the architects orchestrate openings and opaque surfaces to create a powerful and yet unobtrusive presence in the park.

Unter Verwendung zweier äußerst schlichter, sich überschneidender Rechtecke orchestrieren die Architekten offene und geschlossene Oberflächen zu einer kraftvollen und dennoch unaufdringlichen Präsenz.

À partir de deux simples volumes rectangulaires sécants, les architectes ont orchestré des ouvertures et des plans opaques pour créer dans le parc une forme d'une présence à la fois puissante et discrète.

Set in the forest, the structures designed by Gigon/Guyer are like singularites, unexpected and largely inexplicable architectural events that guide the visitor in this strange lost world.

Die von Gigon/Guyer gestalteten, im Wald errichteten Baukörper wirken wie solitäre, unerwartete und letztlich unerklärliche Architekturereignisse, die den Besucher durch eine seltsame, vergangene Welt geleiten.

En pleine forêt, les constructions conçues par Gigon/Guyer se présentent comme des événements architecturaux singuliers, inattendus, et en grande partie inexplicables qui guident le visiteur dans cet étrange monde oublié.

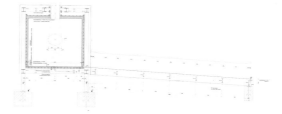

Pavilions are devoted to seeing, hearing and questioning as might almost be obvious from their external forms.

Die Pavillons sind dem Sehen, Hören und Fragen gewidmet, was man an ihren Formen erkennen kann.

Les pavillons sont consacrés à la vision, à l'écoute et aux questions, comme l'illustrent leur forme externe.

# SEAN GODSELL

*Sean Godsell Architects*
*45 Flinders Lane*
*Melbourne*
*Victoria 3000*
*Australia*

*Tel: +61 3 9654 2677*
*Fax: +61 3 9654 3877*
*e-mail: godsell@netspace.net.au*
*Web: www.seangodsell.com*

*Peninsula Ho*

Sean Godsell was born in Melbourne, Australia in 1960. He graduated from the University of Melbourne in 1984 and worked from 1986 to 1988 in London with Sir Denys Lasdun. He created Godsell Associates Pty Ltd. Architects in 1994. After receiving a Masters of Architecture degree from RMIT University in 1999, he was a finalist in the Seppelt Contemporary Art Awards held by the Museum of Contemporary Art in Sydney for his work "FutureShack." He won the RAIA Award of Merit for new residential work for the Carter/Tucker House in 2000. He taught in the RMIT Department of Architecture from 1986 to 1997. His work has been shown at exhibitions in New York, Paris, London and Mendrisio, Switzerland. Recent work includes: Carter/Tucker House (Breamlea, Victoria, Australia, 1999–2000); Peninsula House (Victoria, Australia, 2001–02; ar+d Prizewinner 2002, RAIA Architecture Award 2003); Woodleigh School Science Faculty (Baxter, Victoria, Australia (2002; RAIA William Wardell Award 2003). Current work includes: Lewis House (Dunkeld, Victoria, Australia, 2003); Westwood House (Sydney, Australia, 2003); ACN Headquarters (Victoria, Australia 2003); CIPEA Housing Project (Nanjing, China, 2003).

Sean Godsell, 1960 in Melbourne geboren, schloss 1984 sein Studium an der Universität von Melbourne ab und arbeitete von 1986 bis 1988 bei Sir Denys Lasdun in London. 1994 gründete er Godsell Associates Pty Ltd. Architects. Nachdem er 1999 den Masters of Architecture an der RMIT University erworben hatte, kam er mit seiner Arbeit „FutureShack" in die Endauswahl für die vom Museum of Contemporary Art in Sydney veranstaltete Verleihung der Seppelt Contemporary Art Awards. Im Jahr 2000 wurde Sean Godsell vom Royal Australian Institute of Architects für das Haus Carter/Tucker mit dem RAIA Award of Merit für neue Wohnbauarchitektur ausgezeichnet. Von 1986 bis 1997 lehrte er an der Architekturabteilung der RMIT University. Seine Arbeit wurde in Ausstellungen in New York, Paris, London und Mendrisio, Schweiz, präsentiert. Zu seinen neueren Architekturprojekten zählen: das Haus Carter/Tucker in Breamlea, Victoria (1999–2000), das Peninsula House in Victoria (2001–02), die naturwissenschaftliche Fakultät der Woodleigh School in Baxter, Victoria (2002), das Haus Lewis in Dunkeld, Victoria (2003), das Haus Westwood in Sydney (2003), die ACN-Zentrale in Victoria (2003), alle in Australien, sowie das CIPEA Wohnbauprojekt im chinesischen Nanjing (2003). Sean Godsell ist Träger des ar+d Preises (2002), des RAIA Architecture Award (2003) und des RAIA William Wardell Award (2003).

Sean Godsell est né en 1960 à Melbourne, en Australie. Diplômé de l'Université de Melbourne en 1984, il travaille à Londres de 1986 à 1988 dans l'agence de Sir Denys Lasdun. Il crée Godsell Associates Pty Ltd Architects en 1994. Master of Architecture de la RMIT University en 1999, il est finaliste des Seppelt Contemporary Arts Awards organisés par le Museum of Contemporary Art de Sydney pour son œuvre *FutureShack*. Il remporte le RAIA Award of Merit de création résidentielle pour sa Carter/Tucker House en 2000. Il enseigne au département d'architecture de la RMIT de 1986 à 1997. Son œuvre a été présentée dans des expositions à New York, Paris, Londres et Mendrisio (Suisse). Parmi ses réalisations récentes : Carter/Tucker House (Breamlea, Victoria Australie, 1999/2000) ; Peninsula House (Victoria, Australie, 2001–02, prix ar+d 2002, RAIA Architecture Award 2003) ; faculté des Sciences de Woodleigh School (Baxter, Victoria, Australie, 2002 ; RAIA William Wardell Award 2003), Lewis House (Dunkeld, Victoria, Australie, 2003) ; Westwood House (Sydney, Australie, 2003) ; le siège de CAN (Victoria, Australie, 2003) ; projet d'immeuble de logements CIPEA (Nankin, Chine, 2003).

# PENINSULA HOUSE

*Victoria, Australia, 2001–02*

*Client: private. Total floor area: 210 m². Costs: not specified.*

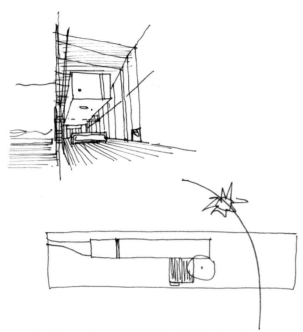

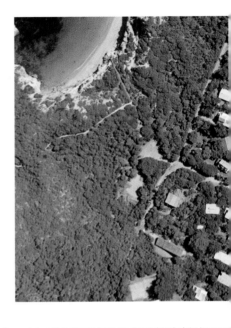

This 30-meter x 7-meter oxidized steel "portal structure" was embedded into the side of a sand dune. This element forms the "exoskeleton" of the house on which the outer skin – operable Jarrah timber shutters, glass roof and walls – are mounted. The house consists of a living/dining room, library and bedroom. The bedroom is accessed by a private stairway. As Sean Godsell says, "the house itself is the nurturing inner room, protected from the elements by a coarse outer hide." The verandah has become further abstracted in this work to become the protective outer layer of the building. The architect goes on to say, "this is a further investigation into the similarities between the enclosed verandah of the traditional Japanese house and the 'sun room' of the Australian house. My interest lies in the iconic nature of these elements to both cultures – Asian and European – and the common architectural ground which they afford to the region." Godsell had already explored the ideas of the closed verandah and inner room in his Carter/Tucker House (Breamlea, Victoria, Australia, 1999-2000).

Die 30 x 7 m messende Portalrahmenkonstruktion aus oxidiertem Stahl wurde in die Seitenfläche einer Sanddüne eingebettet. Diese Konstruktion bildet das „Exoskelett" des Hauses, auf das die Außenhaut – bewegliche Jalousien aus Dscharrah-Holz, Wände und Dach aus Glas – montiert sind. Im Innern besteht das Haus aus Wohn- und Essbereich, einer Bibliothek und einem Schlafzimmer, in das man über eine Treppe gelangt. „Das Haus selbst ist der nährende Innenraum", so Jean Godsell, „der durch eine raue Schale vor den äußeren Elementen geschützt ist." Dabei wurde das Gestaltungsthema Terrasse hier so weit abstrahiert, dass diese zur schützenden Außenhaut des Gebäudes wurde. Dazu der Architekt: „Das ist eine Weiterführung meiner Beschäftigung mit den Parallelen zwischen der umschlossenen Veranda des traditionellen japanischen Hauses und dem ,sun room' des australischen Hauses. Dabei gilt mein Interesse den zu Ikonen gewordenen Elementen der beiden unterschiedlichen Kulturen und den architektonischen Gemeinsamkeiten, die sich daraus ableiten lassen." Godsell hat diese Ideen bereits in seinem 2000 fertig gestellten Haus Carter/Tucker im australischen Breamlea, Victoria, verarbeitet.

Cette « structure en portique » de 30 x 7 m est incrustée dans le flanc d'une dune. Elle forme l'exosquelette de la maison sur lequel s'applique une peau composée de volets mobiles en bois de jarrah, d'une couverture et de murs de verre. La maison comprend un séjour/zone de repas, une bibliothèque et une chambre, accessible par un escalier direct. Pour Sean Godsell : « La maison est une pièce intérieure de ressourcement, protégée des éléments par une peau rugueuse. » La véranda traitée de manière abstraite, constitue la totalité de la protection externe. « C'est une nouvelle exploration des similarités entre la maison japonaise traditionnelle et la *sun room*, la véranda, de la maison australienne. Je m'intéresse à la nature iconique de ces éléments dans ces deux cultures – asiatique et européenne – et la richesse architecturale qu'elles apportent ensemble à la région. » Godsell avait déjà exploré l'idée de véranda fermée et de pièce intérieure dans sa Carter/Tucker House (Breamlea Victoria, Australie, 1999--2000)

*The Peninsula House benefits from a splendid, isolated natural setting, into which its forms have been set without undue destruction of the environment.*

*Das Peninsula House profitiert von seiner wunderbaren und abgeschiedenen Umgebung, in die seine Formen gesetzt wurden, ohne die Natur unnötig zu belasten.*

*La Peninsula House bénéficie d'un cadre isolé et splendide, dans lequel elle s'insère sans porter d'atteinte inutile à l'environnement.*

With its light, wooden slat exterior and relatively low profile, the house fits into the topography and even the coloring of the existing site.

Mit seinen Außenwänden aus hellen Holzlatten und relativ niedrigen Konturen fügt sich das Haus in die Topografie und sogar die Farben seiner Umgebung ein.

Par sa façade extérieure habillée de lattes de bois et son profil relativement bas, la maison s'intègre à la topographie et même aux couleurs du lieu.

The fine, wooden slats visible from the exterior of the house bring to mind some Japanese designs.

Die schmalen Holzstreifen der Außenwände erinnern an einige japanische Designs.

Le lattis de bois visibles de l'extérieur de la maison rappelle certaines conceptions japonaises.

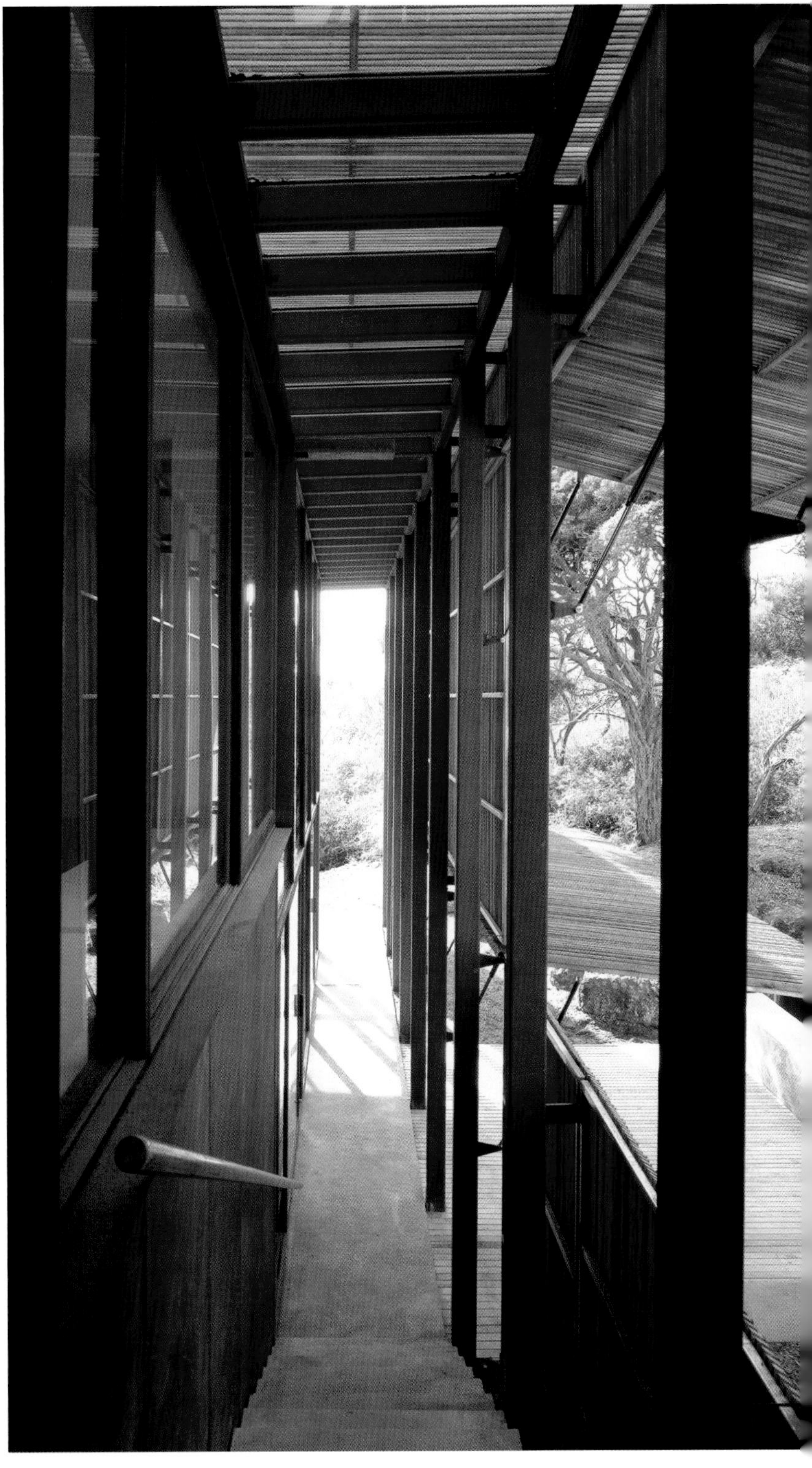

Airy and open, the Peninsula House
has many adjustable surfaces, like
other residences designed by Sean
Godsell.

Das luftig und offen angelegte Peninsula House ist wie frühere Wohnhäuser von Sean Godsell mit verstell-
baren Oberflächen ausgestattet.

Aérée et ouverte la Peninsula House
s'ouvre par de nombreuses ouvertures ajustables, comme d'autres
résidences conçue par Sean Godsell.

A bathroom opening out into an enclosed garden or interior light modulated by overhead slats give an unusual warmth and brightness to the house.

Eine Öffnung im Badezimmer oder das Licht, das durch ein Holzraster gefiltert wird, verleihen dem Haus Wärme und Helligkeit.

La salle-de-bains ouvre sur un jardin clos, ou l'éclairage modulé par le lattis en toiture introduit une luminosité et une chaleur inhabituelles.

# ALEXANDER GORLIN

*Alexander Gorlin Architects*
*137 Varick Street*
*New York, NY 10013*
*USA*

*Tel: +1 212 229 1199*
*Fax: +1 212 260 3590*
*e-mail: agorlin@gorlinarchitects.com*
*Web: www.gorlinarchitects.com*

*House in the Rocky Mounta*

Alexander Gorlin received his Bachelor's degree from the Cooper Union School of Architecture (1978), his Masters from Yale (1980) and then worked in the offices of I. M. Pei and Partners (1981–82) and Kohn Pederson Fox (1984–85) before founding his own firm. He has designed housing in Santa Fe, Chicago, Nova Scotia and Miami; synagogues in New York and Tulsa, Oklahoma; a new boathouse at Yale (1998); the Gravesend Community Center in Brooklyn (2002); and participated in the competitions for the Berlin Spreebogen district (1993) and Madrid's Prado (1995). He has done residential work for such prestigious clients as Alexander Liberman, Grace Mirabella and S. I. Newhouse. He has been an Adjunct Professor at Yale (1982–1990) and a Visiting Professor of Architecture at the Cooper Union (1999, 2000). Current work includes the Aqua Apartment Tower in Miami, and the Liberty Harbor townhouses in Jersey City, New Jersey. His World Trade Center Memorial proposal was exhibited at the 2002 Venice Biennale and he is working presently on the apartment of Daniel Libeskind in New York.

Alexander Gorlin erwarb 1978 seinen Bachelor of Architecture an der Cooper Union School of Architecture in New York und 1980 seinen Master of Architecture an der Yale University. Von 1981 bis 1982 arbeitete er bei I. M. Pei and Partners und von 1984 bis 1985 bei Kohn Pederson Fox, bevor er seine eigene Firma gründete. Zu seinen Projekten gehören Wohnhäuser in Santa Fe, Chicago, Nova Scotia und Miami, Synagogen in New York und Tulsa, Oklahoma, ein neues Bootshaus für Yale (1998), das Gravesend Gemeindezentrum in Brooklyn (2002) sowie seine Wettbewerbsbeiträge für den Bezirk Berlin Spreebogen (1993) und den Madrider Prado (1995). Außerdem hat er Wohnungen für so namhafte Klienten wie Alexander Liberman, Grace Mirabella und S. I. Newhouse gestaltet. Daneben war er von 1982 bis 1990 als außerordentlicher Professor an der Yale University tätig und hatte 1999 und 2000 eine Gastprofessur für Architektur an der Cooper Union inne. Derzeit arbeitet er unter anderem am Aqua Apartment Tower in Miami und den Liberty Harbor Terrassenhäusern in Jersey City, New Jersey. Sein Entwurf für ein World Trade Center Mahnmal wurde 2002 auf der Biennale in Venedig ausgestellt. Zu den aktuellen Projekten gehört außerdem die Wohnung von Daniel Libeskind in New York.

Alexander Gorlin est Bachelor of Architecture de la Cooper Union School of Architecture (1978) et Master of Architecture de Yale (1980). Il a travaillé dans les agences de I. M. Pei and Partners (1981–82) et Kohn Pederson Fox (1984–85) avant de créer sa propre structure. Il a conçu des logements à Santa Fe, Chicago, en Nouvelle-Écosse et à Miami ; des synagogues à New York et Tulsa (Oklahoma) ; un nouveau garage à bateaux à Yale (1998) ; le Gravesend Community Center à Brooklyn (2002) et a participé aux concours pour le quartier du Spreebogen à Berlin (1993) et le musée du Prado à Madrid (1995). Il a conçu les résidences de clients prestigieux dont Alexander Liberman, Grace Mirabella et S. I. Newhouse. Professeur adjoint à Yale (1982–1990) et professeur d'architecture invité à la Cooper Union (1999, 2000). Il travaille actuellement à la tour d'appartements Aqua à Miami et à des maisons urbaines à Libert Harbor (Jersey City, New Jersey). Sa proposition pour le Mémorial du World Trade Center a été exposée à la Biennale de Venise 2002, et il travaille actuellement à un appartement pour Daniel Libeskind à New York.

# HOUSE IN THE ROCKY MOUNTAINS

*Genesee, Colorado, USA, 2000–01*

*Client: Stuart and Chris Allen. Floor area: 1 000 m². Costs: $ 2 500 000.*

This 1 000-square-meter house is built on a two-hectare mountainside site between two streams and within view of 4 200-meter Mount Evans. It is made of concrete block with moss rock stone veneer (a local stone that changes with the humidity, becoming greener with the morning dew) and a steel frame structure. It uses geothermal heating, and is oriented to the mountain winds, obviating the need for air conditioning. Alexander Gorlin states, "this house is conceived as both an abstraction of the rugged landscape of the Colorado Rockies and as a re-inhabited ruin, inspired but the Anasazi stone constructions of the Southwest in Chaco Canyon… There is a constant interplay between inside and outside, blurring the boundary between the two so that one feels part of the wooded site." The entry of the house is by way of a steel bridge over a ravine, sheltering an elk path that runs through the site. Terraces provide flat outside space that otherwise would be missing from the steep site. Sliding steel doors open into a curved entry hall with the dining room overlooking, the living room below and the kitchen and family room beyond. The children's area is separate from the parents' tower with the husband's office above. In a poetic vein, the architect says: "The terraced site, with its stone walls, recalls Dante's ascent in Purgatory, 'Now we were drawing closer; we had reached the part from where first I'd seen a breach, precisely like a gap that cleaves a wall. He led us to a cleft in the rock… approach, the steps are close at hand; from this point on one can climb easily.'"

Das 1 000 m² umfassende Wohnhaus liegt auf einem 2 ha großen Hanggrundstück, zwischen zwei Wasserläufen und mit Blick auf den 4 200 m hohen Mount Evans. Es besteht aus einer Stahlrahmenkonstruktion und einer Kombination aus Beton- und Moosstein (ein lokaler Stein, dessen Farbe sich je nach Feuchtigkeitsgrad ändert, und der mit dem Morgentau grün wird). Für die Klimatisierung des Gebäudes werden Erdwärme und Bergwinde genutzt, wodurch sich eine Klimaanlage erübrigt. Alexander Gorlin sagt über seinen Entwurf, er sei sowohl von der Felslandschaft der Colorado Rockies als auch von den in die Steilhänge des Chaco Canyon eingebauten Wohnanlagen der Anasazi-Indianer inspiriert: „Es herrscht ein ständiges Wechselspiel zwischen Innen und Außen, was die Grenzen zwischen beiden Elementen verwischt, so dass man sich als Teil der bewaldeten Umgebung fühlt." Der Zugang zum Haus verläuft über eine Stahlbrücke. Damit wird ein Pfad durch die darunter liegende Schlucht geschützt, der regelmäßig von Elchen genutzt wird. Terrassen sind die einzigen horizontalen Außenflächen auf diesem ansonsten steil abfallenden Grundstück. Hinter den stählernen Schiebetüren öffnet sich ein geschwungener Eingangsbereich, vom Esszimmer überblickt man den darunter liegenden Wohnraum und die angrenzende Küche. Der Bereich für die Kinder ist vom turmartigen Trakt der Eltern mit dem Büro des Hausherrn im obersten Stock abgetrennt. In der poetischen Deutung des Architekten soll die terrassenförmige Anordnung der Steinwände an Dantes Abstieg ins Fegefeuer und besonders jene Stelle erinnern, an der sich in der Felswand ein Spalt auftut, von wo aus sich leichter herabklettern lässt.

Cette maison de 1000 m² est édifiée en pleine montagne dans la perspective du Mount Evans (4 200 m d'altitude), sur un terrain de deux hectares, pris entre deux torrents. Elle fait appel à une ossature en acier et à des parpaings de béton parés de *moss rock*, une pierre locale qui change de couleur avec l'humidité et tourne au vert sous l'effet de la rosée matinale. Chauffée par géothermie, elle est orientée face aux vents venus de la montagne, ce qui évite la climatisation. Pour Alexander Gorling : « Cette maison est conçue à la fois comme une abstraction du paysage sauvage des Colorado Rockies et comme une ruine qui aurait été ré-habitée, inspirée des constructions en pierre des Ansazi du sud-ouest du Caco Canyon… Un jeu permanent intervient entre l'intérieur et l'extérieur, qui perturbe leurs relations et donne l'impression de faire partie de cet environnement boisé. » On accède par une passerelle d'acier lancée au-dessus d'un petit ravin, pour respecter un passage de rennes. Des terrasses offrent des espaces extérieurs plats dont le site escarpé était dénué. Des portes coulissantes en acier ouvrent sur un hall d'entrée arrondi. La salle à manger domine le séjour en contrebas et la cuisine et le séjour familial plus loin. La zone des enfants est séparée de la tour des parents occupée en partie supérieure par un bureau. Pour l'architecte, épris de poésie, « ce site en terrasses, avec ses murs de pierre, évoque la montée de Dante vers le Purgatoire : Maintenant, nous nous rapprochions ; nous avions atteint l'endroit d'où j'avais déjà aperçu une ouverture, exactement comme une fissure dans un mur… des marches furent bientôt à notre portée, et de là nous pouvions aisément monter. »

*The large, flat expanses of this house allow it to fit into its natural setting as does the moss rock facing.*

*Mit der Wandverkleidung aus Moosstein fügt sich das Haus harmonisch in seine natürliche Umgebung ein.*

*Les terrasses de la maison et son habillage de moss rock contribuent à son intégration dans le cadre naturel.*

*Rather than a massive central volume, the house is laid out as "an abstraction" of the local landscape.*

*Statt als massiver und zentraler Baukörper ist das Haus als eine „Abstraktion" der lokalen Landschaft angelegt.*

*Plutôt qu'un volume massif qui s'impose, la maison est une « abstraction » du paysage dans lequel elle se trouve.*

The architect plays on a contrast between the rough stone façade and the open glazed surfaces with their metal fittings.

Der Architekt setzt spielerische Kontraste zwischen der rauen Stein fassade und den offenen Glasfläch mit ihren Metalleinfassungen.

L'architecte joue de contrastes entre la façade de pierre brute et les surfaces vitrées prises dans une menuiserie métallique.

On a downhill slope, the house steps with the land, allowing for the creation of a double height living room that does not project above the other alignments of the structure.

Indem die Anlage dem abschüssigen Gelände folgt, wurde ein Wohnraum möglich, der sich über zwei Stockwerke erstreckt, ohne über die anderen Bauteile hinauszuragen.

Établie sur une pente, la maison se sert du profil du terrain pour créer un séjour double hauteur qui ne se projette pas pour autant au-dessus des autres alignements.

The spacious, almost fully-glazed living room offers generous views over the surroundings. Rough stone, also seen as an outside cladding continues within, near the fireplace for example.

Der geräumige, fast zur Gänze verglaste Wohnraum bietet weite Ausblicke auf die Umgegend. Grob gearbeitete Steine, die auch als Außenverkleidung dienen, setzen sich im Innern fort, wie hier beim Kamin.

Le séjour spacieux, presque entièrement vitré, offre de généreuses perspectives sur l'environnement. La pierre brute, vue dans l'habillage extérieur, se retrouve dans le mur de la cheminée, par exemple.

The house is a combination of architectural sophistication and a rough natural setting. Within its walls the resident can observe nature without being submitted to any of the inconveniences of survival in the wilderness.

Das Haus wirkt durch die Kombination aus architektonischer Raffinesse und einer rauen natürlichen Umgebung. Die Bewohner in seinem Innern können an der Natur teilhaben, ohne den Unannehmlichkeiten eines Lebens in der Wildnis ausgesetzt zu sein.

La maison est une combinaison entre une architecture sophistiquée et la nature intacte. De ses murs, le résident peut observer la nature sauvage sans être soumis à ses contraintes.

*The bathrooms offer one of the most spectacular contrasts between the roughness of the natural setting and the refinement of the interior.*

*Einer der spektakulärsten Kontraste zwischen der urwüchsigen Umgebung und der schlichten Eleganz der Innenräume stellt das Badezimmer dar.*

*L'un des contrastes les plus spectaculaires entre le cadre naturel et le raffinement des intérieurs est donné par les salles-de-bains.*

# GOULD EVANS

*Gould Evans Associates*
*3136 North 3rd Avenue*
*Phoenix, AR 85013*
*USA*

*Tel: +1 602 234 1140*
*Fax: +1 602 234 1156*
*e-mail: info@gouldevans.com*
*Web: www.gouldevans.com*

Gould Evans is a comprehensive design firm of 200 employees providing architecture, interior design, landscape architecture, planning, and graphic design services to public and private clients. The firm was founded in 1974 and has offices in Phoenix, Arizona; Kansas City, Missouri; Lawrence, Kansas; San Antonio, Texas; Salt Lake City, Utah; Tampa, Florida; and Sausalito, California. These offices operate as a network of affiliated organizations with strong local and regional ties yet have access to a national knowledge base and talent pool. Recent and current projects include the University of Arizona Stevie Eller Dance Theater (Tucson, Arizona, published here); Snow College Performing Arts Center (Ephraim, Utah); Cerner Corporation World Headquarters (Kansas City, Missouri); Community Health Facility (Lawrence, Kansas); and University of Florida Rinker Hall (Gainesville, Florida). Amongst those working on the Stevie Eller Theater, Trudi Hummel received her Bachelor of Architecture from the University of Texas in Austin and is one of the founding principals of the Phoenix office, while Jose D. Pombo received his Bachelor of Science degree from the Arizona State University in Tempe (1994) and his Master of Architecture from UCLA (1997). He worked in the office of Mark Mack in Los Angeles (1996–97) before joining Gould Evans. Donna Barry received her degrees from the Georgia Institute of Technology (BA, 1986; MArch, 1989). She worked with Kohn Pederson Fox (New York, 1994–95), William Bruder (Phoenix, 1996–97) and Peter Eisenman (New York, 1989–1994) before joining Gould Evans in 1998.

Gould Evans, eine Firma mit 200 Angestellten, ist für öffentliche und private Auftraggeber in den Bereichen Architektur, Innenarchitektur, Landschaftsarchitektur, Planung und Grafikdesign tätig. Das Unternehmen wurde 1974 gegründet und hat Niederlassungen in Phoenix (Arizona), Kansas City (Missouri), Lawrence (Kansas), San Antonio (Texas), Salt Lake City (Utah), Tampa (Florida) und Sausalito (Kalifornien). Diese Büros fungieren als ein Netzwerk von Einheiten, die einerseits lokal und regional stark verwurzelt sind, aber gleichzeitig jederzeit auf den landesweiten Unternehmenspool an Wissen und Talent zugreifen können. Zu ihren neueren und aktuellen Projekten zählen: das hier vorgestellte Stevie Eller Dance Theatre der University of Arizona in Tucson, Arizona, das Snow College Performing Arts Center in Ephraim, Utah, die internationale Zentrale der Cerner Corporation in Kansas City, Missouri, das Gemeindegesundheitszentrum in Lawrence, Kansas und die Rinker Hall der University of Florida in Gainesville. Am Stevie Eller Theater arbeiteten unter anderem Trudi Hummel, Jose D. Pombo und Donna Barry mit. Trudi Hummel erwarb ihren Bachelor of Architecture an der University of Texas in Austin und ist eines der leitenden Gründungsmitglieder des Büros in Phoenix. Jose D. Pombo erwarb 1994 seinen Bachelor of Science an der Arizona State University in Tempe und 1997 seinen Master of Architecture an der University of California in Los Angeles (UCLA). Bevor er bei Gould Evans eintrat, arbeitete er von 1996 bis 1997 im Büro von Mark Mack in Los Angeles. Donna Barry erwarb 1986 ihren Bachelor und 1989 den Master of Architecture am Georgia Institute of Technology. Sie arbeitete bei Kohn Pederson Fox in New York (1994–95), bei William Bruder in Phoenix (1996–97) und bei Peter Eisenman in New York (1989–1994), bevor sie 1998 bei Gould Evans eintrat.

Gould Evans est une agence de conception globale de 200 collaborateurs intervenant en architecture, architecture intérieure, architecture du paysage, urbanisme et graphisme pour des clients publics ou privés. L'agence a été fondée en 1974 et possède des bureaux à Phoenix (Arizona), Kansas City (Missouri), Lawrence (Kansas), San Antonio (Texas), Salt Lake City (Utah), Tampa (Floride) et Sausalito (Californie). Ces bureaux travaillent en réseau à implantation locale et régionale forte Parmi ses projets récents et actuels : le Stevie Eller Dance Theater pour l'Université de l'Arizona (Tucson, Arizona, publié ici) ; le Performing Arts Center du Snow College (Ephraim, Utah) ; le siège mondial de la Cerner Corporation (Kansas City) ; un dispensaire (Lawrence) et le Rinker Hall pour l'Université de Floride (Gainesville). Parmi les concepteurs du Stevie Eller Theater figurent : Trudi Hummel, B. Arch de l'University of Texas in Austin et un des associés-fondateurs de l'agence de Phoenix ; Jose D. Pombo, Bachelor of Architecture, Arizona State University in Tempe, en 1994, Master of Architecture de UCLA, en 1997. Il a travaillé pour l'agence de Mark Mack à Los Angeles (1996–97) avant de rejoindre Gould Evans. Donna Barry est B. A. (1986) et Master of Architecture (1989) du Georgia Institute of Technology. Elle a travaillé pour Kohn Pederson Fox (New York, 1994–95), William Bruder (Phoenix, 1996–97) et Peter Eisenman (New York, 1989–1994) avant de rejoindre Gould Evans en 1998.

# STEVIE ELLER DANCE THEATER

*University of Arizona, Tucson, Arizona, USA, 2000–2003*

*Client: University of Arizona. Floor area: 2 790 m². Costs: $ 9 000 000.*

Built for the College of Fine Arts, School of Music and Dance at the University of Arizona, the Stevie Eller Dance Theater includes a 300-seat theater, dance studio and facilities for an outdoor stage, scene shop and costume shop. Proud of the collaborative process that allowed workers to contribute to the project in the construction phase, Gould Evans calls this "a built work of art that works." The building was initially conceived out of a father and daughter's quest to find a distinguished college dance program. During their search, they found the University of Arizona had the BEST dance program with the WORST facility. The father went to the University President, Peter Likins, and Dean of Fine Arts, Maurice Sevigny, with an offer of a large monetary gift, but stipulating that the University and the College of Fine Arts each match his gift. Three years later, this building was born and the man's daughter will dance Ballanchine's "Serenade" with her graduating class in the spring. The design process clearly included reference to "Serenade." As the architects say, "for the design of the Stevie Eller Dance Theater, we learned about dance, about movement, about graphically representing dance through notation formally called 'labanotation.' We immersed ourselves in the IDEA of movement. The faculty taught us about dance, and we taught them about structure and together we created 'dancing columns.' We asked the client to tell us about 'Serenade,' Ballanchine's first ballet written for the students of the American Ballet. We contacted the Dance Notation Bureau and the Ballanchine Foundation in New York and we acquired the labanotation and score for 'Serenade.' We overlaid the 'plans' of the starting positions for each movement of 'Serenade' and created a matrix from which emerged the 'grid' of tilted columns that support the glass encased dance studio on the second floor of the building."

Das Stevie Eller Dance Theater wurde für das College of Fine Arts, School of Music and Dance der University of Arizona gebaut und enthält ein Theater mit 300 Sitzen, ein Tanzstudio, eine Freilichtbühne sowie eine Kostüm- und Kulissenwerkstatt. Auf der Suche nach einem ausgezeichneten College mit Tanzausbildung für seine Tochter stellte der Vater fest, dass die University of Arizona zwar das BESTE Ausbildungsprogramm, aber die SCHLECHTESTEN Räumlichkeiten dafür hatte. Daraufhin bot er dem Universitätspräsidenten, Peter Likins, und dem Dekan der schönen Künste, Maurice Sevigny, eine große Spende an, machte jedoch zur Bedingung, dass von Seiten der Hochschule eine Gegenleistung erbracht wird. Diese erfolgte drei Jahre später in Form des Stevie Eller Dance Theater. Und inzwischen hat die Tochter dort mit ihrer Abschlussklasse Ballanchines ‚Serenade' aufgeführt. Im Gestaltungsprozess, so die beteiligten Architekten, finden sich deutliche Bezüge auf dieses Stück. Sie betonen, dass sie im Zuge der Planung des Gebäudes viel über den Tanz gelernt haben und darüber, wie man Bewegungen durch ein Bezeichnungssystem, das nach dem Tanzpädagogen Rudolf von Laban „Laban-Notation" genannt wird, grafisch darstellen kann: „Dabei beschäftigten wir uns intensivst mit der IDEE von Bewegung. Die Mitglieder der Tanzabteilung lehrten uns Tanz, wir lehrten sie Bauformen und zusammen schufen wir die ‚tanzenden Säulen'. Wir baten die Bauherren, uns von ‚Serenade' zu erzählen, dem ersten Ballett, das Ballanchine für die Studenten der School of American Ballet geschrieben hatte. Wir setzten uns mit dem Dance Notation Bureau und der Ballanchine Foundation in New York in Verbindung und erwarben die Laban-Notation und Partitur für ‚Serenade'. Dann übertrugen wir die Ausgangspositionen für jede Bewegung in diesem Stück in eine Matrix, aus der das ‚Gitterwerk' der schrägen Säulen entstand, die das mit Glas ummantelte Studio im zweiten Stock des Theaters tragen."

Construit pour le College of Fine Arts, School of Music and Dance of the University of Arizona, le Stevie Eller Dance Theater comprend un théâtre de 300 places, un studio de danse, une scène en plein air, un atelier pour les décors et un pour les costumes. Fier du processus de collaboration qui a permis aux ouvriers de contribuer au projet au cours de la phase de chantier, Gould Evans parle d'une « œuvre d'art construite et qui fonctionne ». Ce bâtiment est né de la quête d'un père et sa fille qui recherchaient une école de danse supérieure au programme élitaire. Pendant leur recherche, son père et elle découvrent que l'Université de l'Arizona possède le MEILLEUR programme, et les PIRES installations. Le pére va voir le président de l'Université, Peter Likins, et le doyen des Beaux Arts, Maurice Sevigny, pour leur proposer un don important à condition que l'Université et le College of Fine Arts en fassent autant. Trois ans plus tard, le bâtiment est né et sa fille dansera le ballet *Serenade* de Ballanchine avec sa classe de diplôme au printemps. » Le processus de conception comprenait à l'évidence une référence à *Serenade*. « … Nous avons beaucoup appris sur la danse, le mouvement, la représentation graphique de la danse sous forme d'une notation appelée labanotation. Nous nous sommes immergés dans l'idée du mouvement. L'université nous a enseigné la danse, nous lui avons appris la structure, et ensemble nous avons créé des ‹ colonnes dansantes. › Nous avons demandé au client de nous parler de *Serenade*, la première chorégraphie écrite par Ballanchine pour les élèves de l'American Ballet. Nous avons contacté le Dance Notation Bureau de la Ballanchine Foundation à New York et avons acquis la labanotation et la partition de *Serenade*. Nous avons superposé les ‹ plans › de positions de départ de chaque mouvement du ballet pour créer une matrice d'où a émergé la ‹ grille › de colonnes inclinées qui soutiennent le studio de danse en verre installé au second niveau du bâtiment. »

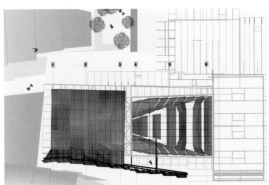
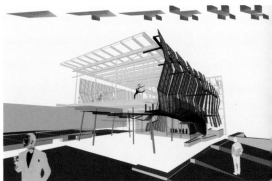

The movement of dancers that in-spired the architectural design can be clearly understood in the drawing above and the photo below.

Wie die Bewegung von Tänzern das architektonische Design inspiriert hat, lässt sich in obiger Zeichnung und untenstehendem Foto klar erkennen.

Les mouvements de danse à l'origine de la conception architecturale sont clairement exprimés par le dessin ci-dessus et la photo ci-dessous.

*With its successive shells and volumes raised on thin pilotis, the Stevie Eller Dance Theater is animated by its interior lighting and the dancers who are visible even from the exterior.*

*Mit seinen aufeinanderfolgenden Verschalungen und auf zierlichen Säulen ruhenden Baukörpern wird das Stevie Eller Dance Theater durch seine Innenbeleuchtung und die Tänzer belebt, die sogar von außen zu sehen sind.*

*Composé de coques et d'une succession de volumes sur pilotis, le Stevie Eller Dance Theater est animé par son éclairage intérieur et même par les danseurs que l'on aperçoit de l'extérieur.*

Bright open rehearsal spaces and outside terraces sheltered by façade elements give a feeling of freedom and openness that is entirely appropriate to dance.

*Helle, offene Proberäume und Außenterrassen, die durch Fassadenelemente geschützt sind, vermitteln ein Gefühl von Freiheit und Weite, das sehr gut zum Thema Tanz passt.*

*Les salles de répétitions largement ouvertes et les terrasses extérieures donnent un sentiment de liberté ou d'ouverture qui correspond parfaitement à l'idée même de danse.*

*Behind the scenes, spaces seem to be treated with the same respect for detail and spaciousness that is usually reserved for public areas.*

*Auch die Nebenräume wurden mit viel Respekt für Details und Raumwirkung behandelt, wie er üblicherweise öffentlichen Bereichen zukommt.*

*Derrières les scènes, les espaces fonctionnels semblent traités avec le même sens du détail et de l'espace que les zones publiques.*

Tilted columns and irregularly aligned
metal plates carry the sense of
movement created by the outside into
the interior of the structure.

Schräggestellte Säulen und unregelmäßig ausgerichtete Metallplatten
setzen das Gefühl von Bewegung im
Gebäudeinnern fort.

Des colonnes inclinées et des parois
métalliques alignées irrégulièrement
introduisent dans les espaces intérieurs le sentiment de mouvement.

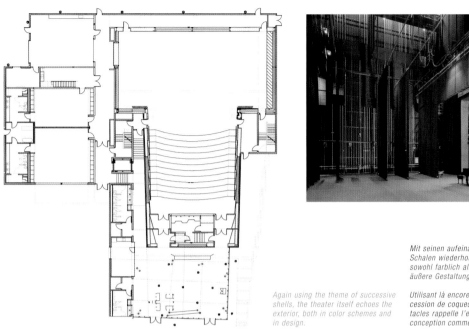

Mit seinen aufeinanderfolgenden
Schalen wiederholt der Theaterraum
sowohl farblich als auch formal die
äußere Gestaltung.

Again using the theme of successive
shells, the theater itself echoes the
exterior, both in color schemes and
in design.

Utilisant là encore le thème de la succession de coques, la salle de spectacles rappelle l'extérieur, dans sa
conception comme dans sa coloration.

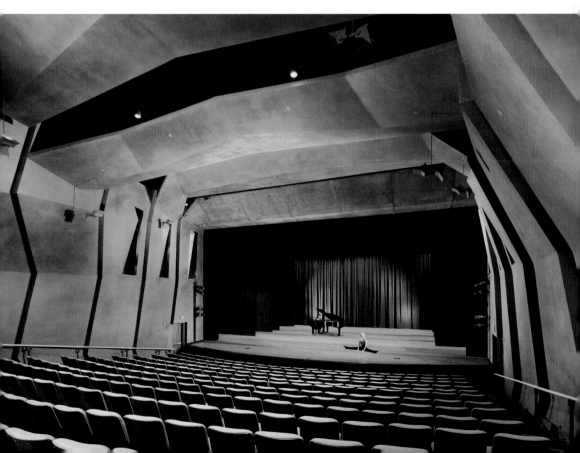

# ZAHA HADID

*Zaha Hadid Architects*
*Studio 9, 10 Bowling Green Lane*
*London EC1R OBQ*
*UK*

*Tel: +44 20 7253 5147*
*Fax: +44 20 7251 8322*
*e-mail: mail@zaha-hadid.com*
*Web: www.zaha-hadid.com*

Zaha Hadid studied architecture at the Architectural Association in London (AA) beginning in 1972 and was awarded the Diploma Prize in 1977. She then became a partner of Rem Koolhaas in the Office for Metropolitan Architecture (OMA) and taught at the AA. She has also taught at Harvard, the University of Chicago, in Hamburg and at Columbia University in New York. Well known for her paintings and drawings she has had a substantial influence, despite having built relatively few buildings. She has completed the Vitra Fire Station, Weil am Rhein, Germany, 1990–1994 and exhibition designs such as that for "The Great Utopia," Solomon R. Guggenheim Museum, New York, 1992. Significant competition entries include her design for the Cardiff Bay Opera House, 1994–1996; the Habitable Bridge, London, 1996; and the Luxembourg Philharmonic Hall, Luxembourg, 1997. More recently, Zaha Hadid has entered a phase of active construction with such projects as the Innsbruck Ski Jump and the Cincinatti Arts Center published here. In 2004, Zaha Hadid became the first woman to win the coveted Pritzker Prize.

Zaha Hadid studierte ab 1972 an der Architectural Association (AA) in London und erhielt 1977 den Diploma Prize. Danach wurde sie Partnerin von Rem Koolhaas im Office for Metropolitan Architecture (OMA). Sie lehrte an der AA in Harvard, an der University of Chicago, in Hamburg und an der Columbia University in New York. Hadid ist besonders durch ihre Gemälde und Zeichnungen bekannt geworden. Obwohl nur wenige ihrer Entwürfe realisiert wurden, so das Vitra-Feuerwehrhaus in Weil am Rhein (1990–1994), gehört sie zu den einflussreichsten Vertreterinnen ihrer Zunft. 1992 entwarf sie das Ausstellungsdesign für „The Great Utopia" im New Yorker Solomon R. Guggenheim Museum. Zu ihren bedeutendsten Wettbewerbsbeiträgen gehören Entwürfe für das Cardiff Bay Opera House (1994–1996), für die Habitable Bridge in London (1996) und die Philharmonie in Luxemburg (1997). In jüngster Zeit ist Zaha Hadid in eine Phase aktiven Bauens eingetreten, so mit den hier vorgestellten Projekten der Sprungschanze in Innsbruck und dem Cincinnati Arts Center. Anfang 2004 wurde sie als erste Frau mit dem begehrten Pritzker Prize ausgezeichnet.

Zaha M. Hadid a étudié l'architecture à l'Architectural Association (AA) de Londres de 1972 à 1977, date à laquelle elle reçoit le Prix du diplôme. Elle est ensuite associée de l'agence de Rem Koolhaas, Office for Metropolitan Architecture, et enseigne à l'AA, Harvard, University of Chicago, la Columbia University, et l'Université de Hambourg. Très connue pour ses peintures et dessins, elle exerce une réelle influence, même si elle n'a que peu construit. Parmi ses réalisations : le poste d'incendie de Vitra (Weil am Rhein, Allemagne, 1990–1994), et des projets pour expositions comme « La Grande Utopie », Solomon R. Guggenheim Museum (New York, 1992). Elle a participé à des concours dont les plus importants sont le projet de la Cardiff Bay Opera House (Pays-de-Galles, 1994–1996), un Pont habitable (Londres, 1996) et la salle de concerts philharmoniques de Luxembourg (1997). Plus récemment, elle est entrée dans une phase de chantiers concrets avec des projets comme un tremplin de ski à Innsbruck (Autriche) et le Cincinnati Arts Center, reproduit ici. En 2004, elle est la première femme à recevoir le Pritzker Prize.

# BERGISEL SKI JUMP

*Innsbruck, Austria, 2001–02*

*Client: Austrian Ski Federation, Innsbruck. Length: 90 m, height: 48 m. Costs: not specified.*

Created in 1926, the Bergisel ski jump has been well known almost since its construction, and was the site of the 1964 and 1976 Winter Olympic competitions. The schedule of international ski jumping events is such that local authorities could allow only one year from demolition to opening of the new facility. Cleverly, the Ski Jump includes a steel plate clad café situated ten meters above the jumping ramp, and it is apparent in the design that the Austrian Ski Federation wanted to create a monument as much as they sought a high-quality sports facility. Seating 150 persons, the café boasts a 360° view of the city and mountain scenery. In spite of local resistance to contemporary architecture of notable quality, both Hadid and Dominique Perrault (Innsbruck Town Hall) have succeeded in breaking into this Tyrolean stronghold of traditionalism. Forty-eight meters tall and seven by seven meters on the ground, the concrete structure has already permitted long flights over the snowy slopes such as the 134.5-meter jump achieved here by Sven Hannawald in January 2002. Hadid has described the structure as an "organic hybrid" – a sort of mixture of a tower and a bridge, but it succeeds in abstracting the speed of motion and flight that characterizes the most spectacular of winter sports events.

Die historische, 1926 gebaute Skisprungschanze Bergisel im Innsbrucker Stadtteil Wilten war Austragungsort der Olympischen Winterspiele 1964 und 1976. Aufgrund programmtechnischer Besonderheiten der internationalen Skisprungwettbewerbe konnten die lokalen Behörden erst ein Jahr nach Abriss der alten Konstruktion die Eröffnung der neuen Schanze genehmigen. Diese ist nun mit einem 10 m über der Absprungstelle liegenden Café ausgestattet, das mit Stahlplatten ummantelt ist. Insgesamt wird aus der Gestaltung deutlich, dass der österreichische Skiverband mit einer anspruchsvollen Sportanlage auch ein Monument schaffen wollte. Das Café mit 150 Sitzen bietet einen vollständigen Rundblick über die Stadt Innsbruck und die umliegende Berglandschaft. Trotz lokaler Vorbehalte gegenüber zeitgenössischer Architektur ist es Zaha Hadid wie schon Dominique Perrault mit seinem Innsbrucker Rathaus gelungen, diese Tiroler Hochburg des Traditionalismus einzunehmen. Ausgehend von einem 7 x 7 m messenden Sockel ragt die Betonkonstruktion 48 m hoch und hat sportliche Höchstleistungen wie den 134,5 m weiten Sprung von Sven Hannawald im Januar 2002 ermöglicht. Hadid hat sie als einen „organischen Hybriden" bezeichnet – eine Mischung aus Turm und Brücke. In jedem Fall artikuliert sich in ihrem Bauwerk auf gelungene Weise die Geschwindigkeit von Bewegung und Flug, die diesen spektakulärsten aller Wintersportwettbewerbe kennzeichnet.

Célèbre depuis sa construction en 1926, le tremplin de saut à ski de Bergisel a été le siège de compétitions olympiques en 1964 et 1976. Le calendrier des compétitions est si serré que les autorités locales ne pouvaient accorder qu'une année entre la démolition et l'inauguration d'un nouveau tremplin. La Fédération autrichienne de ski souhaitait autant un monument qu'une installation sportive. La nouvelle installation comprend un café de 150 places habillé de panneaux d'acier, suspendu à 10 m au-dessus de la rampe de départ, qui offre une vue à 360° sur la ville et la montagne. Malgré une certaine résistance locale à l'architecture contemporaine de qualité, Zaha Hadid comme Dominique Perrrault (Hôtel de ville d'Innsbruck) ont réussi à s'imposer dans ce haut lieu du traditionalisme tyrolien. De 48 m de haut pour une emprise au sol de 7 x 7 m, la structure en béton a déjà enregistré des records comme le saut de 134,5 m de Sven Hannawald en janvier 2002. Hadid décrit ce projet comme « un hybride organique », sorte de mélange de pont et de tour, mais réussit à symboliser la vitesse et le vol qui caractérisent l'une des disciplines olympiques d'hiver les plus spectaculaires.

*Jutting out of its wooded mountain setting, the Ski Jump tower appears to be poised to launch the athletes into the air.*

*Der Turm der Sprungschanze reckt sich aus dem bewaldeten Berghang in die Höhe, wie um die Skispringer in die Luft zu katapultieren.*

*Surgissant de son cadre montagneux et boisé, le tremplin de ski semble voué à la projection de skieurs dans les airs.*

Like a launch ramp, the actual ski run looks as though it winds out of the head of the tower.

*Die eigentliche Sprungschanze sieht aus wie eine spiralförmige Abschussrampe, die sich aus der Turmspitze windet.*

*Comme une rampe de lancement, la piste donne l'impression de se dérouler à partir du sommet de la tour.*

Given its location and its design, the tower offers spectacular views of the mountain and woodland scenery in every direction.

*Dank seines Standorts und Designs bietet der Turm phantastische Ausblicke auf die Berge und Wälder ringsum.*

*Par sa position, la tour offre naturellement des vues panoramiques spectaculaires sur les montagnes et les forêts avoisinantes.*

A curved back makes the tower look as though the ski ramp is tightly wound around it and about to spring into action. The normally static nature of a tower is thus adapted to the sport for which it is intended.

*Die geschwungene Rückseite lässt den Turm aussehen, als sei die Sprungschanze um ihn herumgewickelt und entfalte sich wie im Absprung. Die für einen Turm gegebene Statik richtet sich hier nach der Sportart, für die er konzipiert ist.*

*La face arrière incurvée de la tour donne l'impression que la rampe l'entoure étroitement, parée pour la compétition. La nature normalement statique d'une tour est ainsi adaptée au sport pour lequel elle a été prévue.*

# LOIS & RICHARD ROSENTHAL CENTER FOR CONTEMPORARY ART

*Cincinnati, Ohio, USA, 1999–2003*

*Client: Contemporary Arts Center. Floor area: 7 900 m². Costs: $ 34 100 000.*

*In an institution and a city that may be more famous for censorship than for an open attitude to the arts, the presence of the Rosenthal Center in downtown Cincinnati is nothing short of a triumph for Zaha Hadid.*

*In einer Stadt, die vielleicht eher für Zensurversuche als für Aufgeschlossenheit gegenüber der Kunst bekannt ist, stellt das Rosenthal Center in Downtown Cincinnati geradezu einen Triumph für Zaha Hadid dar.*

*Dans une institution et une ville qui fit parler d'elle pour son esprit de censure artistique, la présence du Rosenthal Center au centre de Cincinnati constitue presque un triomphe pour le projet de Zaha Hadid.*

With the opening of the Rosenthal Center, Zaha Hadid became, surprisingly enough, the first woman to design an American art museum. Even more surprising for the usually angular and complicated Hadid, her new museum fits nicely into a city street of mixed architectural merit. Indeed the only thing that signals the presence of an architectural "star" in this unlikely location is the closed succession of cantilevered boxes that faces on 6th Street. True, Marcel Breuer's Whitney Museum on Madison Avenue presents similarly blind volumes of stone to the street. Then, too, this is the very institution that dared to defy the strictures of Puritan America by exhibiting the controversial photographs of Robert Mapplethorpe, becoming embroiled in a famous obscenity trial. Measuring about 7 900 square meters, this is not a very large building, but it does signal the arrival of Hadid as a serious builder as opposed to a largely theoretical designer. Poured-in-place concrete floors seem to curve effortlessly into walls near the entrance, and visitors see heavy painted black steel ramp-stairs that rise almost 30 meters up to skylights. Each flight of stairs weighs 15 tons, as much as the construction cranes could carry. This staircase is the central mediating feature of the Center, leading to the exhibition space and providing a continuous focal point for the movement of visitors. This is actually more of a "kunsthalle" than it is a museum because the Center has no permanent collection. Hadid's architecture relies on the art it will exhibit to bring its exhibition spaces to life, even if some artists may find her spaces challenging or difficult.

Zaha Hadid, die als erste Frau ein amerikanisches Kunstmuseum entworfen hat, übernahm für das Rosenthal Center nicht ihre meist kantige und komplizierte Formensprache, sondern fügte es in die benachbarte Stadtarchitektur ein, die von durchaus gemischter Qualität ist. Tatsächlich ist das einzige Merkmal für die Handschrift einer „Stararchitektin" an diesem Ort die geschlossene Abfolge von kastenförmigen Bauteilen, die über die 6th Street auskragen. Zugegeben, Marcel Breuers Whitney Museum auf der Madison Avenue präsentiert sich zur Straßenseite hin mit ähnlich blinden Steingebilden. Und das ist eben jene Institution, die es wagte, mit der umstrittenen Ausstellung der Fotografien von Robert Mapplethorpe der scharfen Kritik des puritanischen Amerika zu trotzen und dafür wegen Obszönität in einen berühmt gewordenen Prozess verwickelt wurde. Zurück zum Rosenthal Center: Es ist zwar mit 7 900 m² kein besonders großformatiger Bau. Aber es zeigt, dass sich Hadid von einer eher im theoretischen Bereich wichtigen Gestalterin zur ernsthaften Praktikerin entwickelt hat. Im Inneren scheinen die vor Ort gegossenen Betonböden mit sanftem Schwung mühelos in die Wände beim Eingang überzuziehen, während sich massive, rampenförmige Treppen aus schwarzgestrichenem Stahl fast 30 m bis zu den Oberlichtern hochziehen. Jeder dieser Treppenaufgänge wiegt 15 Tonnen, so viel wie die Baukräne maximal tragen konnten. Die Treppen sind außerdem das zentrale Bindeglied des Museumsgebäudes: Sie führen zu den Ausstellungsräumen und bündeln den Besucherstrom. Es handelt sich hier übrigens mehr um eine „Kunsthalle" als um ein Museum, da das Center über keine permanente Sammlung verfügt. Hadids Gestaltung verlässt sich daher auf die ausgestellte Kunst, um ihre Räume zum Leben zu erwecken, selbst wenn einige Künstler diese herausfordernd oder schwierig finden könnten.

L'inauguration du Rosenthal Center a fait de Zaha Hadid la première femme à avoir conçu un musée en Amérique. Son style anguleux et complexe s'est plaisamment intégré dans une rue très fréquentée mais d'intérêt architectural moyen. Le seul élément qui signale la présence d'une « star » architecturale dans ce lieu improbable est l'effet d'empilement de boîtes en porte à faux qui donne sur la 6th Street. Il est vrai que le Whitney Museum de Marcel Breuer, sur Madison Avenue, offre lui aussi des volumes aveugles similaires. Le Rosenthal Center est l'institution qui avait osé défier les blocages de l'Amérique puritaine en exposant des photographies controversées de Robert Mapplethorpe, déclenchant un célèbre procès pour obscénité. Mesurant environ 7 900 m², le bâtiment n'est pas très vaste, mais annonce l'arrivée de Hadid parmi les constructeurs après son long cantonnement dans la théorie. Les sols en béton coulé in situ semblent s'incurver sans effort le long des murs de l'entrée d'où partent de lourdes rampes-escaliers en béton peint en noir qui s'élèvent jusqu'à 30 m de haut sous une verrière zénithale. Chaque volée d'escalier pèse 15 tonnes, la limite de portée des grues utilisées. Cet escalier est l'élément central du Centre et conduit aux espaces d'exposition tout en focalisant la circulation des visiteurs. Le centre est davantage une galerie qu'un musée car il ne possède pas de collection permanente. L'architecture de Hadid compte sur l'art exposé pour donner vie aux volumes, même si certains artistes les trouveront sans doute difficiles à occuper.

*Although its interlocking block façade creates a surprising contrast to the heterogeneous and traditional downtown street, exterior and interior views of the Center show that it echoes the movement and even the architecture of its surroundings.*

*Obwohl die ineinandergreifenden Fassadenblöcke einen Kontrast zu dem heterogenen Straßenbild bilden, spiegeln die Innen- und Außenansichten des Gebäudes die Dynamik und sogar die Architektur seiner Umgebung wieder.*

*Bien que la façade composée de blocs imbriqués crée un contraste avec le cadre traditionnel d'une rue de centre-ville, les vues extérieures et intérieures rappellent cependant l'animation et même l'architecture de son environnement.*

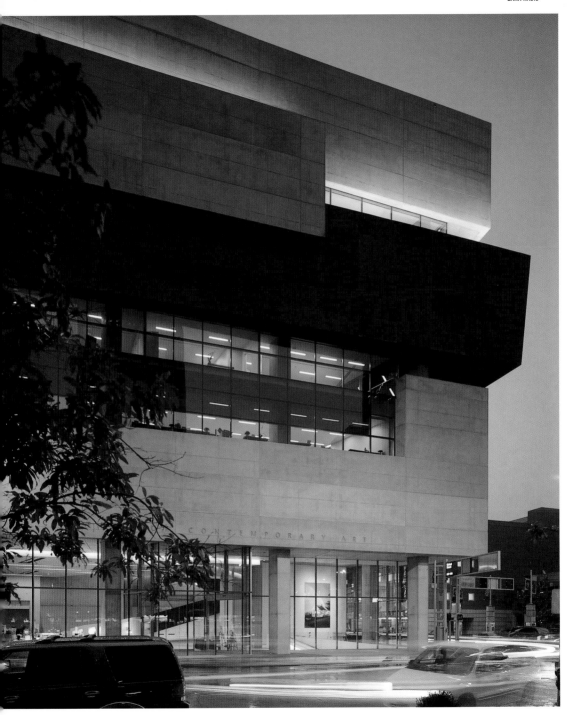

*By alternating the opaque and seemingly more weighty blocks with glazed surfaces below them, Hadid animates the surface of the building in a surprising way.*

*Durch den Wechsel von opaken und scheinbar massiven Blöcken mit darunter liegenden verglasten Oberflächen, belebt Hadid die Fassade des Gebäudes auf ungewöhnliche Weise.*

*En positionnant des surfaces vitrées entre des blocs opaques apparemment plus lourds, Zaha Hadid anime l'enveloppe de son musée de façon surprenante.*

# HERZOG & DE MEURON

*Herzog & de Meuron*
*Rheinschanze 6*
*4056 Basel*
*Switzerland*

*Tel: +41 61 385 57 57*
*Fax: +41 61 385 57 58*
*e-mail: info@herzogdemeuron.com*

Jacques Herzog and Pierre de Meuron were both born in Basel in 1950. They received degrees in architecture at the Swiss Federal Institute of Technology (ETH) in Zurich in 1975 after studying with Aldo Rossi, and founded their firm Herzog & de Meuron Architecture Studio in Basel in 1978. Harry Gugger and Christine Binswanger joined the firm in 1991, while Robert Hösl and Ascan Mergenthaler became partners in 2004. Their built work includes the Antipodes I Student Housing at the Université de Bourgogne, Dijon (1991–92), the Ricola Europe Factory and Storage Building in Mulhouse (1993) and a gallery for a private collection of contemporary art in Munich (1991–92). Most notably they were chosen early in 1995 to design the new Tate Gallery extension for contemporary art in London, situated in the Bankside Power Station, on the Thames, opposite St. Paul's Cathedral that opened in May 2000. They were also shortlisted in the competition for the new design of the Museum of Modern Art in New York (1997). More recently, they have built the Forum 2004 Building and Plaza (Barcelona, 2002–2004), and plan to build the Caixa Forum-Madrid; the Davines Head Office (Parma); and the National Stadium, main stadium for the 2008 Olympic Games in Beijing.

Jacques Herzog und Pierre de Meuron wurden beide 1950 in Basel geboren. Sie studierten bei Aldo Rossi an der Eidgenössischen Technischen Hochschule (ETH) in Zürich, wo sie 1975 ihr Diplom machten. 1978 gründeten sie in Basel ihre Firma Herzog & de Meuron. 1991 traten Harry Gugger und Christine Binswanger der Firma bei, während Robert Hösl und Ascan Mergenthaler 2004 Partner wurden. Zu ihren Bauten gehören das Studentenwohnheim Antipodes I der Université de Bourgogne in Dijon (1991–92), das Ausstellungsgebäude für eine Privatsammlung moderner Kunst in München (1991–92) und das Fabrik- und Lagergebäude der Firma Ricola Europe in Mülhausen (1993). 1995 erhielten sie ihren bedeutendsten Auftrag: das Tate Modern genannte Museum für zeitgenössische Kunst, das im Mai 2000 in der umgebauten Bankside Power Station an der Themse, gegenüber St. Paul's Cathedral, eröffnet wurde. Beim Wettbewerb für die Umgestaltung des Museum of Modern Art in New York (1997) kamen Herzog & de Meuron in die engere Wahl. Zu den aktuellen Projekten zählen das Forum 2004 Building and Plaza in Barcelona (2004–2004) sowie die Entwürfe für das Caixa Forum in Madrid, das Davines Head Offices in Parma und das Hauptstadion für die Olympischen Spiele in Peking (2008).

Jacques Herzog et Pierre de Meuron sont tous deux nés à Bâle en 1950. Diplômés en architecture de l'institut fédéral suisse de technologie (ETH) de Zurich (1975), ils étudient auprès d'Aldo Rossi et fondent leur agence, Herzog & de Meuron Architecture Studio, à Bâle, en 1978. Harry Gugger et Christine Binswanger rejoignent l'agence en 1991, tandis que Robert Hösl et Ascan Mergenthaler deviennent partenaires en 2004. Parmi leurs réalisations : le foyer d'étudiants Antipodes 1 pour l'Université de Bourgogne, à Dijon (1991–1992), l'usine-entrepôt Ricola Europe, à Mulhouse (1993) et une galerie pour une collection privée d'art contemporain, à Munich (1991–92). Ils ont été sélectionnés en 1995 pour l'extension de la Tate Gallery of Modern Art de Londres, installée dans une ancienne centrale électrique, Bankside Power Station, au bord de la Tamise, face à la cathédrale Saint-Paul, et inaugurée en mai 2000. Ils ont fait partie des architectes retenus pour le concours de la transformation du Museum of Modern Art de New York (1997). Plus récemment, ils ont réalisé le bâtiment du Forum 2004 et la Plaza (Barcelone, 2002–2004) et planifié la construction du Caixa Forum-Madrid, le bureau Davines Head (Parme) et le stade national, principal stade olympique pour les Jeux à Pékin en 2008.

# PRADA AOYAMA TOKYO

*Minato-ku, Tokyo, Japan, 2001–2003*

Client: Prada Japan Co. Ltd. Floor area: 2 860 m². Costs: not specified.

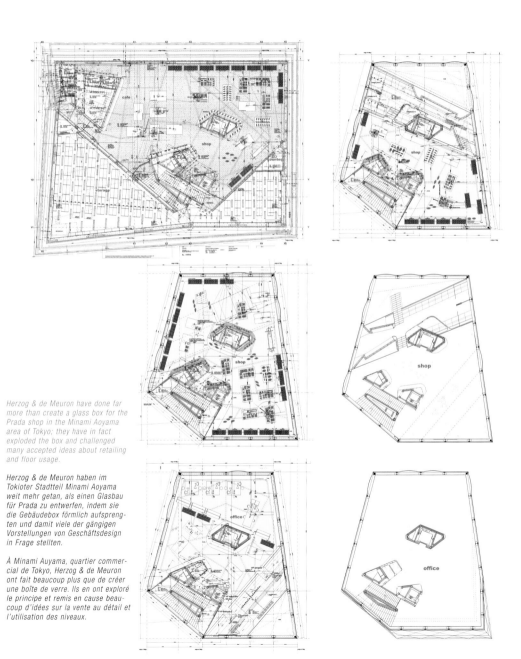

*Herzog & de Meuron have done far more than create a glass box for the Prada shop in the Minami Aoyama area of Tokyo; they have in fact exploded the box and challenged many accepted ideas about retailing and floor usage.*

*Herzog & de Meuron haben im Tokioter Stadtteil Minami Aoyama weit mehr getan, als einen Glasbau für Prada zu entwerfen, indem sie die Gebäudebox förmlich aufsprengten und damit viele der gängigen Vorstellungen von Geschäftsdesign in Frage stellten.*

*À Minami Auyama, quartier commercial de Tokyo, Herzog & de Meuron ont fait beaucoup plus que de créer une boîte de verre. Ils en ont exploré le principe et remis en cause beaucoup d'idées sur la vente au détail et l'utilisation des niveaux.*

Built on a 953-square-meter site in the heart of the Omotesando shopping district, this structure has a 369-square-meter footprint and is 32 meters high. The gross floor area is 2860 square meters. The area contains densely packed low-rise buildings of no particular distinction, aside perhaps from the Collezione Building by Tadao Ando just down the street. This fact freed the architects of many of the usual contextual requirements, although local zoning laws distinctly limited possible forms. Within the zoning framework, Herzog & de Meuron imagined a fairly tall structure as compared to the neighborhood, and an unusual outdoor plaza. They settled on a simple, immediately recognizable shape clad in 840 glass panes, 205 of which have a spherical, convex shape and 16 (ground floor) a concave shape. Inside the structure, the architects put an emphasis on openings between floors that give an impression of continuous, flowing space. As they say, "the Prada Aoyama store is the first building by Herzog & de Meuron in which the structure, space and façade form a single unit. The vertical cores, the horizontal tubes, the floor slabs and the façade grilles define the space, but at the same time, they are the structure and the façade." This aspect of the design as well as its internal fluidity resulted, together with the stringent fire and earthquake rules, in making this one of the more complex small buildings recently erected in Japan. Within, the architects consciously referred to the famous pictures by Andreas Gursky of other Prada boutiques and decided that they wanted "to develop a slightly more 'primitive' or 'archaic' form of presentation, somewhat like a market stall." As for the interiors and material choices, the architects have said, "the fittings with lamps and furniture for the presentation of Prada products and for visitors were designed especially for this location. The materials are either hyper-artificial, like resin, silicon and fiberglass, or hyper-natural, like leather, moss or porous planks of wood. Such contrasting materials prevent fixed stylistic classifications of the site, allowing both traditional and radically contemporary aspects to appear as self-evident and equal components of today's global culture."

Das neue Prada-Gebäude steht im Herzen des Tokioter Geschäftsviertels Omotesando auf einem 953 m² großen Grundstück. Es hat eine Aufstandsfläche von 369 m², ist 32 m hoch und bietet eine Nutzfläche von 2860 m². Abgesehen von Tadao Andos Collezione Building, das nur wenige Meter entfernt in derselben Straße liegt, besteht die dicht bebaute Umgebung aus niedrigen, unauffälligen Gebäuden. Innerhalb des vorgeschriebenen Rahmens entwarfen Herzog & de Meuron ein im Vergleich zur Nachbarschaft ziemlich hohes Gebäude und einen ungewöhnlichen Vorplatz. Sie entschieden sich für eine schlichte, dennoch charakteristische Außenform, die mit 840 Glasplatten ummantelt ist, von denen 205 nach außen und 16 im Erdgeschoss nach innen gewölbt sind. Im Inneren haben die Architekten Wert auf eine durchgehende, fließende Raumwirkung zwischen den Stockwerken gelegt. Sie erläutern: „Das Prada-Aoyama Gebäude ist der erste Entwurf von Herzog & de Meuron, in dem Baukörper, Innenraum und Fassade eine Einheit bilden. Die vertikalen Kernelemente, die horizontalen Röhren, die Bodenplatten und die Fassadengitter definieren den Raum und bilden gleichzeitig die Gesamtkonstruktion." Dieser Aspekt der Gestaltung führte zusammen mit der durchlässigen Innenraumgestaltung und den strengen Feuer- und Erdbebenschutzbestimmungen dazu, dass hier eins der komplexesten in jüngster Zeit in Japan realisierten kleineren Bauwerke entstanden ist. Sich bewusst auf die berühmten Bilder beziehend, die Andreas Gursky von anderen Prada-Boutiquen gemacht hat, beschlossen die beiden Architekten, eine etwas primitivere oder archaischere Form der Präsentation zu wählen – mehr in der Art eines Marktstands. Über die Materialauswahl für das Interieur sagen sie: „Die Ausstattungsstücke wie Lampen und Verkaufsmöbel wurden speziell für dieses Projekt entworfen. Die Materialien sind entweder hyper-künstlich so wie Kunstharz, Silikon und Glasfaser oder hyper-natürlich wie Leder, Moos oder poröse Holzplanken. Derart kontrastierende Materialien verhindern eine bestimmte stilistische Klassifizierung und lassen sowohl traditionelle wie auch radikal zeitgenössische Gestaltungsmittel als selbstverständliche und gleichwertige Elemente der globalen Kultur von heute bestehen."

Édifié sur un terrain de 953 m² au cœur du quartier commercial d'Omotesando, cet immeuble de 32 m de haut occupe une emprise au sol de 369 m², pour une surface totale de 2860 m². Le quartier se compose de petits immeubles sans grand intérêt, en dehors peut-être du Collezione Building de Tadao Ando, un peu plus bas dans la rue. Dans le cadre du zonage existant, Herzog & de Meuron ont imaginé une structure assez haute, comparée à son voisinage, et une curieuse plazza. La forme simple mais à forte identité est habillée de 840 panneaux de verre, dont 205 sont semi-sphériques convexes et 16 (au rez-de-chaussée) concaves. À l'intérieur, les architectes ont mis l'accent sur les liaisons entre les niveaux, ce qui donne l'impression d'un espace en flux continu : « Le magasin Prada Aoyama est le premier immeuble de Herzog & de Meuron dans lequel la structure, l'espace et la façade forment un seul tout. Les noyaux verticaux, les tubes horizontaux, les dalles des planchers et les grilles de façade définissent l'espace, tout en étant à la fois structure et façade. » Cet aspect de la conception et la fluidité interne qui en résultent, associées à la stricte réglementation sur les incendies et les tremblements de terre, en fait l'un des plus complexes petits immeubles récemment érigés au Japon. Pour l'aménagement intérieur, les architectes se sont volontairement référés à de célèbres photographies prises par Andreas Gursky dans d'autres magasins Prada et décidé « qu'ils voulaient mettre au point une forme de présentation plus primitive ou archaïque, un peu comme un étal de marché... Les équipements, dont les lampes et les meubles de présentation des produits Prada, ont été spécialement dessinés pour le lieu. Les matériaux sont soit hyper artificiels, comme la résine, le silicone et la fibre de verre, soit hyper naturels, comme le cuir, la mousse ou les planches de bois brut. Le contraste entre ces matériaux fait échapper l'endroit aux classifications stylistiques rigides, et fait que des aspects à la fois traditionnels et radicalement contemporains semblent devenir des composants évidents et égaux de la culture globale d'aujourd'hui. »

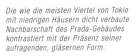

*Crowded with low buildings like most of Tokyo, the neighborhood of the Prada building contrasts with its jutting glass presence.*

*Die wie die meisten Viertel von Tokio mit niedrigen Häusern dicht verbaute Nachbarschaft des Prada-Gebäudes kontrastiert mit der Präsenz seiner aufragenden, gläsernen Form.*

*Par sa présence transparente et dynamique l'immeuble Prada contraste avec son voisinage saturé de constructions basses, comme presque partout à Tokio.*

Unlike any of its neighbors, the Prada building has a small outdoor plaza.

*Im Gegensatz zu seinen Nachbarn ist das Prada-Gebäude mit einem kleinen Vorplatz ausgestattet.*

À la différence de ses voisins, l'immeuble Prada est précédé d'une petite place.

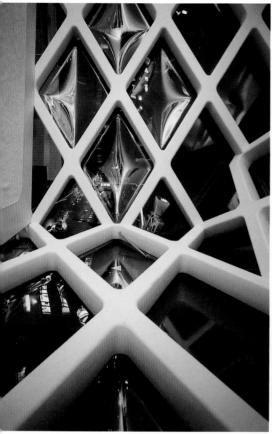

The web of glass blocks that characterizes the façade as seen from the outside also animates and defines the unusual interior spaces.

Das Netzwerk aus Glassegmenten, das die Außenfassade charakterisiert, belebt und definiert auch die ungewöhnlichen Innenräume.

La trame de blocs de verres si caractéristique de cette façade vue de l'extérieur, définit et anime des volumes intérieurs inhabituels.

Determined to create an architectural "event", client and designers have made the rather staid image of Prada evolve toward the cutting edge of current architecture.

Mit dem Ziel, ein architektonisches „Ereignis" zu schaffen, haben Auftraggeber und Planer das eher gesetzte Image von Prada mit der Avantgarde zeitgenössischer Architektur in Zusammenhang gebracht.

Déterminé à créer un « événement » architectural, le client et les architectes ont fait évoluer l'image assez rigide de Prada aux confins de l'architecture contemporaine.

# TOYO ITO

*Toyo Ito & Associates, Architects*
*1-19-4 Shibuya, Shibuya-ku,*
*Tokyo 150-0002*
*Japan*

*Tel: +81 3 3409 5822*
*Fax: +81 3 3409 5969*
*e-mail: mayumi@toyo-ito.co.jp*
*Web: www.toyo-ito.co.jp*

Born in 1941 in Seoul, Korea, Toyo Ito graduated from the University of Tokyo in 1965, and worked in the office of Kiyonori Kikutake until 1969. He created his own office in 1971, assuming the name of Toyo Ito & Associates, Architects in 1979. His completed work includes the Silver Hut residence (Tokyo, 1984); Tower of the Winds (Yokohama, Kanagawa, 1986); Yatsushiro Municipal Museum (Yatsushiro, Kumamoto, 1989–1991); and the Elderly People's Home (1992–1994) and Fire Station (1992–1995) both located in the same city on the island of Kyushu. He participated in the Shanghai Luijiazui Center Area International Planning and Urban Design Consultation in 1992, and has built a Public Kindergarten (Eckenheim, Frankfurt, Germany, 1988–1991). Recent projects include his Odate Jukai Dome Park (Odate, Japan, 1995–1997); Nagaoka Lyric Hall (Nagaoka, Niigata, Japan, 1995–1997); and Ota-ku Resort Complex (Tobu-cho, Chiisagata-gun, Nagano, 1996–1998). One of his most successful and widely published projects, the Mediatheque in Sendai, was completed in 2001.

Toyo Ito, geboren 1941 in Seoul, Korea, schloss 1965 sein Studium an der Universität Tokio ab und arbeitete bis 1969 im Büro von Kiyonori Kikutake. 1971 gründete er sein eigenes Architekturbüro, das seit 1979 unter dem Namen Toyo Ito & Associates, Architects firmiert. Zu seinen Bauten gehören das Wohnhaus Silver Hut in Tokio (1984), der Turm der Winde in Yokohama, Kanagawa (1986), das städtische Museum in Yatsushiro, Kumamoto (1989–1991) sowie ein Seniorenwohnheim (1992–1994) und eine Feuerwehrstation (1992–1995) auf der Insel Kyushu. 1992 nahm Toyo Ito an der internationalen Konferenz für Planung und Entwicklung des Gebiets um das Luijiazui Center in Shanghai teil. Ferner baute er einen städtischen Kindergarten in Frankfurter Stadtteil Eckenheim (1988–1991). Zu seinen jüngsten Projekten zählen der Odate Jukai Dome Park in Odate (1995–1997), die Nagaoka Lyric Hall in Nagaoka, Niigata (1995–1997) und der Freizeitkomplex Ota-ku in Tobu-cho, Chiisagata-gun, Nagano (1996–1998), alle in Japan. Eines seiner erfolgreichsten und bekanntesten Werke, die Mediathek im nordjapanischen Sendai, wurde 2001 fertiggestellt.

Né en 1941 à Séoul, en Corée, Toyo Ito est diplômé de l'Université de Tokyo en 1965 et travaille dans l'agence de Kiyonori Kikutaké jusqu'en 1969. Il crée sa propre agence en 1971, qui prend le nom de Toyo Ito & Associates, Architects en 1979. Parmi ses réalisations : la maison Silver Hut (Tokyo, 1984) ; la Tour des vents (Yokohama, Kanagawa, 1986) ; le Musée municipal de Yatsushiro (Yatsushiro, Kumamoto, 1989–1991) ; une maison de retraite (1992–1994) et une caserne de pompiers (1992–1995) dans une ville de l'île de Kyushu. Il a participé au concours international d'urbanisme de la zone de Luijiazui à Shangaï (1992), et a dessiné un jardin d'enfants (Eckenheim, Francfort, Allemagne 1988–1991). Parmi ses récents projets : le Odate Jukai Dome Park (Odate, Japon, 1995–1997) ; la salle de concerts lyriques de Nagaoka (Nagaoka, Niigata, Japon, 1995–1997) et le complexe touristique Ota-ku (Tobu-Cho, Chiisagata-gun, Nagano, 1996–1998). L'un de ses projets les plus réussis et les plus médiatisés est la médiathèque de Sendai, achevée en 2001.

# SERPENTINE GALLERY PAVILION 2002

*Kensington Gardens, London, UK, 2002*

*Client: Serpentine Gallery, Kensington Gardens. Floor area: 310 m². Costs: £ 600 000.*

Each year, the Serpentine Gallery in London's Kensington Park commissions international architects to design a pavilion for the Gallery. Toyo Ito's 2002 participation was the third in the series, following Zaha Hadid (2000) and Daniel Libeskind with Arup (2001). His single story structure was covered in aluminum panels and glass. The 5.3-meter-high structure was formed by a steel grillage of flat bars. The concept was to create a columnless structure that was not dependent on an orthogonal grid system, making an open space to be used during the summer months as a café and event space. The seemingly random structure was determined by an algorithm derived from the rotation of a single square. Each piece of the structure functioned not only as a beam, but also to absorb vibrations so that all elements combined to form a complex, mutually interdependent whole. The point, as explained by the architect, was "to render visible again the systems that make the most basic conditions of architecture possible, but which were being obscured by a rationalism obsessed with uniformity." The £600 000 pavilion, designed with the engineering firm Arup, had painted structural plywood floors and 3mm aluminum panels for the walls and ceiling and was left in place for three months.

Jedes Jahr beauftragt die im Londoner Park Kensington Gardens gelegene Serpentine Gallery einen Architekten mit der Gestaltung eines Pavillons. Toyo Itos Beitrag aus dem Jahr 2002 war der dritte in dieser Serie, dem die Arbeiten von Zaha Hadid (2000) und Daniel Libeskind (2001) vorangegangen waren. Seine knapp 5,3 m hohe, eingeschossige Konstruktion bestand aus einem Trägerrost aus Flachstahl, umhüllt von unregelmäßig geformten Aluminiumplatten und Glas. Die Grundidee war ein Bauwerk, das ohne tragende Säulen und rechtwinkliges Rastersystem auskommen und als offener Raum gestaltet werden sollte. Dabei kam den einzelnen Elementen der Konstruktion nicht nur die Funktion eines Trägers zu, sondern auch die, Schwingungen zu absorbieren, so dass alle Teile zusammen ein komplexes und ineinandergreifendes Ganzes bildeten. Dabei ging es ihm darum, jene Systeme wieder sichtbar zu machen, auf denen die einfachsten Grundformen der Architektur aufbauen, die aber von einem Rationalismus verdeckt worden sind, der von der Idee der Uniformität besessen ist. Der zusammen mit Arup für die Summe von 600 000 Pfund gestaltete Pavillon war im Inneren mit Böden aus gestrichenem Furnierholz und 3 mm starken Aluminiumtafeln für Wände und Decken ausgestattet.

Chaque année, la Serpentine Gallery à Kensington Park à Londres commande un pavillon à un architecte connu. La participation de Toyo Ito en 2002 était la troisième de la série, après Zaha Hadid (2000) et Daniel Libeskind (2001). Ce pavillon sans étage était habillé de panneaux d'aluminium et de verre. La structure de 5,3 m de haut, était constituée d'une grille composée de barres de section plate. L'idée était de créer une structure sans colonne qui ne dépende pas d'une trame orthogonale. La forme apparemment aléatoire avait été déterminée par un algorithme issu de la rotation d'un carré. Chaque élément de la structure fonctionnait non seulement à la manière d'une poutre mais absorbait les vibrations pour que les éléments combinés constituent un tout complexe et interdépendant. Pour l'architecte, l'idée était de « rendre de nouveau visibles les systèmes qui ont rendu possibles les conditions de base de l'architecture mais qui ont été masqués par un rationalisme obsédé par l'uniformité ». Ce pavillon, qui a coûté 600 000 livres sterling, conçu en collaboration avec l'agence d'ingénierie Arup, faisait appel à des planchers de contreplaqué structurel peint, de murs et de plafonds en panneaux d'aluminium de 3 mm d'épaisseur. Il est resté trois mois en place.

*The exploded appearance of Ito's pavilion is a demonstration of his inventiveness. It is difficult to guess that he had designed this pavilion.*

*Das in Segmente aufgebrochene äußere Design des Pavillons ist eine Demonstration von Itos kaum zu erratendem Ideenreichtum.*

*L'apparence explosée du pavillon de Ito est une démonstration de son inventivité. Il serait difficile de deviner qu'il a conçu cette forme.*

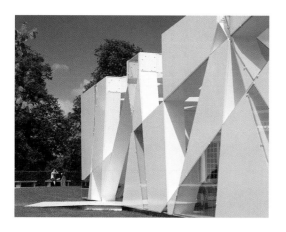

Trotz seiner im Wesentlichen recht-
eckigen Form wirkt der Pavillon, als
würden seine massiven Baukörper in
der Luft schweben.

*Despite its essentially rectangular
form, the pavilion seems to make
solid volumes float in the air.*

Bien que de forme essentiellement
rectangulaire, le pavillon donne l'impression que ses volumes aveugles
flottent dans les airs.

*The angular, white structural
elements give ample openings for
the interior space that is bright,
cheerful and airy.*

Die winkelförmigen weißen Konstruk-
tionselemente sorgen für zahlreiche
Öffnungen im Innenraum, was diesen
hell, fröhlich und luftig wirken lässt.

Les grands éléments anguleux blancs
dégagent de vastes ouvertures qui
éclairent un volume intérieur lumineux, animé et aéré.

# WES JONES

*Jones, Partners: Architecture*
*141 Nevada Street*
*El Segundo, CA 90245*
*USA*

*Tel: +1 310 414 0761*
*Fax: +1 310 414 0765*
*e-mail: info@jonespartners.com*
*web: www.jonespartners.com*

*Rob Brill Reside.*

Wes Jones, born in 1958 in Santa Monica, attended the United States Military Academy at West Point, the University of California at Berkeley (BA) and the Harvard Graduate School of Design where he received a Masters of Architecture degree. A recipient of the Rome Prize in Architecture, he has served as a visiting Professor at Harvard, Rice, Tulane and Columbia Universities. He worked with Eisenman/Robertson, Architects, in New York before becoming Director of Design at Holt Hinshaw Pfau Jones in San Francisco. As partner in charge of design at Holt Hinshaw Pfau Jones, he completed the Astronauts' Memorial at Kennedy Space Center in Florida and the South Campus Chiller Plant for UCLA. Recent projects include the Brill, Stieglitz, Arias-Tsang, and San Clemente residences, Union Square, Golden Plate, San Francisco, and Offices for Andersen Consulting in Kuala Lumpur. Current work includes: Redondo Beach Duplex; private residence, Hollywood; private residence, Mulholland; townhouse, Channel District, Tampa; private compound, Yucca Valley; Editing suites, Venice CA.

Wes Jones, 1958 in Santa Monica geboren, studierte an der United States Military Academy in West Point, der University of California in Berkeley (BA-Abschluss) und an der Harvard Graduate School of Design, wo er den Master of Architecture erwarb. Er erhielt den Prix de Rome in Architektur und war als Gastprofessor an den Universitäten Harvard, Rice, Tulane und Columbia tätig. Wes Jones arbeitete im New Yorker Büro Eisenman/Robertson, Architects, bevor er Director of Design bei Holt Hinshaw Pfau Jones in San Francisco wurde. Als Planungspartner führte er dort das Astronauts' Memorial am Kennedy Space Center in Florida und die Anlage South Campus Chiller Plant für die University of California in Los Angeles (UCLA) aus. Zu seinen jüngsten Projekten gehören die Wohnhäuser Brill, Stieglitz, Arias-Tsang und San Clemente, Union Square, Golden Plate in San Francisco sowie Büros für Andersen Consulting in Kuala Lumpur. Derzeit arbeitet er am Redondo Beach Doppelhaus, Villen in Hollywood und Mulholland sowie Wohnungen und Häusern im Channel District von Tampa, im Yucca Valley und in Venice, Kalifornien.

Wes Jones, né en 1958 à Santa Monica, étudie à l'École militaire de West Point, à l'Université de Californie à Berkeley (B. A.) et à l'Harvard Graduate School of Design dont il est Master of Architecture. Titulaire du prix de Rome d'architecture, il a été professeur invité à Harvard, Rice, Tulane et Columbia. Il a travaillé avec Eisenman/Robertson, architectes à New York, avant de devenir directeur de la conception chez Holt Hinshaw Pfau Jones à San Francisco. Associé en charge de la conception pour eux, il réalise le Mémorial des astronautes au Kennedy Space Center de Floride et l'unité de réfrigération du campus sud de UCLA. Parmi ses récents projets : les maisons Brill, Stieglitz, Arias-Tsang et San Clemente, Union Square/Golden Plate à San, Francisco et des bureaux pour Andersen Consulting à Kuala Lumpur. Il travaille actuellement au projet de Redondo Beach Duplex, une résidence privée à Hollywood, une autre à Mulholland, une maison de ville à Tampa (Channel District) ; un domaine privé dans la Yucca Valley ; les Editing suites à Venice, le tout en Californie.

# ROB BRILL RESIDENCE AND STUDIO

*Silverlake, California, USA, 1998–2000*

*Client: Eric and Nanette Brill. Floor area: 241 m². Costs: $ 300 000.*

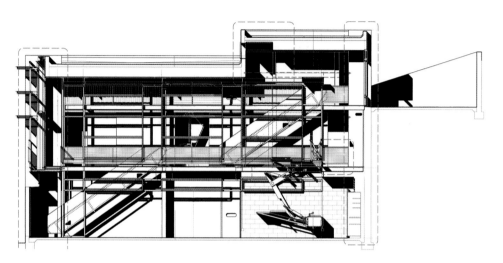

This 241-square-meter residence for a musician is a remodeled martial arts studio located in a fashionable Los Angeles neighborhood. The house was commissioned by Eric and Nanette Brill for Eric's brother Rob Brill. The architect views this as a case study in the efficient use of technology. As he writes, "the difference between using technology as a symbol, and more visibly being technology itself, as an expression arising from within technology rather than one that merely borrows technological form to illustrate some other non-technological interest, is the distinction between the work of Jones, Partners and others who might be considered technologically oriented. Since technology does not admit an author other than nature, the signature architect must make non-or anti-technological adjustments in order to assert authorship." Features he cites to justify this position are the moving gantry, which also serves as a stage for musical performances, and sliding wall panels that serve as acoustic mediators between private and public space. The multiple opaque and translucent wall panels also serve as a flexible division between private and public space. The remodeling was actually more of a reconstruction, because the original structure was "leveled down to the retaining walls," and the "floor separating the studio's workout area from the garage level was removed, creating a three-story living space in one half of the resulting volume, and a stacked tier of private spaces in the other half, above a new garage."

Das 241 m² umfassende Haus für einen Musiker liegt in einer vornehmen Wohngegend von Los Angeles und war vor dem Umbau ein Studio für Kampfsportarten. Es wurde von Eric und Nanette Brill für Eric's Bruder Rob Brill in Auftrag gegeben. Der Architekt betrachtet seinen Entwurf als Fallstudie für die effiziente Nutzung neuer Technologien. Dazu führt er aus: „Der Unterschied zwischen der *Anwendung* von Technologie als Symbol und dem sichtbareren *Sein* von Technologie, als Ausdruck, der von der Technik selbst hervorgebracht wird, anstatt sich technologische Formen nur auszuleihen, um ein anderes, nicht-technologisches Anliegen zu illustrieren, entspricht dem Unterschied zwischen der Arbeit von Jones, Partners und anderen, die man als technologisch orientiert betrachten könnte. Da *Technologie* keinen anderen Urheber zulässt als die Natur, muss der schöpferische Architekt nicht-technologische oder anti-technologische Anpassungen vornehmen, um seine Urheberschaft geltend zu machen." Bauliche Merkmale dieses Wohnhauses sind der bewegliche Stützblock, der auch als Bühne für Konzerte dient, Schiebewände, welche die Räume akustisch verbinden und etliche opake sowie durchscheinende Wandpaneele, welche die privaten von den öffentlichen Räumen des Hauses abgrenzen. Der Umbau war eigentlich mehr ein Wiederaufbau, denn das ursprüngliche Gebäude wurde bis auf die Stützmauern abgerissen.

Cette résidence de 241 m² construite pour un musicien est un studio d'arts martiaux remodelé dans un quartier à la mode de Los Angeles. Il s'agit d'une commande d'Eric et Nanette Brill pour Rob Brill, le frère d'Eric. L'architecte le considère comme une étude sur la mise en œuvre efficace des technologies : « La différence entre *utiliser* une technologie comme symbole, et de façon plus visible *être* la technologie elle-même, comme une expression venue de la technologie même plutôt qu'empruntant tout au plus la forme technologique pour illustrer une quelconque autre intention non technologique, est ce qui distingue le travail de Jones, Partners de celui d'autres praticiens qui se considèrent sensibles à la technologie. Puisque la technologie n'admet pas d'autre auteur que la nature, l'architecte célèbre doit pratiquer des ajustements non- ou anti-technologiques pour affirmer sa signature. » Pour justifier sa position, il cite le pont mobile qui sert aussi de scène à des spectacles musicaux, ou les panneaux de mur coulissants qui font office de médiateurs acoustiques entre les espaces privatifs et de réception. De multiples panneaux opaques et translucides font également fonction de cloisonnements souples entre ces deux zones. La rénovation a surtout pris l'aspect d'une reconstruction, car la structure originale a été « arasée aux murs de soutènement ».

*Jones has long been interested in a mechanistic and rather esthetically "harsh" approach to his buildings. This is visible both in the section above and in the images to the right.*

*Jones hat seit langem einen mechanistischen und ästhetisch „kantig strengen" Zugang zu seinen Gebäuden, was sowohl im Querschnitt als auch auf den Fotos deutlich wird.*

*Jones s'est longtemps intéressé à une approche mécaniste, esthétiquement assez « brute ». C'est visible à la fois dans la coupe ci-dessus et les images de droite.*

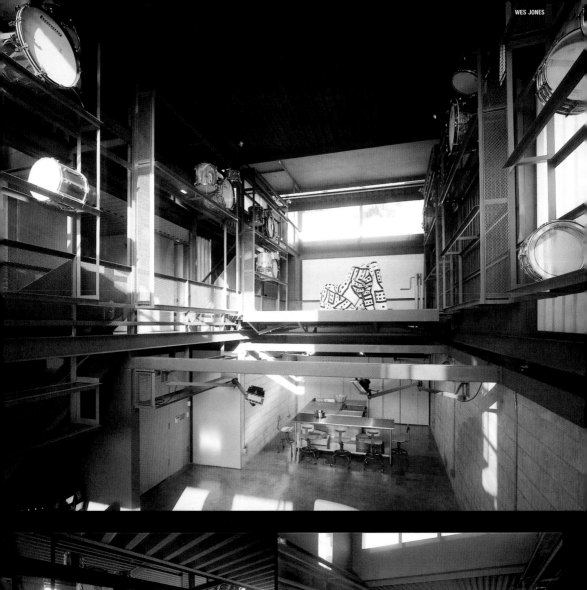

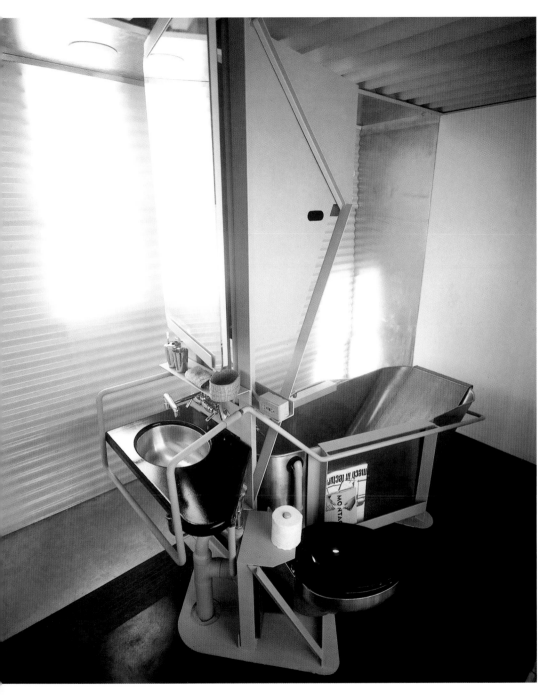

Inspired by industrial space and design, Wes Jones goes so far as to create a bathroom design that looks completely mechanical, almost the opposite of the sleek white lines sought by many architects.

Inspiriert von Industriearchitektur und -design wirkt das Badezimmer nahezu maschinenartig und verkörpert das Gegenteil der eleganten, weißen Linien, nach denen viele Architekten streben.

Inspiré par la conception et les espaces industriels, la salle-de-bains a un aspect entièrement technique, presque à l'opposé de l'approche lisse et des couleurs blanches pratiquées par de nombreux architectes.

# ANISH KAPOOR

*Mar.*

Anish Kapoor was born in Bombay in 1954 and has lived and worked in London since the early 1970s. Not an architect, but a sculptor, he studied at the Hornsey College of Art (1973–1977) and the Chelsea School of Art (1977–78), and his first solo exhibition followed in 1980. His early work centered on lightweight materials and bright colors. Subsequent to moving into a ground-floor studio space in the late 1980s, he began to experiment with stone sculpture, but in almost all cases he deals with the ambiguities of perception. As he says, "I don't want to make sculpture about form… I wish to make sculpture about belief, or about passion, about experience that is outside of material concern." His work has been exhibited all over the world and is held in many major international collections. He represented Britain at the XLIV Biennale in Venice and won the Turner Prize in 1991. He has been commissioned to create a large-scale stainless-steel work for Chicago's Millennium Park, scheduled for completion in 2004.

Anish Kapoor, 1954 in Bombay geboren, lebt und arbeitet seit den frühen 1970er Jahren in London. Er ist kein Architekt, sondern Bildhauer, der von 1973 bis 1977 am Hornsey College of Art und von 1977 bis 1978 an der Chelsea School of Art studierte. Seine erste Einzelausstellung hatte er 1980. Seine frühen Arbeiten waren durch die Verwendung leichter Materialien und heller Farben gekennzeichnet. Nachdem er Ende der 1980er Jahre ein geräumiges Erdgeschossatelier bezog, begann er mit Steinskulpturen zu experimentieren. Aber auch hier gilt sein besonderes Interesse der Vieldeutigkeit von Wahrnehmung. Er selbst sagt, dass er keine Skulpturen machen wolle, bei denen es um die Form geht, sondern Skulpturen, die etwas über Glauben oder Leidenschaft, jedenfalls über eine Erfahrung aussagen, die über das Materielle hinaus geht. Seine Arbeiten wurden in der ganzen Welt ausgestellt und sind Teil bedeutender internationaler Sammlungen. 1991 vertrat er Großbritannien auf der Biennale in Venedig und wurde mit dem Turner Prize ausgezeichnet. Derzeit arbeitet er an einer großformatigen Stahlplastik für den Millennium Park in Chicago, die 2004 fertig gestellt sein soll.

Anish Kapoor, né à Bombay en 1954, vit et travaille à Londres depuis le début des années 1970. Sculpteur, et non architecte, il a étudié au Hornsey College of Art (1973–1977) et à la Chelsea School of Art (1977–78). Sa première exposition personnelle s'est tenue en 1980. Ses premières œuvres font appel à des matériaux légers et aux couleurs vives. Après avoir emménagé dans un atelier en rez-de-chaussée, il s'essaye à la sculpture sur pierre, mais continue à s'intéresser aux ambiguités de la perception. « Je ne veux pas faire de la sculpture sur la forme, je veux faire des sculptures sur la croyance, la passion, l'expérience, extérieures à la matérialité. » Ses œuvres ont été exposées dans le monde entier et figurent dans les plus grandes collections. Il a représenté la Grande-Bretagne à la XLIV Biennale de Venise et remporté le Turner Prize en 1991. Il a reçu commande d'une importante pièce en acier inoxydable pour le Millenium Park de Chicago, qui devrait être achevée en 2004.

# MARSYAS

*Turbine Hall, Tate Modern, London, UK, October 9, 2002–April 6, 2003*

*Client: Tate Modern/Unilever. Size: 155 x 23 x 35 m. Costs: not specified.*

After Louise Bourgeois and Juan Muñoz, Anish Kapoor was the third artist to participate in The Unilever Series of commissions for the Turbine Hall at Tate Modern. He was, though, the first to make use of the entire length of Tate Modern's enormous Turbine Hall, which measures 155 meters long, 23 meters wide and 35 meters high. Marsyas was comprised of three steel rings joined by a single span of PVC membrane. The geometry generated by these three rigid steel structures determined the sculpture's overall form, a shift from vertical to horizontal and back to vertical again. As Kapoor stated, "the Turbine Hall at Tate Modern is an enormously difficult space, the great problem is that it demands verticality. This is contrary to every notion about sculpture that I've ever engendered in my work. So I felt that the only way to deal with the vertical is to deal with the full horizontal." The title of the work refers to Marsyas, a satyr in Greek mythology, who was flayed alive by Apollo. Unsurprisingly, Anish Kapoor described the impression he intended with the choice of dark red PVC as being "rather like flayed skin." Because of its large dimensions and positioning, it was impossible to view the entire sculpture from any one vantage point, but the artist succeeded not only in altering the architectural space itself, but in creating a new, almost anti-geometric volume suspended in the void of the Turbine Hall.

Anish Kapoor war nach Louise Bourgeois und Juan Muñoz der dritte Künstler, der an der von Unilever organisierten Serie von Auftragsarbeiten für die Turbinenhalle der Tate Modern teilnahm. Er war jedoch der Erste, der mit seiner Arbeit den gesamten Raum der riesigen Halle in Anspruch nahm. Die Installation mit dem Titel „Marsyas" bestand aus drei Stahlringen, die durch eine durchgehende Haut aus PVC-Folie miteinander verbunden waren. Die Geometrie, die durch die drei feststehenden Stahlringe entstand, bestimmte die Gesamtform der Skulptur, die durch eine Verlagerung vom Vertikalen ins Horizontale und wieder zurück gekennzeichnet war. Dazu Anish Kapoor: „Die Turbinenhalle in der Tate Modern ist ein ungeheuer schwieriger Raum, wobei das größte Problem darin besteht, dass sie Vertikalität verlangt. Und das steht im Widerspruch zu allen Vorstellungen über Skulptur, die ich jemals in meinen Arbeiten zum Ausdruck gebracht habe." Der Titel des Werks bezieht sich auf Marsyas, einen Satyr aus der griechischen Mythologie, der von Apollo bei lebendigem Leib enthäutet wurde. Wenig überraschend sagt Anish Kapoor über die Wirkung, die er mit der Wahl der dunkelroten PVC-Folie erzielen wollte, dass sie einer abgezogenen Haut ähneln sollte. Obwohl die Skulptur wegen ihrer riesigen Dimensionen und ihrer Anordnung im Raum von keinem einzigen Punkt aus zur Gänze überschaubar war, ist es dem Künstler dennoch gelungen, nicht nur den Raum selbst zu verändern, sondern einen neuen, beinahe anti-geometrischen Baukörper durch die Leere der Turbinenhalle schweben zu lassen.

Après Louise Bourgeois et Juan Muñoz, Anish Kapoor a été le troisième artiste à bénéficier d'une commande Unilever pour le Turbine Hall de la Tate Modern. Cependant, il a été le premier à utiliser intégralement cet énorme volume. *Marsyas* était constitué de trois anneaux d'acier entre lesquels était tendue une membrane de PVC. La géométrie issue des rapports de ces éléments rigides déterminait la forme d'ensemble de la sculpture, qui passait de la verticale à l'horizontale pour revenir à la verticale. Comme Kapoor l'explique : « Le Turbine Hall est un espace extrêmement difficile, le grand problème étant qu'il demande une verticalité, ce qui était contraire à toute notion de sculpture rencontrée dans mes travaux jusqu'à présent. » Le titre de l'œuvre renvoie à Marsyas, satyre de la mythologie grecque, qui fut écorché vif par Apollon. Kapoor décrit l'impression recherchée par le choix de PVC rouge sombre comme un effet de « peau d'écorché ». Du fait de ses grandes dimensions et du positionnement de l'œuvre, il était impossible de la voir en totalité d'un seul point de vue. L'artiste a réussi non seulement à modifier le volume architectural, mais à créer un volume presque anti-géométrique suspendu dans le vide de ce hall gigantesque.

*Filling the vast space of the Tate Modern Turbine Hall has been a challenge that artists have risen to with varying success. Anish Kapoor managed to reconfigure the space in the image of his own new geometry.*

*Den riesigen Raum der Turbinenhalle in der Tate Modern haben die beauftragten Künstler mit unterschiedlichem Erfolg ausgefüllt. Anish Kapoor gestaltete den Raum nach dem Bild seiner eigenen, neuen Geometrie um.*

*Occuper l'énorme espace du hall de la turbine de la Tate Modern est un défi que quelques artistes ont relevé avec un succès varié. Anish Kapoor a réussi à reconfigurer l'espace par une géométrie originale.*

# REM KOOLHAAS/OMA

*Office for Metropolitan Architecture*
*Heer Bokelweg 149*
*3032 AD Rotterdam*
*The Netherlands*

*Tel: +31 10 243 8200*
*Fax: +31 10 243 8202*
*e-mail: office@oma.nl*
*Web: http://www.oma.nl*

Rem Koolhaas was born in Rotterdam in 1944. Before studying at the Architectural Association in London, he tried his hand as a journalist for the Haagse Post and as a screenwriter. He founded the Office for Metropolitan Architecture in London in 1975, and became well known after the 1978 publication of his book *Delirious New York*. OMA is led by four partners: Rem Koolhaas, Ole Scheeren, Ellen van Loon and Joshua Ramus. Their built work includes a group of apartments at Nexus World, Fukuoka (1991), and the Villa dall'Ava, Saint-Cloud (1985–1991). Koolhaas was named head architect of the Euralille project in Lille in 1988, and has worked on a design for the new Jussieu University Library in Paris. His 1400 page book *S,M,L,XL* (Monacelli Press, 1995) has more than fulfilled his promise as an influential writer. He won the 2000 Pritzker Prize and the 2003 Praemium Imperiale Award for architecture. Recent work of OMA includes a house, Bordeaux, France, 1998; the campus center at the Illinois Institute of Technology, published here; the new Dutch Embassy in Berlin; the Guggenheim Las Vegas; and the recent Prada boutique in the Soho area of New York. Current work has included the design of OMA's largest project ever: the 575 000-square-meter Headquarters and Cultural Center for China Central Television (CCTV) in Beijing; the 1 850-seat Porto Concert Hall; and the New City Center for Almere, The Netherlands.

Rem Koolhaas, 1944 in Rotterdam geboren, arbeitete vor seinem Studium an der Architectural Association in London als Journalist für die Haagse Post und als Drehbuchautor. 1975 gründete er in London das Office for Metropolitan Architecture (OMA) und wurde mit seinem 1978 erschienenen Buch *Delirious New York* weithin bekannt. OMA wird von vier Partnern geführt: Rem Koolhaas, Ole Scheeren, Ellen van Loon und Joshua Ramus. Zu ihren Bauten gehören die Villa dall'Ava im französischen Saint-Cloud (1985–1991) und Wohnungen in Nexus World im japanischen Fukuoka (1991). 1988 wurde Rem Koolhaas die Leitung des Euralille-Projekts in Lille übertragen; außerdem erarbeitete er einen Entwurf für die neue Bibliothek der Universität Jussieu in Paris. Mit seinem 1 400 Seiten starken Buch *S,M,L,XL* (Monacelli Press, 1995) hat er seinen Status als einflussreicher Theoretiker und Autor bestätigt. Im Jahr 2000 erhielt Koolhaas den Pritzker Prize und 2003 den Architekturpreis Praemium Imperiale. Zu den neueren Projekten gehören ein Wohnhaus in Bordeaux (1998), das hier vorgestellte Campus-Zentrum des Illinois Institute of Technology, das neue Gebäude für die Niederländische Botschaft in Berlin, das Guggenheim Museum in Las Vegas und die neue Prada Boutique im New Yorker Stadtteil Soho. Zu den derzeitigen Projekten zählen der bislang größte Auftrag für OMA, das 575 000 m² umfassende Verwaltungs- und Kulturgebäude für China Central Television (CCTV) in Peking, der Porto Konzertsaal mit 1 850 Plätzen sowie das neue Citycenter für Almere, Niederlande.

Rem Koolhaas naît à Rotterdam en 1944. Avant d'étudier à l'Architectural Association de Londres, il s'essaye au journalisme pour le *Haagse Post* et à l'écriture de scénarii. Il fonde l'Office for Metropolitan Architecture à Londres en 1975 et devient célèbre par la publication en 1978 de son ouvrage *Delirious New York*. OMA est dirigé par quatre partenaires, Rem Koolhaas, Ole Scheeren, Ellen van Loon et Joshua Ramus. Parmi leurs réalisations : un ensemble d'appartements à Nexus Next World (Fukuoka, Japon, 1991) ; la villa dall'Ava (Saint-Cloud, France, 1985–1991). Koolhaas est nommé architecte en chef du projet Euralille à Lille en 1988 et propose un projet de bibliothèque pour la Faculté de Jussieu à Paris. Son livre de 1400 pages *S,M,L,XL* (Monacelli Press, 1995) confirme son influence et son impact de théoricien. Il a remporté le Pritzker Prize en 2000 et le Praemium Imperiale en 2003. Parmi les réalisations récentes : une maison à Bordeaux (1998), le Campus Center de l'Illinois Institute of Technology, publiée ici, la nouvelle ambassade des Pays-Bas à Berlin, le Guggenheim Las Vegas, et tout récemment, la boutique Prada à Soho, New York. Actuellement son agence travaille sur son plus important projet à ce jour, le siège et centre culturel de la télévision centrale chinoise (CCTV) à Pékin (575 000 m²) ; une salle de concert de 1850 places à Porto et le Nouveau centre-ville d'Almere (Pays-Bas).

# McCORMICK TRIBUNE CAMPUS CENTER

*Illinois Institute of Technology, Chicago, Illinois, USA, 2000–2003*

*Client: Illinois Institute of Technology. Floor area: 10 690 m². Total costs: $ 48 200 000.*

*True to his own concept of urban density, OMA took on this project, which runs a train tube right through a campus building, with an obvious relish.*

*Seinem eigenen Konzept urbaner Dichte treu bleibend, übernahm OMA dieses Projekt, bei dem ein Eisenbahntunnel geradewegs durch ein Campusgebäude verläuft.*

*Fidèle à ses idées sur la densité urbaine, OMA a entrepris avec une satisfaction évidente ce projet qui fait passer les trains dans un tube en plein milieu d'un campus.*

In 1938, the Armour Institute of Technology, a modest technical training school located on the south side of Chicago, hired Ludwig Mies van der Rohe (1886–1969) to take over its architectural program. Two years later, Armour and the Lewis Institute merged to form the Illinois Institute of Technology. Armour's original two-hectare campus could not accommodate the combined schools' requirements and Mies was encouraged to press ahead with plans for a new 50-hectare campus. Following the war, the IIT campus developed at the rate of two buildings a year until 1968. Rem Koolhaas and the Office for Metropolitan Architecture were chosen over Zaha Hadid, Peter Eisenman, the team of Werner Sobek and Helmut Jahn and Kazuyo Sejima to design a new campus center in 1998. One extremely unusual element of the Koolhaas design is a reinforced concrete-supported acoustical tube, encased in corrugated stainless steel and enveloping 160 meters of existing Chicago Transit Authority elevated commuter train track. This tube sits directly above the building's concrete roof, and is designed to significantly reduce train noise and vibration (to about 70 decibels when a train passes through the tube). The other element of the design is the 10 690-square-meter, one-story Campus Center building, housing the IIT Welcome Center, dining facilities, the campus radio station, auditorium and meeting rooms, university bookstore, coffee bar, convenience store, post office and student activity offices. Construction began in July 2000 at a total cost of $48.2 million: $34.6 million for the building and $13.6 million for the tube. The new Campus Center is located between 32nd and 33rd Streets, east of State Street and the Mies van der Rohe Campus, unifying the residential (east) side of the Main Campus with the educational (west) side and integrating key student services and facilities in one structure. Its interior circulation patterns are based on OMA's observation of student movements through the site before construction. As the *Chicago Tribune* pointed out in a very critical article ("Details mar the extraordinary in Koolhaas' IIT campus center," by Blair Kamin, Tribune architecture critic, September 28, 2003) budgetary constraints and difficulties building the overhanging tube delayed completion and made the finished result somewhat less convincing than advertised.

Im Jahr 1938 stellte das Armour Institute of Technology, eine bescheidene technische Lehranstalt im Süden Chicagos, Ludwig Mies van der Rohe (1886–1969) als Leiter der Architekturabteilung ein. Zwei Jahre später fusionierten Armour und Lewis Institute und bildeten gemeinsam das Illinois Institute of Technology. Da der ursprüngliche, 2 ha große Armour Campus den Anforderungen nicht mehr entsprach, wurde van der Rohe mit der Planung eines neuen, 50 ha umfassenden Campus beauftragt. Zwischen 1945 und 1968 wuchs der IIT-Campus um jährlich zwei neue Gebäude. Den 1998 veranstalteten Wettbewerb zur Gestaltung eines neuen Campuskomplexes, an dem unter anderen Zaha Hadid, Peter Eisenman, das Team von Werner Sobek und Helmut Jahn sowie Kazuyo Sejima teilnahmen, gewann Rem Koolhaas mit seinem Office for Metropolitan Architecture. Außergewöhnlichstes Element seines Entwurfs ist eine Röhre aus Stahlbeton mit einer Haut aus geriffeltem Edelstahl, die einen 160 m langen Abschnitt der Chicago Transit Hochbahngleise umgibt. Diese Röhre verläuft direkt über dem Betondach des Campusgebäudes und ist so konzipiert, dass sie den bis zu 70 Dezibel starken Lärm und die Vibrationen der durchfahrenden Züge beträchtlich reduziert. Der andere Teil des Entwurfs besteht aus dem eingeschossigen Gebäude des Campus Centers, das auf einer Nutzfläche von 10 690 m² das IIT Welcome Center, Mensa und Cafeteria, die universitätseigene Radiostation, ein Auditorium, Sitzungsräume, eine Universitätsbuchhandlung, Geschäfte, ein Postamt und Studentenbüros beherbergt. Die Bauarbeiten begannen im Juli 2000, die Kosten betrugen 48,2 Millionen Dollar, wobei 34,6 Millionen auf das Gebäude und 13,6 Millionen auf die Schallschutzröhre entfielen. Das neue Campus Center liegt zwischen der 32nd und 33rd Street, östlich der State Street und dem von Mies van der Rohe angelegten Campus. Es verbindet den östlichen Teil des Hauptcampus, auf dem sich Wohnbauten befinden, mit dem von Unterrichtsgebäuden eingenommenen westlichen Teil sowie wichtige Serviceeinrichtungen für Studenten zu einem Gesamtkomplex. Die Wege und Gänge basieren auf Studien, die OMA vor dem Bau im Hinblick darauf erstellt hatte, wie sich die Studenten auf dem Areal bewegen. Der Architekturkritiker Blair Kamin hat in seinem äußerst kritischen Artikel, der am 28. September 2003 in der *Chicago Tribune* erschien, darauf hingewiesen, dass budgetäre Zwänge und technische Schwierigkeiten bei der Konstruktion der Röhre zu Verzögerungen bei der Fertigstellung führten und das Endresultat dadurch weniger überzeugend ausfiel als erwartet wurde.

En 1938, l'Armour Institute of Technology, modeste école de formation au sud de Chicago, chargea Ludwig Mies van der Rohe (1886–1969) de son programme d'architecture. Deux ans plus tard, l'Armour et le Lewis Institute fusionnèrent pour former l'Illinois Institute of Technology. Les deux hectares de l'Armour ne pouvant accueillir les deux écoles, Mies fut pressé de dessiner les plans d'un nouveau campus de 50 hectares. Après la guerre, celui-ci se développa au rythme de deux bâtiments par an jusqu'en 1968. Rem Koolhaas et son agence, l'Office for Metropolitan Architecture, ont été choisis devant Zaha Hadid, Peter Eisenman, l'équipe de Werner Sobek et Helmut Jahn et Kazuyo Sejima pour créer le nouveau centre du campus en 1998. Un élément extrêmement curieux du projet de Koolhaas est un tube acoustique sur piliers en béton armé, gainé de tôle d'acier inoxydable nervurée et enveloppant sur 160 mètres la voie ferrée surélevée, de la Chicago Transit Authority. Il est directement posé sur le toit de béton du bâtiment et doit réduire de façon importante le bruit et les vibrations des trains (environ 70 décibels). L'autre élément du projet est le bâtiment du Campus Center de 10 690 m², qui abrite le Centre d'accueil de l'IIT, un restaurant, la station de radio du campus, un auditorium, des salles de réunion, la librairie de l'université, un café, une boutique, une poste et des bureaux pour les activités étudiantes. La construction qui a débuté en juillet 2000 a coûté 48,2 millions de dollars : 34,6 millions pour le bâtiment et 13,6 pour le tube. Le nouveau Campus Center est situé entre 32nd et 33rd Streets, à l'est de State Street et du Mies van der Rohe Campus. Il réunit la partie résidentielle (est) du campus principal à la partie d'enseignement (ouest) et intègre les principaux services destinés aux étudiants en une seule structure. Les circulations intérieures ont tenu compte d'une étude sur les déplacements des étudiants réalisée avant la construction. Comme le *Chicago Tribune* l'a fait remarquer dans un article très critique du 28 septembre 2003 (« Des détails gâchent ce qu'il y a d'extraordinaire dans l'IIT Campus Center de Koolhaas », selon Blair Kamin, critique d'architecture du *Chicago Tribune*), les contraintes budgétaires et les difficultés à construire le tube en porte-à-faux ont retardé le chantier et donné un résultat final un peu moins convaincant que ce qui avait été annoncé.

*Much of the IIT building carries the distant echo of Miesian modernism, even if the fact that a train runs through it does create quite a detour from the Modernist legacy of the master of this campus.*

*Ein Großteil des IIT-Gebäudes erinnert von Ferne an den Modernismus eines Mies van Rohe, selbst wenn die Röhre eine beträchtliche Abweichung vom modernistischen Vermächtnis des Baumeisters dieses Campus darstellt.*

*Les bâtiments de l'IIT renvoient encore l'écho distant du modernisme miésien, même si l'irruption du train bouscule le legs du grand maître allemand.*

Assemblages of sometimes hard
materials and unexpected angles dif-
ferentiate OMA from the tradition that
Mies established in the United States
during his tenure at IIT.

Die Zusammenstellung von teils har-
ten Materialien und unerwarteten
Blickwinkeln trennt OMA von der
Tradition, die van der Rohe während
seiner Amtsdauer am IIT etabliert hat.

Les assemblages de matériaux parfois bruts et les compositions inattendues différencient OMA de la tradition établie par Mies aux États-Unis
au cours de sa présence au IIT.

The presence of the train tube is marked inside the building as well as outside, recalling the layered complexity that OMA has long espoused, sometimes at the expense of a certain simplicity and directness.

Die Präsenz des Bahntunnels kennzeichnet sowohl das Innere als auch das Äußere des Gebäudes und erinnert an die schichtweise aufgebaute Komplexität, die OMA seit langem präferiert.

La présence du tube est aussi forte vue de l'extérieur que de l'intérieur. Elle rappelle la complexité des strates que OMA a longtemps pratiquées, parfois aux dépens d'une certaine simplicité et franchise.

# KENGO KUMA

Kengo Kuma & Associates
2-24-8 Minami Aoyama
Minato-ku
Tokyo 107-0062
Japan

Tel: +81 3 3401 7721
Fax: +81 3 3401 7778
e-mail: kuma@ba2.so-net.ne.jp
Web: www02.so-net.ne.jp/~kuma/

*Great Bamboo W*

Born in 1954 in Kanagawa, Japan, Kengo Kuma graduated in 1979 from the University of Tokyo with a Masters in Architecture. In 1985–86, he received an Asian Cultural Council Fellowship Grant and was a visiting scholar at Columbia University. In 1987 he established the Spatial Design Studio, and in 1991 he created Kengo Kuma & Associates. His work includes: the Gunma Toyota Car Show Room (Maebashi, 1989); Maiton Resort Complex (Phuket, Thailand); Rustic, Office Building, Doric, Office Building; M2, Headquarters for Mazda New Design Team (all in Tokyo 1991); Kinjo Golf Club, Club House (Okayama, 1992); Kiro-san Observatory (Ehime, 1994); Atami Guest House, Guest House for Bandai Corp (Atami, 1992–1995); Karuizawa Resort Hotel (Karuizawa, 1993); Tomioka Lakewood Golf Club House (Tomioka, 1993–1996); Toyoma Noh-Theater, (Miyagi, 1995–96); and the Japanese Pavilion for the Venice Biennale (Venice, Italy, 1995). He has recently completed the Stone Museum (Nasu, Tochigi) and a Museum of Ando Hiroshige (Batou, Nasu-gun, Tochigi).

Kengo Kuma, geboren 1954 in Kanagawa, Japan, schloss 1979 sein Studium an der Universität Tokio mit dem Master of Architecture ab. Von 1985 bis 1986 arbeitete er mit einem Stipendium des Asian Cultural Council als Gastwissenschaftler an der Columbia University in New York. 1987 gründete Kuma das Spatial Design Studio und 1991 das Büro Kengo Kuma & Associates in Tokio. Zu seinen Bauten gehören: der Gunma Toyota Car Showroom in Maebashi, Japan (1989), die Ferienanlage Maiton in Phuket, Thailand, die Bürogebäude Rustic und Doric sowie M2, der Hauptsitz für die Designabteilung von Mazda, alle 1991 in Tokio ausgeführt; ferner das Klubhaus des Kinjo Golf Club in Okayama (1992), das Gästehaus für die Firma Bandai Corporation in Atami (1992–1995), ein Hotel in Karuizawa (1993), das Klubhaus des Lakewood Golf Club in Tomioka (1993–1996), das Observatorium Kiro-san in Ehime (1994), der Japanische Pavillon auf der Biennale in Venedig (1995) und das Noh-Theater in Toyama, Miyagi (1995–96). Seine neuesten Projekte sind das Steinmuseum in Nasu, Tochigi, sowie ein Museum für die Werke von Ando Hiroshige in Batou, Nasu-gun, Tochigi.

Né en 1954 à Kanagawa, Japon, Kengo Kuma est Master of Architecture de l'Université de Tokyo (1979). En 1985–86, il bénéficie d'une bourse de l'Asian Cultural Council et est chercheur invité à la Columbia University. En 1987, il crée le Spatial Design Studio, et en 1991 Kengo Kuma & Associates. Parmi ses réalisations : le Car Show Room Toyota de Gunma (Maebashi, 1989) ; le Maiton Resort Complex (Phuket, Thaïlande, 1991) ; le Rustic Office Building (Tokyo, 1991) ; l'immeuble de bureaux Doric (Tokyo, 1991) ; le siège du département de design de Mazda (Tokyo, 1991) ; le Kinjo Golf Club, Club House (Okayama, 1992) ; l'Observatoire Kiro-san (Ehime, Japon, 1994) ; l'Atami Guest House pour Bandaï Corp (Atami, 1992–1995) ; le Karuizawa Resort Hotel (Karuizawa, 1993) ; le Club House du Tomioka Lakewood Golf (Tomioka, 1993–1996) ; le Théâtre Nô Toyoma (Miyagi, 1995–96) et le pavillon japonais de la Biennale de Venise en 1995. Il vient d'achever le Musée de la pierre (Nasu, Tochigi) et le Musée Ando Hiroshige (Batou, Nasu-gun, Tochigi).

# GREAT BAMBOO WALL

*Badaling, China, 2000–2002*

*Client: SOHO China Ltd. Floor area: 528 m². Costs: not specified.*

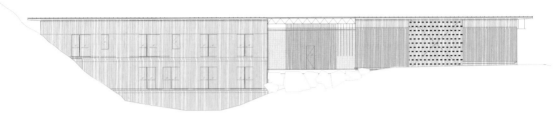

In October 2002, the SOHO (Small Office, Home Office) China group inaugurated the first 11 of 59 planned guest houses located near the Great Wall of China. Created by the young couple Pan Shiyi and his wife Zhang Xin, respectively 39 and 36 years old, SOHO China has called on a number of well-known architects for this project, including Shigeru Ban. Their intention is to make a weekend community mainly for wealthy Chinese clients, and aside from the first 11 villas they have created a 4 000-square-meter club with pools, restaurants, cinemas and art galleries. The cost of the houses ranges from 500 000 to one million euros and they are between 330 and 700 square meters in size. Each house has its own style, or rather that of its architect, though the complex does not give the impression of being a kind of architectural "zoo." The structure designed by Kengo Kuma, called the Great Bamboo Wall, is set on a 1 930-square-meter site and has a total floor area of 528 square meters. Intended as a small hotel unit, it is a reinforced concrete one-story structure (and basement) with a partly steel frame. The partial basement takes advantage of a natural dip in the site under part of the structure. An extensive use of glass and bamboo walls with fairly large openings between each pole and bamboo cladding on pillars gives an impression of lightness and a relationship to the traditional architecture of Asia. Kuma attains a simplicity and a modernity that have more to do with the most recent trends in architecture than with the ancient past, however. As he says about bamboo, "skin and outer surface are different. Concrete has an outer surface, but not skin. On top of that, I don't find concrete to be particularly attractive. That's because without skin, the soul within never appears. Bamboo has particularly beautiful skin. And, bamboo has a soul residing within. In Japan there is a famous children's tale about how 'Princess Kakuyahime,' the Moon Goddess, was born inside a stalk of bamboo. People believed the story that she was born inside a stalk of bamboo because bamboo has a peculiar type of skin and possesses a soul." After this structure, Kuma has undertaken the realization of seven houses in the same project area.

Im Oktober 2002 eröffnete die Firmengruppe SOHO (Small Office, Home Office) China in einem Gebiet nahe der Chinesischen Mauer die ersten elf von insgesamt 59 geplanten Gästehäusern. Das von dem 39-jährigen Pan Shiyi und seiner 36-jährigen Frau Zhang Xin gegründete Unternehmen SOHO China beauftragte eine Reihe bekannter Architekten mit der Planung, darunter auch Shigeru Ban. Die Zielgruppe sind Wochenendgäste, hauptsächlich wohlhabende Chinesen, für die neben den Villen ein 4 000 m² großes Clubareal mit Schwimmbädern, Restaurants und Kunstgalerien angelegt wurde. Die zwischen 330 und 700 m² großen Häuser kosten 500 000 bis eine Million Euro. Zwar hat jedes von ihnen seinen eigenen Stil, oder besser gesagt, den seines Architekten, trotzdem macht die Anlage nicht den Eindruck, als würde hier eine Art „Architektur-Zoo" entstehen. Das von Kengo Kuma entworfene Great-Bamboo-Wall-Gebäude steht auf einem 1 930 m² großen Grundstück und hat eine Nutzfläche von 528 m². Es ist als kleines Hotel gedacht und besteht aus einem eingeschossigen Bauteil aus Stahlbeton mit einem Stahlrahmenteilstück. Der zusätzliche Untergeschossraum ergab sich durch Ausnutzung einer natürlichen Senke, die sich unter einem Teil des Gebäudes befindet. Das Haus selbst vermittelt durch die großzügige Ausstattung mit Glas und Bambus den Eindruck von Leichtigkeit und Nähe zur traditionellen Architektur Asiens. Kuma überzeugt hier jedoch mit einer Schlichtheit und Modernität, die mehr mit den neuesten Architekturtrends als mit der Vergangenheit zu tun haben. Zum Thema Bambus erläutert er: „Es gibt einen Unterschied zwischen Haut und Außenfläche. Beton hat eine Außenfläche, aber keine Haut. Außerdem finde ich Beton nicht besonders attraktiv. Und zwar deshalb, weil ohne Haut die Seele nicht zum Vorschein kommt. Bambus dagegen hat eine besonders schöne Haut. Und Bambus besitzt eine Seele. In Japan gibt es ein berühmtes Kindermärchen, in dem erzählt wird, wie Prinzessin Kakuyahime, die Mondgöttin, aus einem Bambusrohr geboren wurde. Die Menschen glaubten diese Geschichte, eben weil Bambus so eine charakteristische Haut hat und eine Seele besitzt." Nach der Fertigstellung dieses Gebäudes hat Kuma die Planung von weiteren sieben Häusern für dasselbe Projekt übernommen.

En octobre 2002, le SOHO (Small Office, Home Office) China group a inauguré les onze premières maisons d'hôtes sur les 59 qu'il compte édifier près de la Grande muraille de Chine. Créé par un jeune couple, Pan Shiyi et son épouse Zhang Xin, respectivement âgés de 39 et 36 ans, SOHO China a fait appel pour ce projet à un certain nombre d'architectes connus, dont Shigeru Ban. Leur programme est de réaliser des résidences de week-end, principalement destinées à de riches clients chinois. En dehors des onze villas, ils ont déjà créé un club de 4 000 m² comprenant des piscines, des restaurants, des cinémas et des galeries d'art. Le coût des maisons s'élève de 500 000 à 1 million d'euros pour des surfaces de 330 à 700 m². Chacune possède son style propre, ou plutôt celui de son architecte, mais l'ensemble ne donne pas pour autant l'impression de zoo architectural. Le projet de Kengo Kuma, appelé « La grande muraille de bambou » est érigé sur un terrain de 1 930 m² pour 528 m² utiles. Ce petit ensemble hôtelier est une construction en béton armé d'un seul niveau (+ sous-sol) et ossature partiellement en acier. Le sous-sol profite d'un creux naturel du sol. Le recours extensif au verre et aux murs de bambou avec d'assez grandes ouvertures entre chaque pilier de bambou et des espacements marqués entre les lattes du même bois donne une impression de légèreté et rappelle l'architecture traditionnelle de l'Asie. Kuma atteint à une simplicité et une modernité néanmoins plus en rapport avec les tendances récentes de l'architecture qu'avec un passé lointain. Il explique à propos du bambou : « Peau et surface extérieure sont différentes. Le béton possède une surface, pas une peau. De plus, je ne trouve pas le béton particulièrement séduisant. Quand il n'y a pas de peau, l'âme est absente. Le bambou possède précisément une peau magnifique. Et il a une âme en lui. Un célèbre conte japonais pour enfants parle de la Princesse Kakuyahime, déesse de la lune née dans une âme de bambou. Les gens croient qu'elle est née dans une âme de bambou parce que celui-ci possède une peau particulière et une âme. » Après ce projet, Kuma a entrepris la construction de sept résidences dans la même région.

*The Great Bamboo Wall building fits naturally into its site, as can be seen in the elevation on the left and in the photos.*

*Das Great-Bamboo-Wall-Gebäude fügt sich harmonisch in seine Umgebung ein, wie im Querschnitt links und in den Fotos zu sehen ist.*

*La maison d'hôtes s'intègre naturellement dans son site, comme le montre l'élévation à gauche, et les photos.*

A light, open structure permits views to the hilly setting and a basin brings an unexpected freshness into the building itself. Though far less durable than the stones of the Great Wall, bamboo is of course a very popular Asian building material.

Eine helle, offene Raumaufteilung ermöglicht Ausblicke auf die umliegende Berglandschaft und bringt eine überraschende Frische in das Gebäude. Wenn auch weit weniger dauerhaft als die Steine der chinesischen Mauer, ist Bambus in Asien ein sehr beliebtes Baumaterial.

La structure légère et ouverte favorise les vues sur le cadre montagneux environnant, tandis qu'un bassin apporte une fraîcheur inattendue dans le bâtiment lui-même. Moins résistant que les pierres de la Grande muraille, le bambou n'en reste pas moins un matériau de construction très populaire en Asie.

The simplicity and directness of the design might reveal the architect's effort to mediate the divide that exists between the architecture of his own country and that of China.

*Mit der Einfachheit und Geradlinigkeit des Designs stellte der Architekt eine Verbindung zwischen der Architektur seines eigenen Landes und der Chinas her.*

*La simplicité et la franchise de conception révèlent cependant un effort pour trouver une voie entre l'architecture de son propre pays et celle de la Chine.*

# DANIEL LIBESKIND

*Studio Daniel Libeskind*
*2 Rector Street, 19th Floor*
*New York, NY 10006*
*USA*

*Tel: +1 212 497 9110*
*Fax: +1 646 452 6198*
*e-mail: info@daniel-libeskind.com*
*Web: www.daniel-libeskind.com*

*World Trade Cen*

Born in Poland in 1946 and now a US citizen, Daniel Libeskind studied music in Israel and New York before taking up architecture at the Cooper Union in New York. He has taught at Harvard, Yale, Hanover, Graz, Hamburg, and UCLA. His work includes the Jewish Museum in Berlin, which is an extension to the Berlin Museum, 1992–1999; numerous proposals such as his 1997 plan to build an extension to the Victoria & Albert Museum in London; and his prize-winning scheme for the Bremen Philharmonic Hall, 1995. Like Zaha Hadid, Libeskind has had a considerable influence through his theory and his proposals, rather than his limited built work. The Felix Nussbaum Museum in Osnabrück, Germany is in fact one of his first built, completed works. His recent work includes the Imperial War Museum, published here; the Shoah Center in Manchester, England; the Jewish Museum, San Francisco, California; and the JVG University-Colleges of Public Administration, Guadalajara, Mexico. Libeskind's victory in the complex competition for the World Trade Center site in Manhattan places him at the forefront of contemporary architecture.

Der amerikanische Architekt Daniel Libeskind wurde 1946 in Polen geboren. Er studierte zunächst Musik in Israel und New York, bevor er an der Cooper Union in New York mit Architektur begann. Er hat in Harvard, Yale, Hannover, Graz, Hamburg und an der UCLA gelehrt. Zu seinen Arbeiten gehören das Jüdische Museum in Berlin, eine Erweiterung des Berlin Museums (1992–1999), zahlreiche Entwürfe wie der zur Erweiterung des Victoria & Albert Museums in London (1997) und der preisgekrönte Wettbewerbsbeitrag für die Philharmonie in Bremen (1995). Wie Zaha Hadid ist Libeskind einflussreicher durch seine Theorien und Entwürfe als durch seine wenigen realisierten Bauten, von denen das Felix Nussbaum Museum in Osnabrück zu den ersten gehört. Zu seinen neuesten Projekten zählen das hier präsentierte Imperial War Museum, das Shoah Center in Manchester, England, das Jewish Museum in San Francisco und die JVG University-Colleges of Public Administration in Guadalajara, Mexiko. Libeskinds Sieg im diffizilen Wettbewerb für die Neugestaltung des World-Trade-Center-Geländes in Manhattan gibt ihm einen Platz in der ersten Reihe der Architekten unserer Zeit.

Né en Pologne en 1946 et aujourd'hui citoyen américain, Daniel Libeskind étudie la musique en Israël et à New York avant de suivre des cours d'architecture à la Cooper Union, à New York. Il a enseigné à Harvard, Yale, Hanovre, Graz, Hambourg et UCLA. Ses réalisations comprennent, entre autres, le musée juif de Berlin, extension du Berlin Museum (1992–1999), et de nombreux projets comme celui de l'extension du Victoria & Albert Museum à Londres et la Philharmonie de Brême qui lui valut un prix en 1995. Comme Zaha Hadid, son influence considérable s'exerce plus à travers son enseignement et ses propositions théoriques que par son œuvre construite relativement limitée. Le Felix Nussbaum Museum à Osnabrück (Allemagne) est en fait l'une de ses premières réalisations. Il a récemment achevé l'Imperial War Museum à Manchester, publié ici, et le Shoah Center, dans la même ville, le Jewish Museum (San Francisco, Californie, USA) et le Collège d'administration publique de l'Université JVG (Guadalajara, Mexique). Sa victoire au concours du World Trade Center à Manhattan l'a placé au premier plan de la scène architecturale contemporaine.

# IMPERIAL WAR MUSEUM NORTH

*Manchester, UK, 2000–2002*

*Client: The Trustees of the Imperial War Museum, London. Total floor area: 6 500 m². Costs: £ 15 600 000.*

The Imperial War Museum was established by an Act of Parliament in 1920. Its purpose is to collect, preserve and display material and information connected with military operations in which Britain or the Commonwealth have been involved since August 1914. With four branches in the South East, the Imperial War Museum had wanted for some time to offer the population in the north access to its exceptionally rich collections of films, photographs, art, documents, objects, and services. The aluminum-clad building, Daniel Libeskind's first structure in the UK, is based on the concept of a world shattered by conflict, a fragmented globe reassembled in three interlocking shards. These shards represent conflict on land, in the air and on water. Visitors enter through the Air Shard, which is 55 meters high and open to the elements. It houses a viewing platform at 29 meters with views across the Manchester Ship Canal toward the city center. The Earth Shard is curved and houses the main public areas of the Museum, exhibition space and the special exhibitions gallery. The Water Shard, overlooking the Manchester Ship Canal, accommodates a 160-seat restaurant. In his project text, the architect writes, "Paul Valéry pointed out the world is permanently threatened by two dangers: order and disorder. This project develops the realm of the in between, the inter-est, the realm of democratic openness, plurality and potential. By navigating the course between rigid totalities on one hand, and the chaos of events on the other, this building reflects an evolving identity open to profound public participation, access and education. The Museum is therefore a catalyst for focussing energies, both entrepreneurial and spiritual, and moulding them into a creative expression."

Das Imperial War Museum wurde 1920 gegründet. Seine Aufgabe ist es, Material und Informationen über Militäroperationen, in die Großbritannien oder das Commonwealth seit August 1914 involviert waren, zu sammeln, zu konservieren und auszustellen. Die Verantwortlichen des Museums, das mit vier Außenstellen im Südosten von England vertreten war, wollten schon seit längerem, dass auch die Bevölkerung im Norden des Landes Zugang zu seinen äußerst umfangreichen Sammlungen von Filmen, Fotos, Kunstwerken, Dokumenten, Objekten und Dienstleistungen erhält, und beauftragte Daniel Libeskind mit diesem Projekt. Libeskind hat sein erstes in Großbritannien realisiertes Gebäude mit Aluminium verkleidet. Es basiert auf dem bildhaften Gestaltungskonzept einer durch Konflikte in Trümmer gegangenen Welt, einer fragmentierten Erdkugel, die in drei Bruchstücken, die sich gegenseitig durchdringen, wieder zusammenfindet. Diese Bruchstücke repräsentieren den bewaffneten Konflikt zu Land, in der Luft und auf See. Der Eintritt ins Museum erfolgt durch den 55 m hohen, offenen Luft-Teil, der in 29 m Höhe mit einer Aussichtsplattform ausgestattet ist. Im gewölbten Baukörper, der die Erde symbolisiert, sind die öffentlichen Bereiche des Museums mit den Räumen für die permanente und die Sonderausstellungen untergebracht, während der wiederum den Kanal überblickende Wasser-Teil ein Restaurant mit 160 Plätzen beherbergt. In seiner Projektbeschreibung erklärt Libeskind: „Paul Valéry hat einmal bemerkt, dass die Welt ständig von zwei Gefahren bedroht sei: Ordnung und Unordnung. Dieses Projekt entwickelt das Reich, das dazwischen liegt, das *inter-est*, das Reich der demokratischen Offenheit, der Pluralität und des Potentials. Indem es den Kurs hält zwischen starrer Totalität auf der einen Seite und dem Chaos der Ereignisse auf der anderen Seite, entfaltet dieses Gebäude eine Identität, die offen ist für die Beteiligung der Öffentlichkeit."

L'Imperial War Museum a été créé par un acte du Parlement de 1920. Son objectif est de réunir, préserver et exposer les matériaux et informations liés aux opérations militaires auxquelles ont participé la Grande-Bretagne et le Commonwealth depuis août 1914. Disposant de quatre installations dans le Sud-Est de l'Angleterre, le musée voulait depuis un certain temps offrir aux populations du nord un accès à ses collections exceptionnellement riches en films, photographies, œuvres d'art, documents, objets et à ses services. Première réalisation de Daniel Libeskind au Royaume-Uni, le bâtiment habillé d'aluminium repose sur un concept de monde bouleversé par les conflits, que traduit la forme d'un globe éclaté en trois fragments imbriqués. Ils représentent les conflits sur terre, dans l'air et sur mer. Les visiteurs pénètrent dans l'« Air Shard », de 55 m de haut, ouvert sur le ciel, qui abrite un belvédère à 29 m de haut donnant sur le Ship Canal de Manchester et le centre-ville. Le « Earth Shard » incurvé accueille les principales zones ouvertes au public, un espace d'exposition et la galerie des expositions spéciales. Le « Water Shard », au-dessus du canal, contient un restaurant de 160 couverts. Dans sa présentation du projet, l'architecte écrivait : « Paul Valéry a fait remarquer que le monde est en permanence menacé par deux dangers : l'ordre et le désordre. Ce projet développe le domaine de l'entre-deux, le *inter est*, celui de l'ouverture démocratique, la pluralité et le potentiel. En navigant entre des entités rigides d'un côté et le chaos des événements de l'autre, ce bâtiment reflète une identité en évolution, ouverte à la participation, à l'accès et à l'éducation approfondie du public. Le musée est ainsi un catalyseur qui concentre les énergies à la fois spirituelles et d'esprit d'entreprise pour en faire une expression créative. »

Though less abruptly fragmented than many of Libeskind's other designs, the Imperial War Museum nonetheless does evoke the ferocity of war.

Wenn auch auf weniger schroffe Weise fragmentarisch als viele andere Entwürfe von Libeskind, evoziert das Imperial War Museum dennoch die Grausamkeit von Krieg.

Bien que moins abruptement fragmenté que beaucoup d'autres projets de Libeskind, le Imperial War Museum évoque à sa façon la férocité de la guerre.

The metal-sheathed forms of the Museum appear sculptural, in a sometimes ominous way. This is certainly not a tribute to war as some military people might imagine it.

Die mit Metall ummantelten, skulpturalen Formen des Museums wirken manchmal bedrohlich. Das ist keinesfalls als Tribut an den Krieg zu verstehen, wie einige Militärbegeisterte vielleicht meinen könnten.

Les formes gainées de métal du Musée sont d'un caractère sculptural parfois inquiétant. Il ne s'agit certainement pas d'une ode à la guerre telle que certains militaires auraient pu l'imaginer.

Overhanging forms and sweeping curves characterize the design in a flux of movement, where cutting edges are more common than soothing esthetics.

Überhängende Formen und Bogenlinien sind kennzeichnend für die Dynamik der Gestaltung, die sich mehr durch Kanten als eine glättende Ästhetik auszeichnet.

Les formes suspendues et les courbes généreuses créent des flux de mouvements, d'une esthétique plus abrupte et agressive qu'apaisante.

As he did in the Jewish Museum in Berlin, Libeskind shows a mastery here of the evocative power of color and lighting.

*Wie in seinem Jüdischen Museum in Berlin demonstriert Libeskind auch hier seine Meisterschaft im Umgang mit Farbe und Licht.*

*Comme pour le Musée juif de Berlin, Libeskind témoigne ici d'une maîtrise de la puissance évocatrice de la couleur et de l'éclairage.*

Angled walls and interrupted lines of light seem to imply that there is no clear way forward in conflict.

*Schräge Wände und unterbrochene Lichtstreifen deuten auf Konflikte ohne klaren Ausweg.*

*Les murs inclinés et les traits de lumière interrompus semblent impliquer qu'il n'existe pas d'issue claire aux conflits.*

*A somber atmosphere assures that that the architect does not participate here in a glorification of war, but in an explanation.*

*Die düstere Atmosphäre macht deutlich, dass es dem Architekten hier nicht um eine Glorifizierung von Krieg, sondern um eine Erklärung geht.*

*L'atmosphère sombre montre que l'architecte ne participe pas à une quelconque glorification de la guerre mais à son explication.*

*Streaks of light and vehicles and aircraft hanging at odd angles have more to do with the effects of explosion than of any ordered march to victory.*

*Die Zickzacklinien der Lichtstreifen und die aufgehängten Luft- und anderen Fahrzeuge implizieren eher Auswirkungen einer Explosion als einen geordneten Marsch zum Sieg.*

*Des éclairs lumineux, des véhicules et des avions suspendus selon des angles étranges évoquent davantage les effets d'une explosion qu'une marche victorieuse.*

# RICHARD MEIER

*Richard Meier & Partners, Architects LLP*
*475 Tenth Avenue, 6th Floor*
*New York, NY 10018*
*USA*

*Tel: +1 212 967 6060*
*Fax: +1 212 967 3207*
*e-mail: mail@richardmeier.com*
*Web: www.richardmeier.com*

*Restaurant*

Born in Newark, New Jersey in 1934. Richard Meier received his architectural training at Cornell University, and worked in the office of Marcel Breuer (1960–1963) before establishing his own practice in 1963. He won the 1984 Pritzker Prize and the 1988 Royal Gold Medal. His notable buildings include The Atheneum, (New Harmony, Indiana, 1975–1979); Museum of Decorative Arts (Frankfurt, Germany, 1979–1984); High Museum of Art (Atlanta, Georgia, 1980–1983); Canal Plus Headquarters (Paris, France, 1988–1991); City Hall and Library (The Hague, The Netherlands, 1990–1995); Barcelona Museum of Contemporary Art (Barcelona, Spain, 1988–1995); and the Getty Center (Los Angeles, California, 1984–1997). Recent work includes the US Courthouse and Federal Building (Phoenix, Arizona, 1995–2000); 173–176 Perry Street Condominium Towers (New York, NY, 2001–02); Jubilee Church (Rome, 2003); Crystal Cathedral International Center for Possibility Thinking (Garden Grove, CA, 2003); and the Arp Museum (Rolandseck, Germany).

Richard Meier, geboren 1934 in Newark, New Jersey, studierte Architektur an der Cornell University und arbeitete in der Firma von Marcel Breuer (1960–1963), bevor er 1963 sein eigenes Büro eröffnete. Er wurde 1984 mit dem Pritzker Prize und 1988 mit der Royal Gold Medal ausgezeichnet. Zu seinen bedeutendsten Bauten gehören: The Atheneum in New Harmony, Indiana (1975–1979), das Museum für Kunsthandwerk in Frankfurt am Main (1979–1984), das High Museum of Art in Atlanta, Georgia (1980–1983), das Getty Center in Los Angeles (1984–1997), die Zentrale von Canal Plus in Paris (1988–1991), das Museum für zeitgenössische Kunst in Barcelona (1988–1995) und Rathaus und Bibliothek in Den Haag (1990–1995). Zu seinen jüngsten Projekten zählen das US Courthouse and Federal Building in Phoenix, Arizona (1995–2000), Condominium Towers in 173–176 Street, New York (2001-02), die Kirche des Heiligen Jahres in Rom (2003), das Crystal Cathedral International Center for Possibility Thinking im kalifornischen Garden Grove (2003) sowie das Arp Museum im deutschen Rolandseck.

Né à Newark (New Jersey), en 1934, Richard Meier étudie à la Cornell University et travaille dans l'agence de Marcel Breuer (1960–1963), avant de s'installer à son compte en 1963. Il obtient le Prix Pritzker en 1984 et la Royal Gold Medal en 1988. Principales réalisations: The Atheneum, New Harmony (Indiana, USA, 1975–1979); Musée des Arts Décoratifs de Francfort-sur-le-Main (1979–1984); High Museum of Art (Atlanta, Géorgie, 1980–1983); siège de Canal + (Paris, 1988–1991); hôtel de ville et bibliothèque (La Haye, 1990–1995); Musée d'Art Contemporain de Barcelone (1988–1995); Getty Center (Los Angeles, Californie, 1984–1996). Travaux récents: Tribunal fédéral et immeuble de l'administration fédérale à Phoenix (Arizona, USA, 1995–2000); les tours Condominium, 173-176 Perry Street (New York, NY, 2001–02); l'église du Jubilée (Rome, 2003); le Crystal Cathedral International Center for Possibility Thinking (Garden Grove, Californie, USA, 2003) et le Arp Museum (Rolandseck, Allemagne).

# RESTAURANT 66

*New York, New York, USA, 2003*

*Client: Phil Suarez and Jean-Georges Vongerichten. Floor area: 808 m². Costs: not specified.*

Located at 241 Church Street in the Tribeca area of Manhattan, 66 is an open-space restaurant with large frosted glass panes subdividing the dining areas. A 3.5-meter-high curved glass wall marks the entrance and fish tanks separate the dining area for 150 guests from the kitchen. A frosted glass wall marks the bar area. Red silk banners with Chinese ideograms hang above a 13.4-meter epoxy resin communal table. The dining tables also designed by the architect are made of ice blue poured epoxy resin with stainless steel bases. Other furniture is by Eames (Herman Miller), Bertoia (Knoll), and Eero Saarinen (Knoll). Housed in the Textile Building, designed in 1901 by Henry Hardenbergh, the architect of the Plaza Hotel and Dakota apartment building, this restaurant is the sixth opened in New York by the Strasbourg-born chef Jean-Georges Vongerichten. Vongerichten, who worked here as he has elsewhere with Phil Suarez, is also responsible for the Paris restaurant Market. The floor area of the facility is about 808 square meters. Its turn-of-the-century origin is made apparent by leaving visible the original iron columns, painted in Richard Meier's trademark white.

Das Restaurant 66 befindet sich in der Church Street 241 im Manhattaner Stadtteil Tribeca. Sein loftartiger Innenraum wird durch große Mattglasscheiben untergliedert. Eine gewölbte, 3,5 m hohe Glaswand markiert den Eingangsbereich, während Aquarien die Trennlinie zwischen der Küche und dem Speisesaal mit 150 Plätzen bilden. Auch die Bar wird durch eine Wand aus Mattglas abgegrenzt. Rotseidene Banner mit chinesischen Schriftzeichen hängen über einem 13,4 m langen, durchgehenden Tisch aus Epoxydharz. Auch die vom Architekten entworfenen Einzeltische sind aus eisblauem, gegossenem Epoxydharz, haben aber einen Sockel aus Edelstahl. Die anderen Einrichtungsgegenstände sind Entwürfe von Eames (Herman Miller), Bertoia (Knoll) und Eero Saarinen (Knoll). Das 808 m² große Restaurant befindet sich in dem 1901 von dem Architekten des Hotel Plaza und des Apartmenthauses Dakota, Henry Hardenbergh, entworfenen Textile Building. Es ist das neueste von insgesamt sechs ebenfalls in New York ansässigen Lokalen des in Straßburg geborenen Chefkochs Jean-Georges Vongerichten, dem auch das Pariser Restaurant Market gehört. Der historische Ursprung des Hauses wurde beim Umbau kenntlich gemacht, indem man die Eisensäulen in ihrer ursprünglichen Form beließ, nur angestrichen in Richard Meiers Markenzeichen, der Farbe Weiß.

Installé au 241 Church Street dans le quartier de Tribeca à Manhattan, le 66 est un restaurant de plan ouvert de 808 m² au sol subdivisés par de grands panneaux de verre givré. Un mur de verre incurvé de 3,5 m de haut marque l'entrée, et des aquariums séparent la salle à manger de 150 couverts de la cuisine. Un autre mur de verre givré met en valeur le bar. Des bannières de soie rouge à idéogrammes chinois sont suspendues au-dessus d'une table d'hôte en résine époxy de 13,4 m de long. Les tables du restaurant, également conçues par l'architecte, sont en résine époxy bleu glacier moulée à piétement en acier inoxydable. D'autres meubles sont signés Eames (Herman Miller), Bertoia (Knoll) et Eero Saarinen (Knoll). Installé dans le Textile Building, conçu en 1901 par Henry Hardenbergh, l'architecte du Plaza Hotel et de l'immeuble Dakota, ce restaurant est le sixième ouvert à New York par le chef strasbourgeois Jean-Georges Vongerichten, qui a travaillé sur ce projet comme pour les autres avec Phil Suarez. Il est également à l'origine du restaurant parisien le Market. L'origine historique de l'immeuble retrouve ses droits dans les colonnes métalliques apparentes, peintes dans le blanc qui est la signature de Richard Meier.

Richard Meier's trademark white design is here applied to a pre-existing iron column while red flags set off the purity of the architect's lines.

Richard Meiers Markenzeichen, das weiße Design, zeigt sich hier an einer originalen Eisensäule, während rote Banner die puristischen Linien des Architekten hervorheben.

Le blanc caractéristique de Richard Meier s'applique ici aux anciennes colonnes métalliques. L'alignement de bannières rouges fait ressortir la pureté des lignes de l'architecte.

Though a wooden floor and the iron column again visible here may not seem very typical of Richard Meier, his crisp delimitation of space and surfaces is everywhere in evidence.

Wenngleich Holzboden und Eisensäulen nicht sehr typisch für Richard Meier sein mögen, ist seine klare Definition von Raum und Oberfläche überall evident.

Si le sol en bois et les colonnes métalliques ne sont pas vraiment typiques du style de Meier, son sens de la délimitation tendue de l'espace et des surfaces est omniprésent.

Black and silver furniture as well as screens and glass surfaces stand out against the white walls of the restaurant.

Möbel in Schwarz und Silber sowie Raumteiler und Glaswände heben sich gut gegen die weißen Wänden des Restaurants ab.

Les meubles en noir et blanc ainsi que les écrans et les plans de verre ressortent sur le fond des murs blancs du restaurant.

Rigorous and rectilinear the 66 Restaurant may show Richard Meier under a less strict angle than some of his new buildings, but the spirit of the architect has surely marked this location.

Im Restaurant 66 zeigt sich Richard Meier vielleicht von einer weniger strengen Seite als in anderen von ihm gestalteten Gebäuden, doch ist auch diese Arbeit stark von seinem Stil und seiner Haltung geprägt.

Rigoureux et d'une stricte géométrie rectiligne, le 66 Restaurant montre Richard Meier sous un angle moins strict que certaines de ses récentes réalisations, même si l'esprit de son architecture marque définitivement ce lieu.

# JUBILEE CHURCH

*(Dio Padre Misericordioso), Tor Tre Teste, Rome, Italy, 1996–2003*

Client: Vicariato of Rome. Floor area: 830 m² (church), 1 450 m² (community center), 10 000 m² (site). Costs: not specified.

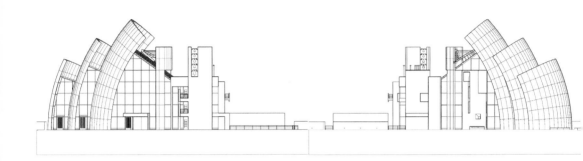

*A succession of shells like sails billowing in the wind marks this church, set up on its platform in Rome to mark the Jubilee year.*

*Eine Abfolge von Schalensegmenten, die wie Segel wirken, kennzeichnet die Kirche, die zum katholischen Jubiläumsjahr in Rom errichtet wurde.*

*Une succession de coques, telles des voiles gonflés par le vent, signalent cette église, édifiée à Rome pour marquer l'année du Jubilée.*

Sitting on its glistening plaza, the Jubilee church at sunset takes on an even more ship-like appearance. Meier has often used nautical metaphors in his work, but in this context the successive sails are surprising.

Die auf einem schimmernden Platz ruhende Jubiläumskirche sieht bei Sonnenuntergang sogar noch schiffsähnlicher aus. Meier hat zwar bereits in früheren Arbeiten nautische Metaphern eingesetzt, aber in diesem Kontext sind die segelartigen Formen neu und ungewöhnlich.

Posée sur une plazza de travertin poli, l'église du Jubilée fait encore plus penser à un bateau au coucher du soleil. Si Meier a souvent utilisé des métaphores nautiques dans son œuvre, l'utilisation de cette succession de voiles n'en est pas moins surprenante.

Commissioned by the Vicariato of Rome, this church is set on a triangular site on the boundary of a public park surrounded by 10-story apartment buildings in a community of approximately 30 000 residents. The project features the use of concrete, stucco, travertine and glass and three dramatic shells or arcs that evoke billowing white sails. Unprecedented in Meier's work, the concrete arcs are graduated in height from 17 to 27 meters. The invited competition to design the structure included Tadao Ando, Günter Behnisch, Santiago Calatrava, Peter Eisenman, and Frank Gehry, as well as Meier, who won in the spring of 1996. Construction began in 1998, and although the architect has designed the Hartford Seminary in Connecticut (1981) and the International Center for Possibility Thinking at the Crystal Cathedral in Southern California (2003), this was his first church. As always, Richard Meier places an emphasis on light. "Light is the protagonist of our understanding and reading of space. Light is the means by which we are able to experience what we call sacred. Light is at the origins of this building," he says. Commenting on the fact that he may be the first Jewish architect asked to design a Catholic church, Meier says, "I feel extremely proud that I was the one chosen to design this church. It is very clear that the Catholic Church chose my design based on its merits, not because of a need to make a statement in regard to their relationship to Jews throughout history. Three of the architects in the competition were Jewish. They were chosen to compete because they were among the top architects of our time." His sources of inspiration, he says, were "the churches in which the presence of the sacred could be felt: Alvar Aalto's churches in Finland, Frank Lloyd Wright's Wayfarer's Chapel in the United States along with the Chapel at Ronchamp and La Tourette by Le Corbusier." The Jubilee Church was inaugurated on October 26, 2003 to mark the 25th anniversary of the Pontificate of John Paul II.

Die Jubiläumskirche gehört zu einer Gemeinde mit circa 30 000 Einwohnern. Sie steht auf einem dreiseitigen Grundstück am Rand eines öffentlichen Parks und ist von zehnstöckigen Wohnblocks umgeben. Ein besonderes Gestaltungsmerkmal des mit Beton, Gipsputz, Travertin und Glas ausgestatteten Bauwerks sind drei dramatisch geformte Bögen, die an Segel denken lassen, die sich im Wind blähen. Diese in Meiers Werk noch nie da gewesenen Betonformen sind der Höhe nach von 17 bis 27 m gestaffelt. Neben Meier wurden auch Tadao Ando, Günter Behnisch, Santiago Calatrava, Peter Eisenman and Frank O. Gehry zu dem Wettbewerb für die Gestaltung dieses Projekts eingeladen, den Meier im Frühjahr 1996 für sich entschied. Mit den Bauarbeiten wurde 1998 begonnen und obwohl der Architekt zuvor das Hartford Priesterseminar in Connecticut (1981) und das International Center for Possibility Thinking der Crystal Cathedral in Südkalifornien (2003) geplant hatte, ist dies sein erster Sakralbau. Wie immer hebt Richard Meier in seinem Entwurf speziell das Licht hervor: „Licht ist der Protagonist unseres Verständnisses und unserer Auffassung von Raum. Das Licht ist das Medium, durch welches wir das erleben können, was wir heilig nennen. Licht liegt am Ursprung dieses Gebäudes." Als Antwort auf die Tatsache, dass er vermutlich der erste jüdische Architekt ist, der mit der Gestaltung einer katholischen Kirche betraut wurde, sagt Meier: „Ich bin ungeheuer stolz darauf, dass ich ausgewählt wurde, um diese Kirche zu entwerfen. Dabei ist ganz klar, dass die Katholische Kirche meinen Entwurf aufgrund seiner Vorzüge wählte, und nicht weil es ihr darum ging, eine Aussage über ihr Verhältnis zu Juden zu machen. Drei der Architekten, die am Wettbewerb teilgenommen haben, sind jüdisch. Und sie wurden zu dem Wettbewerb eingeladen, weil sie zu den besten Architekten unserer Zeit gehören." Seine Quelle der Inspiration, erläutert Meier, waren „Kirchen, in denen man die Präsenz des Heiligen fühlen kann: Alvar Aaltos Kirchen in Finnland, Frank Lloyd Wrights Wayfairer Kapelle in den Vereinigten Staaten und die Wallfahrtskirche zu Ronchamp sowie das Kloster La Tourette von Le Corbusier." Die Jubilee Church wurde zur Feier des 25-jährigen Pontifikats von Johannes Paul II. am 26. Oktober 2003 eingeweiht.

L'église est implantée sur un terrain triangulaire en bordure d'un parc public entouré d'immeubles de logements de 10 étages dans un ensemble qui compte environ 30 000 résidents. Le projet qui fait appel au béton, au stuc, au travertin et au verre se caractérise par trois coques ou arcs spectaculaires qui évoquent des voiles blanches et gonflées. Motif sans précédent dans l'œuvre de Meier, ces arcs de béton s'étagent de 17 à 27 mètres. Le concours sur invitation comprenait Tadao Ando, Günther Behnisch, Santiago Calatrava, Peter Eisenman et Frank Gehry ainsi que Meier qui le remporta en 1996. C'était son premier projet d'église même s'il a déjà conçu le Séminaire de Hartford (Connecticut, 1981), l'International Center for Possibility Thinking de la Crystal Cathedral (Californie du sud, 2003). Le chantier débuta en 1998. Comme toujours, Meier a mis l'accent sur la lumière : « La lumière est le protagoniste qui nous fait comprendre et lire l'espace. La lumière est le moyen par lequel nous sommes en mesure de faire l'expérience de ce que nous appelons le sacré. La lumière est à l'origine de ce projet. » Commentant le fait qu'il est peut-être le premier architecte juif à concevoir une église, il ajoute : « Je me sens extrêmement fier d'avoir été choisi… il est clair que l'Église catholique a retenu mon projet pour ses mérites, et non pas pour marquer une position par rapport à sa relation avec les Juifs au cours de l'histoire. Trois architectes invités étaient juifs. Ils avaient été sélectionnés parce qu'ils faisaient partie des tout premiers architectes de notre temps. » Ses sources d'inspiration ont été « des églises dans lesquelles on peut sentir la présence du sacré : celles de Alvar Aalto en Finlande, la Wayfairer's Chapel de Frank Lloyd Wright aux États-Unis, la chapelle de Ronchamp et le couvent de la Tourette par Le Corbusier ». L'église du Jubilée a été inaugurée le 26 octobre 2003, pour marquer le 25ème anniversaire du pontificat de Jean-Paul II.

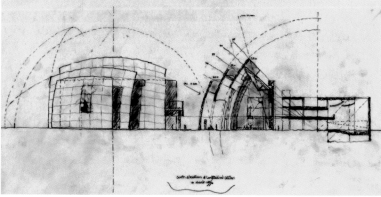

*As always attentive to the effects of light in his architecture, Richard Meier has created a light-filled church with a markedly asymmetrical interior design.*

*Wie immer sorgfältig auf die Wirkung des Lichts in seiner Architektur bedacht, hat Richard Meier eine lichterfüllte Kirche mit einem ausgesprochen asymmetrischen Innenraum entworfen.*

*Toujours attentif aux effets de la lumière dans son architecture, Meier a créé une église extrêmement lumineuse sur un plan intérieur fortement asymétrique.*

# MEYER EN VAN SCHOOTEN

*Meyer en Van Schooten Architecten B. V.*
*P. O. Box 2737*
*1000 CS Amsterdam*
*The Netherlands*

*Tel: +31 20 5319 800*
*Fax: +31 20 53 19 801*
*e-mail: office@meyer-vanschooten.nl*
*Web: www.meyer-vanschooten.nl*

Roberto Meyer was born in 1959 in Bogotá, Colombia, while Jeroen van Schooten was born in Nieuwer Amstel, The Netherlands in 1960. They created their firm Meyer en Van Schooten Architecten B. V. in Amsterdam in 1984. Their work includes housing in Enschede, Apeldoorn, Amsterdam, Rotterdam, Zaandam and Arnhem. They have also built a number of bridges (IJburg, Amsterdam, 1998). Their recent work includes: 60 apartments (Geuzenbaan, Amsterdam); central library/30 apartments/ offices/shops (Almere-Stad); 150 apartments + parking (Verolme terrain, Alblasserdam); 52 apartments in block 11 and 78 apartments in block 14b Gershwin (south axis, Amsterdam); and the 160-apartment Veranda complex in Rotterdam. Their ING building published here won several awards, including the 2002 Netherlands Steel Prize (Nationale Staalprijs 2002) and the 2003 Aluminum Architecture Award 2003 (Nederlandse Aluminium Award Architectuur 2003). Upcoming work includes a Science Center for the University of Amsterdam, to be completed in 2007.

Roberto Meyer wurde 1959 in Bogotá, Kolumbien, und Jeroen van Schooten 1960 im niederländischen Nieuwer Amstel geboren. Zusammen gründeten sie 1984 ihre Firma Meyer en Van Schooten Architecten B.V. in Amsterdam. Zu ihren Arbeiten gehören Wohnbauten in Enschede, Apeldoorn, Amsterdam, Rotterdam, Zaandam und Arnheim. Außerdem planten sie eine Reihe von Brücken, wie die von IJburg, Amsterdam (1998). Zu ihren jüngsten Projekten zählen: 60 Wohnungen in Geuzenbaan, Amsterdam, eine Anlage aus Bücherei, 30 Wohnungen, Büros und Geschäften in Almere-Stad, 150 Wohnungen mit Parkplatz auf dem Verolme Gelände in Alblasserdam, 52 Wohnungen in Block 11 und 78 Wohnungen in Block 14b der Gershwin Südachse in Amsterdam sowie die Anlage Veranda mit 160 Wohnungen in Rotterdam. Ihr hier vorgestelltes ING-Gebäude erhielt zahlreiche Auszeichnungen, wie 2002 den Nationale Staalprijs (Niederländische Stahlpreis) und 2003 den Nederlandse Aluminium Award Architectuur. Zu ihren nächsten Aufgaben gehört ein Wissenschaftszentrum für die Universität Amsterdam, das 2007 fertig gestellt sein soll.

Roberto Meyer est né en 1959 à Bogotá (Colombie) et Jeroen van Schooten à Nieuwer Amstel (Pays-Bas) en 1960. Ils ont créé leur agence Meyer en Van Schooten Architecten B.V. à Amsterdam en 1984. Leurs réalisations comprennent des logements à Enschede, Apeldoorn, Amsterdam, Rotterdam, Zaandam et Arnhem. Ils ont également construit plusieurs ponts (IJburg, Amsterdam, 1998). Parmi leurs travaux récents : 60 appartements (Geuzenbaan, Amsterdam) ; Bibliothèque centrale/30 appartements/bureaux/ commerces (Almere-Stad) ; 150 appartements et parkings (Verolme Terrain, Alblasserdam) ; 52 appartements (bloc 11) et 78 appartements (bloc 14 b Gershwin (Axe sud, Amsterdam), et l'ensemble Veranda de 160 appartements à Rotterdam. L'immeuble ING, publié ici, a remporté plusieurs prix dont le Nationale Staalprijs 2002 (Prix de l'acier) et le Prix néerlandais de l'aluminium 2003. Ils travaillent actuellement au Centre des sciences de l'Université d'Amsterdam, prévu pour 2007.

# ING GROUP HEADQUARTERS

*Amsterdam, The Netherlands, 1998–2002*

*Client: ING Group N.V. Building area: 3 500 m², office floor area: 7 500 m². Costs: not specified.*

Built on a long, narrow site near Amsterdam's Ring Road, the ING headquarters lies between the Zuidas area of high-rise buildings and a green zone called De Nieuwe Meer. The architects intentionally kept the structure low on the "green" side and made it rise in the direction of the city. In order to allow motorists a view toward the green zone and at the same time to give the offices a view over the highway, the building is set up on pilotis ranging in height from 9 to 12.5 meters. A great deal of attention was paid to the energy efficiency of the structure, for example with a double-skin façade that facilitates natural ventilation while providing a sound barrier against traffic noise. A pumping system makes use of an aquifer located 120 meters under the building to provide cold/warm thermal storage. Successive stories within the building "intermingle and offer glimpses from one to another. Atriums, loggias and gardens vary the interior space as well. As the architects have written, "the new headquarters symbolizes the banking and insurance conglomerate as a dynamic, fast-moving international network. Transparency, innovation, eco-friendliness and openness were the main starting points for the design." Another interesting element in the design process is the request of the client that the building last between 50 and 100 years. Set up on V-shaped stilts, the structure looks as though it might just move on before that.

Die ING-Zentrale wurde auf einem lang gestreckten, schmalen Grundstück errichtet, das nahe der Amsterdamer Ringautobahn zwischen der Hochhausgegend Zuidas und dem Naherholungsgebiet De Nieuwe Meer liegt. Bewusst hielten die Architekten das Gebäude zur „grünen Seite" hin niedrig und ließen es zur Stadtseite hin ansteigen. Um den Autofahrern nicht den Blick ins Grüne zu verstellen und den Büros gleichzeitig einen Ausblick über die Schnellstraße hinweg zu gewähren, wurde das Gebäude auf 9 bis 12,5 m hohe Stützpfeiler gesetzt. Große Sorgfalt wurde auch auf ein effizientes Energiesystem verwendet, beispielsweise mit einer doppelwandigen Fassade, die für natürliche Belüftung sorgt und einen Schutz gegen den Verkehrslärm bietet. Außerdem wird durch eine Pumpanlage eine 120 m unterhalb des Gebäudes liegende, wasserführende Schicht als Thermospeicher genutzt. Im Inneren sind die Stockwerke nicht klar abgegrenzt, sondern gehen ineinander über, so dass sich immer wieder Durchblicke von einem Geschoss zum anderen öffnen. Auch Atrien, Loggien und Wintergärten bringen Abwechslung in den Innenraum. Die Architekten über ihr Projekt: „Mit der neuen Zentrale stellt sich der Bank- und Versicherungskonzern als ein dynamisches, internationales Netzwerk dar. Dabei waren die Aspekte Transparenz, Innovation, Umweltfreundlichkeit und Offenheit für uns entwurfsbestimmend." Wichtig war zudem die Anforderung des Auftraggebers, das Gebäude solle eine Lebensdauer von 50 bis 100 Jahren haben. Mit seinen V-förmigen Stelzen sieht es jedoch aus, als könnte es schon vor dieser Zeit einfach weiterziehen.

Édifié sur un long terrain étroit en bordure de l'autoroute périphérique d'Amsterdam, le siège d'ING est situé entre le quartier de tours de Zuidas et une zone verte, De Nieuwe Meer. Sur le côté « vert », les architectes ont volontairement maintenu une faible hauteur qui s'accroît rapidement vers le côté ville. Pour permettre aux automobilistes de conserver une vision de la zone verte et offrir aux bureaux une vue qui passe par-dessus l'autoroute, l'immeuble est posé sur des pilotis dont la hauteur varie de 9 à 12,5 m. Une grande attention a été portée à l'autonomie énergétique du bâtiment, par exemple grâce à une façade à double-peau qui permet une ventilation naturelle et protège du bruit de la circulation. Un système de pompage utilise la nappe phréatique à 120 m de profondeur pour le stockage thermique. Les différents étages « s'imbriquent et offrent des vues l'un sur l'autre ». Atriums, loggia et jardins diversifient l'intérieur de l'espace. Comme le précisent les architectes : « La nouvelle approche internationale, de transparence, d'innovation, de sensibilité écologique et d'ouverture a constitué le principal point de départ du projet. » Un autre élément intéressant, à la demande du client, est que l'immeuble dure de 50 à 100 ans. Posé sur ses pilotis en V, on a l'impression qu'il pourrait bien avoir envie de se transporter ailleurs avant cette date.

Like an apparition out of a "Star Wars" movie, the ING Headquarters building looks almost as though it is ready to move forward on its legs.

Die an ein Wesen aus „Star Wars" erinnernde ING-Zentrale sieht fast so aus, als könne sie sich auf ihren Stelzenbeinen vorwärtsbewegen.

Comme sorti d'un film de la série Star Wars, le siège d'ING donne l'impression d'être prêt à déambuler sur ses grandes jambes inclinées.

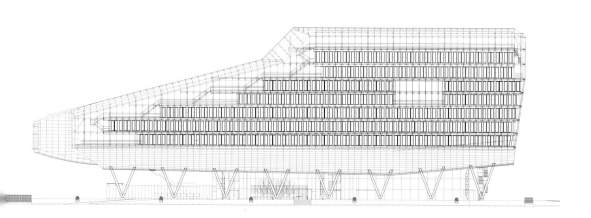

Massive as seen from almost any angle, the weight of the structure seems all the more imposing since it is lifted off the ground.

Das Gewicht des von fast jedem Blickwinkel massiv aussehenden Gebäudes wirkt umso eindrucksvoller, wenn man bedenkt, dass es auf Stützpfeilern ruht.

Massif sous presque tous ses angles, l'immeuble semble d'un poids d'autant plus imposant qu'il est surélevé par rapport au sol.

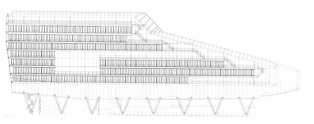

Though the image above gives the impression that the structure spreads wider as it rises, sections show that this is not the case.

Obwohl das Bild oben den Eindruck erweckt, dass das Gebäude nach oben breiter wird, beweist der Querschnitt das Gegenteil.

Contrairement à l'impression donnée par l'image ci-dessus, la structure n'est pas évasée vers le haut comme le montrent les coupes ci-dessous.

Ground level images give an impression of lightness since the weight of the structure is carried on the external tilted "legs."

Die Bilder vom Innenraum im Erdgeschoss vermitteln einen Eindruck von Leichtigkeit, während das Gewicht des Gebäudes von den schräggestellten „Beinen" getragen wird.

Les photos prises au niveau du sol donnent une impression de légèreté du fait de la surélévation sur pilotis.

The glazed airiness of the ground floor is repeated in this space, where a zig-zagging stairway goes up the glass façade.

Die luftige Atmosphäre im Erdgeschoss wiederholt sich in diesem Raum, wo eine Treppe im Zickzack die Glasfassade entlang nach oben führt.

La transparence aérienne du rez-de-chaussée se retrouve à l'intérieur du volume, marqué par un escalier en zigzag qui semble escalader la façade de verre.

*Though the density of the metallic structure gives a technical or mechanical appearance to the whole, the space is filled with light.*

*Obwohl die dichte Metallkonstruktion dem Ganzen eine technische Note verleiht, ist der Innenraum von Licht erfüllt.*

*Si la densité de la présence du métal donne un aspect technique ou mécanique, les volumes sont très lumineux.*

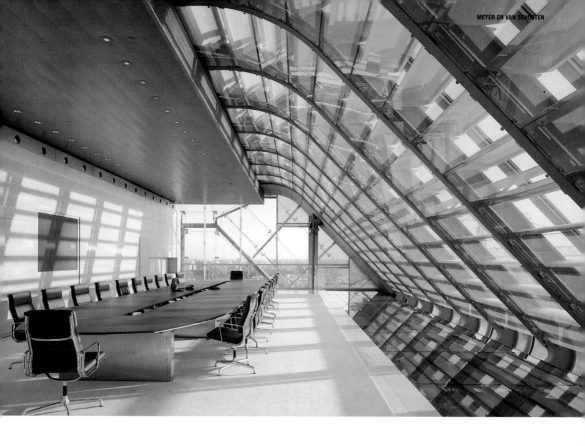

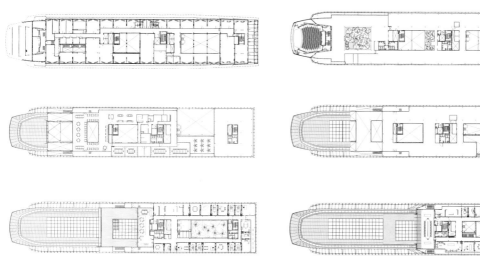

Floor plans show the fundamental regularity of the design and the effect of the progressively increasing area of the glazed roof. Above, a board room in the upper level.

Die Grundrisse zeigen die Regelmäßigkeit der Gestaltung und die mit jedem Stockwerk größer werdende Fläche der Dachverglasung. Oben: ein Sitzungsraum im Obergeschoss.

Les plans des niveaux montrent le parti pris de régularité de la conception et l'effet du toit de verre dont la taille croît peu à peu. Ci-dessus, une salle du conseil au niveau supérieur.

# OSCAR NIEMEYER

*Oscar Niemeyer*
*Avenida Atlantica 3940*
*Rio de Janeiro*
*Brazil*

*Tel: +55 21 5234 890*
*Fax: +55 21 2676 388*
*Web: www.niemeyer.org.br*

*Serpentine Gallery Pavilion 200*

Born in Rio de Janeiro in 1907, Oscar Niemeyer studied at the Escola Nacional de Belas Artes. He graduated in 1934 and joined a team of Brazilian architects collaborating with Le Corbusier on a new Ministry of Education and Health in Rio de Janeiro. It was Lucio Costa, for whom he worked as an assistant, who introduced Niemeyer to Le Corbusier. Between 1940 and 1954, his work was based in three cities: Rio de Janeiro, Sao Paulo and Belo Horizonte. In 1956 Niemeyer was appointed architectural adviser to Nova Cap – an organization responsible for implementing Lucio Costa's plans for Brazil's new capital. The following year, he became its chief architect, designing most of the city's important buildings. In 1964 he sought exile in France for political reasons. There, amongst other structures, he designed the building for the French Communist Party in Paris. With the end of the dictatorship he returned to Brazil, immediately resuming his professional activities. He was awarded the Gold Medal of the American Institute of Architecture in 1970 and the 1988 Pritzker Prize.

Oscar Niemeyer, geboren 1907 in Rio de Janeiro, schloss sich unmittelbar nach seinem Studienabschluss 1934 an der Escola Nacional de Belas Artes einer Gruppe brasilianischer Architekten an, die zusammen mit Le Corbusier das neue Ministerium für Bildung und Gesundheit in Rio de Janeiro planten. Lucio Costa, für den Niemeyer als Assistent arbeitete, stellte ihn Le Corbusier vor. Zwischen 1940 und 1954 war Niemeyer an drei Orten tätig: Rio de Janeiro, Sao Paulo und Belo Horizonte. 1956 wurde er zum architektonischen Berater von Nova Cap ernannt – einer Organisation, die gegründet worden war, um Lucio Costas Pläne für Brasiliens neue Hauptstadt zu realisieren. Im folgenden Jahr wurde er zum leitenden Architekten berufen, der die meisten wichtigen Gebäude der Stadt entwarf. 1964 ging er aus politischen Gründen nach Frankreich ins Exil und plante dort unter anderem das Gebäude der Kommunistischen Partei Frankreichs in Paris. Mit dem Ende der Diktatur kehrte er nach Brasilien zurück und nahm sofort seine Aktivitäten als Architekturprofessor wieder auf. 1970 erhielt er die Gold Medal des American Institute of Architects und 1988 den Pritzker Prize.

Né à Rio de Janeiro en 1907, Oscar Niemeyer étudie à la Escola Nacional de Belas Artes. Diplômé en 1934, il fait partie de l'équipe d'architectes brésiliens qui collabore avec Le Corbusier pour le nouveau ministère de l'éducation et de la santé à Rio. C'est Lucio Costa, dont il est assistant, qui l'introduit auprès de Le Corbusier. De 1940 à 1954, il intervient essentiellement dans trois villes : Rio de Janeiro, Sao Paulo et Belo Horizonte. En 1956, il est nommé conseiller pour l'architecure de Nova Cap, organisme chargé du développement des plans de Costa pour la nouvelle capitale. L'année suivante, il devient son architecte en chef, dessinant la plupart des bâtiments importants de Brasilia. En 1964, il s'exile en France pour des raisons politiques. Là, entre autres, il construit le siège du parti communiste à Paris. À la fin de la dictature, il retourne au Brésil, reprenant immédiatement ses responsabilités professionnelles. Il reçoit la médaille d'or de l'American Institute of Architecture en 1970 et le Pritzker Prize en 1988.

# SERPENTINE GALLERY PAVILION 2003

*Kensington Gardens, London, UK, 2003*

*Client: Serpentine Gallery, Kensington Gardens. Floor area: 250 m². Costs: not specified.*

"I am delighted to be designing the Serpentine Gallery Pavilion, my first structure in the United Kingdom," wrote Oscar Niemeyer. "My idea was to keep this project different, free and audacious. That is what I prefer. I like to draw, I like to see from the blank sheet of paper a palace, a cathedral, the figure of a woman appearing. But life for me is much more important than architecture." In these times of computer-generated architecture, it is a rare privilege to see the recent work of an architect who worked with Le Corbusier in the mid-1930s. The Pavilion he created for the Serpentine Gallery does have very much the spirit of one of his own sketches brought to life. After first refusing to design this small structure, Niemeyer accepted when the director of the Serpentine, Julia Peyton-Jones, went to Rio to meet him. One of his long-time collaborators, the engineer Jose Carlos Sussekind, and Arups in London actually made certain that the Pavilion was built. Made of concrete and steel, the structure looks more like a permanent addition to the Kensington Gardens than it is. "My architecture followed the old examples," said Niemeyer when he received the 1988 Pritzker Prize. "The beauty prevailing over the limitations of the constructive logic. My work proceeded, indifferent to the unavoidable criticism set forth by those who take the trouble to examine the minimum details, so very true of what mediocrity is capable of." It appears that in these circumstances, Niemeyer wanted to create nothing else than a resumé of his own work. "I wanted to give a flavor of everything that characterizes my work," he said to *The Financial Times*. The first thing was to create something floating above the ground. In a small building occupying a small space, using concrete, and few supports and girders, we can give an idea of what my architecture is all about."

„Ich bin hocherfreut, den Serpentine Gallery Pavilion zu entwerfen, mein erstes Bauwerk in Großbritannien", schrieb Oscar Niemeyer. „Meine Idee war, dieses Projekt anders wirken zu lassen – frei und verwegen. Das ist es, was ich bevorzuge. Ich zeichne gern und ich mag es, auf einem weißen Blatt Papier einen Palast, eine Kathedrale, die Gestalt einer näher kommenden Frau entstehen zu sehen. Aber das Leben ist für mich viel wichtiger als die Architektur." In diesen Zeiten computererzeugten Gestaltens ist es ein seltenes Privileg, die neueste Arbeit eines Architekten zu sehen, der schon Mitte der 1930er Jahre mit Le Corbusier zusammengearbeitet hat. Der von Niemeyer entworfene Pavillon hat in der Tat eine spirituelle Energie – er wirkt, als sei seine Zeichnung zum Leben erwacht. Die aus Beton und Stahl bestehende Konstruktion sieht allerdings dauerhafter aus, als sie wirklich ist. Der Architekt sagte 1988 in seiner Dankesrede zur Verleihung des Pritzker Prize: „Meine Architektur folgte den alten Vorbildern. Das heißt, die Ästhetik hat immer die Begrenzungen der konstruktiven Logik überwogen. Meine Arbeit entwickelte sich unabhängig von der unvermeidlichen Kritik derer, die sich die Mühe machen, jedes kleinste Detail zu untersuchen – was so treffend charakterisiert, wozu Mittelmäßigkeit fähig ist." Es scheint, als habe Niemeyer mit dem Serpentine Gallery Pavilion ein Resümee seiner architektonischen Arbeit präsentieren wollen. In einem Interview mit der *Financial Times* fasste er zusammen: „Ich wollte einen Eindruck von all dem vermitteln, was für mein Werk charakteristisch ist. Dabei ging es mir vornehmlich darum, etwas zu gestalten, das über den Erdboden schwebt. Indem wir in einem kleinen Gebäude, das wenig Raum einnimmt, Beton, ein paar Stützen und Träger verwenden, können wir eine Vorstellung davon vermitteln, worum es in meiner Architektur geht."

« Je suis ravi de concevoir le pavillon de la Serpentine Gallery, ma première réalisation au Royaume-Uni », a écrit Oscar Niemeyer. « Mon idée a été de trouver une approche différente, libre et audacieuse. C'est ce que je préfère. J'aime dessiner, j'aime voir apparaître sur la feuille blanche un palais, une cathédrale, la figure d'une femme. Mais pour moi la vie est beaucoup plus importante que l'architecture. » En ces temps d'architecture générée par ordinateur, c'est un privilège rare de voir naître une œuvre récente d'un architecte qui a travaillé avec Le Corbusier au milieu des années 1930. Son pavillon pour la Serpentine Gallery fait penser à l'animation de l'un de ses croquis. En béton et en acier, la structure pourrait être une addition permanente aux Kensington Gardens, ce qu'elle n'est pas. « Mon architecture a suivi des exemples anciens », a déclaré Niemeyer en recevant le Pritzker Prize 1988. « La beauté prend le pas sur les limites de la logique de construction. Mon œuvre a progressé, indifférente aux critiques inévitables avancées par ceux qui perdent leur temps à examiner des détails sans importance, bon exemple de ce dont la médiocrité est capable. » Niemeyer souhaitait créer un résumé de son œuvre. « Je voulais donner le goût de tout ce qui caractérise mon œuvre », a-t-il déclaré au *Financial Times*. « La première étape a été de créer quelque chose qui flotte au-dessus du sol. À travers une petite construction qui occupe une petite parcelle, à partir du béton, de quelques poutres et supports, on peut donner une idée de ce qu'est l'architecture. »

Succeeding Toyo Ito in Kensington Gardens as the architect of the Serpentine's temporary summer pavilion Oscar Niemeyer calls on a typically daring use of wide expanses of white concrete.

Der auf Toyo Ito als Architekt des Sommerpavillons der Serpentine Gallery in Kensington Gardens folgende Oscar Niemeyer präsentiert einen typisch wagemutigen Einsatz großer, weißer Betonflächen.

Succédant à Toyo Ito pour construire le pavillon d'été temporaire de la Serpentine dans les Kensington Gardens, Oscar Niemeyer utilise les grands plans de béton blanc qui lui sont familiers.

Using as few supports and girders as possible, the structure offers light, open spaces that appear more tent-like than solid.

Unter Verwendung so weniger Stützen und Träger wie möglich bietet der Bau helle, offene Räume, die ihn mehr wie ein Zelt als ein massives Gebäude wirken lassen.

À partir d'un nombre aussi réduit que possible de poutres et de poteaux, la structure offre des espaces ouverts et lumineux qui font davantage penser à une tente qu'à une construction lourde.

Oscar Niemeyer clearly still masters the dramatic design that made him famous in Brasilia and elsewhere.

Oscar Niemeyer ist nach wie vor ein Meister der dramatischen Formgebung, die ihn in Brasilia und anderswo berühmt gemacht hat.

Oscar Niemeyer maîtrise toujours le style spectaculaire qui l'a rendu célèbre à Brasilia et dans le monde.

# JEAN NOUVEL

Architectures Jean Nouvel
10, Cité d'Angoulême
75011 Paris
France

Tel: +33 1 49 23 83 83
Fax: +33 1 43 14 81 10

*Monolith, Expo.*

Born in 1945 in Sarlat, France, Jean Nouvel was admitted to the École des Beaux-Arts in Bordeaux in 1964. In 1970, he created his first office with François Seigneur. His first widely noticed project was the Institut du Monde Arabe in Paris (1981–1987, with Architecture Studio). Other works include his Nemausus housing (Nîmes, 1985–1987); offices for the CLM/BBDO advertising firm (Issy-les-Moulineaux, 1988–1992); Lyon Opera House (Lyon, 1986–1993); Vinci Conference Center (Tours, 1989–1993); Euralille Shopping Center (Lille, 1991–1994); Fondation Cartier (Paris, 1991–1995); Galeries Lafayette (Berlin, 1992–1996); and his unbuilt projects for the 400-meter-tall "Tour sans fin," La Défense (Paris, 1989); Grand Stade for the 1998 World Cup (Paris, 1994); and Tenaga Nasional Tower (Kuala Lumpur, 1995). His largest recently completed project is the Music and Conference Center in Lucerne, Switzerland (1998–2000). He won both the competition for the Museum of Arts and Civilizations, Paris, and the competition for the refurbishment of the Reina Sofia Center, Madrid in 1999. Recent work includes the Dentsu advertising agency tower in Tokyo and plans for the Standard Hotel in Soho (New York). In 2003, Jean Nouvel won a competition sponsored by the Aga Khan Trust for Culture for the design of the waterfront Corniche in Doha, Qatar, and was called on to design the new Guggenheim Museum in Rio de Janeiro.

Jean Nouvel, geboren 1945 im französischen Sarlat, studierte ab 1964 an der École des Beaux-Arts in Bordeaux. 1970 gründete er zusammen mit François Seigneur sein erstes Architekturbüro. Weithin bekannt wurde Nouvel mit seinem Institut du Monde Arabe in Paris (1981–1987), bei dem er mit Architecture Studio zusammenarbeitete. Zu seinen weiteren Arbeiten zählen: die Wohnanlage Nemausus in Nîmes (1985–1987), das Opernhaus in Lyon (1986–1993), die Büros der Werbeagentur CLM/BBDO in Issy-les-Moulineaux (1988–1992), das Kongresszentrum Vinci in Tours (1989–1993), das Einkaufszentrum Euralille in Lille (1991–1994), die Fondation Cartier in Paris (1991–1995) und die Galeries Lafayette in Berlin (1992–1996). Außerdem plante Jean Nouvel den 400 m hohen Turm „Tour sans fin" in La Défense, Paris (1989), das Grand Stade für die Fußball-Weltmeisterschaft von 1998 in Paris (1994) und den Tenaga Nasional Tower in Kuala Lumpur (1995), die aber alle nicht realisiert wurden. Sein umfangreichstes, in neuerer Zeit fertig gestelltes Projekt ist das Musik- und Kongresszentrum in Luzern (1998–2000). Im Jahr 1999 gewann er sowohl den Wettbewerb für das Musée des Arts et Civilisations in Paris sowie für die Modernisierung des Reina Sofia Zentrums in Madrid (1999). Zu seinen jüngsten Arbeiten zählen der Turm für die Werbeagentur Dentsu in Tokio und Entwürfe für das Standard Hotel in Soho, New York. 2003 gewann Jean Nouvel den vom Aga Khan Trust for Culture gesponserten Wettbewerb für die Gestaltung der Uferpromenade in Doha auf der arabischen Halbinsel Qatar und wurde mit der Planung des neuen Guggenheim Museums in Rio de Janeiro beauftragt.

Né en 1945 à Sarlat, Jean Nouvel est admis à l'École des Beaux-Arts de Bordeaux en 1964. En 1970, il crée une première agence avec François Seigneur. Son premier projet vraiment remarqué est l'Institut du Monde Arabe, à Paris, (1981–1987, avec Architecture Studio). Parmi ses autres réalisations : les immeubles d'appartements Nemausus, à Nîmes (1985–1987), les bureaux de l'agence de publicité CLM/BBDO (Issy-les-Moulineaux, 1988–1992), l'Opéra de Lyon (1986–1993), le palais des congrès Vinci (Tours, 1989–1993), le centre commercial Euralille (Lille, 1991–1994), la Fondation Cartier (Paris, 1991–1995), les galeries Lafayette (Berlin, 1992–1996). Parmi ses projets non réalisés : une tour de 400 m « La tour sans fin » (La Défense, Paris, 1989), le Grand Stade de la Coupe du monde de football 1998 (Paris, 1994), la Tour nationale Tenaga (Kuala Lumpur, Malaisie, 1995). En 1999, il a remporté les concours du Musée des Arts et Civilisations (Paris) et de la restructuration-extension du Centro Reina Sofia (Madrid). Parmi ses réalisations récentes : la tour du goupe publicitaire Dentsu à Tokyo et le Standard Hotel à Soho (New York). En 2003, il a remporté un concours organisé par l'Aga Khan Trust for Culture pour la nouvelle corniche de Doha au Qatar, et a été choisi pour le nouveau Guggenheim Museum de Rio de Janeiro.

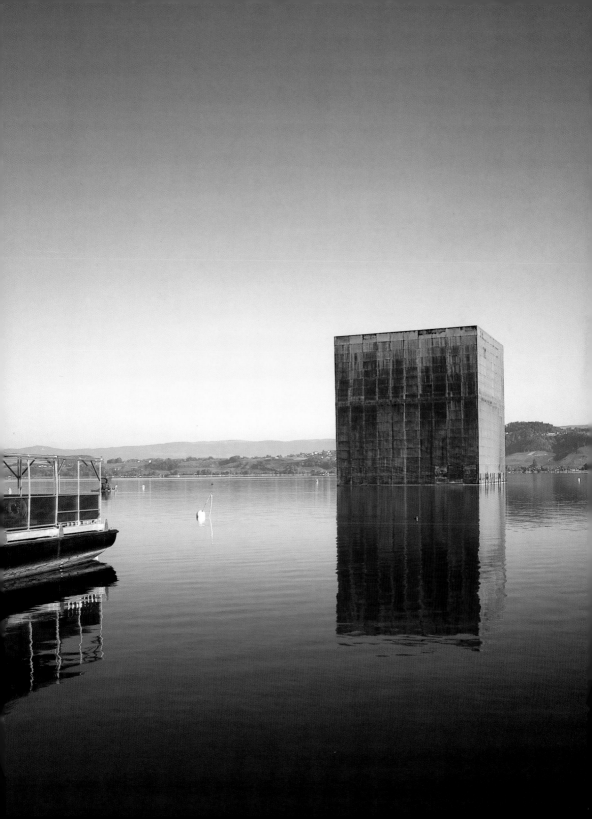

# MONOLITH, EXPO.02

*Morat, Switzerland, 2000–01*

Client: Swiss Expo.02. Dimensions: 34 x 34 x 34 m. Costs: € 36 000 000 (all interventions).

For the Swiss National Exhibition, in principle organized every 25 years, it was decided in 2002 to situate the pavilions in four different cities near Neuchatel. In each case, the buildings had to be temporary and situated whenever possible on the lakes of Neuchatel and Morat. Jean Nouvel was chosen as the main architect involved in the attractive historic city of Morat. He conceived a series of interventions, the most visible of which was a monolithic block of rusting steel sitting off the shore in the lake. Another unexpected structure was an exhibition area occupied by the Fondation Cartier and made of stacks of logs. Actually, with its reference to logging, this structure may have had more to do with Switzerland than some of the other elements of the exhibitions. Using tents, containers and military camouflage, Nouvel occupied Morat with his temporary designs in a manner and style that in some cases approached installation art more than architecture. Unlike the other cities involved in Expo.02, Morat, at Nouvel's instigation, did not create a closed-off area for the pavilions – rather the different elements were dispersed in proximity to the lake, with a simple ticketing system allowing entry to each area in whatever order the visitor preferred. This spreading of the Expo throughout the city was in part due to the relatively dense town configuration but it also permitted a real discovery of the city. For those interested in Nouvel, seeking out and recognizing his interventions became a part of the adventure of visiting the Expo. Nouvel's Expo.02 became part of Morat rather than being an incoherent addition. Although Expo.02 in Morat has not been as widely published as many other recent works by Jean Nouvel, it is amongst his most inventive and surprising efforts. He showed in particular that he was sensitive to changing circumstances, where astonishing new buildings may not be as much in the spirit of the times as an ability to use simple materials and designs to redefine space and serve a specific purpose.

Die Organisatoren der Schweizer Landesausstellung, die in der Regel alle 25 Jahre stattfindet, beschlossen für das Jahr 2002, die Ausstellungspavillons auf vier verschiedene Standorte nahe der Kantonshauptstadt Neuchâtel zu verteilen. Die Bauten sollten temporär sein und, wenn möglich, direkt auf dem Neuenburger oder Murtensee liegen. Jean Nouvel, der als leitender Architekt für die historische Gemeinde Murten ausgewählt worden war, entwarf eine Reihe von Arbeiten, deren hervorstechendste ein monolithischer Block aus rostigem Stahl war, der in einiger Entfernung vom Ufer aus dem Wasser ragte. Ebenfalls sehr ungewöhnlich war eine andere Arbeit, eine Ausstellungsfläche für die Fondation Cartier, die aus übereinander gestapelten Holzstämmen bestand. Mit ihrem Bezug auf die Holzindustrie hatte diese Konstruktion mehr mit der Schweiz zu tun als viele andere Beiträge. Einige von Nouvels Konstruktionen waren mit Bestandteilen wie Zelten, Containern und Tarnnetzen der Installationskunst näher als der Architektur. Im Gegensatz zu anderen Standorten der Expo.02 verzichtete Murten – auf Nouvels Betreiben – auf einen abgegrenzten Bereich für die Pavillons. Stattdessen wurden die einzelnen Objekte in Seenähe verteilt. Ein unkompliziertes Kartensystem erlaubte den Besuchern, alle Ausstellungsbereiche in beliebiger Reihenfolge zu besichtigen. Dass sich die Expo so über die ganze Stadt ausbreiten konnte, ergab sich aus Murtens relativ dichtem Stadtgefüge, das den Ausstellungsbesuchern die Gelegenheit bot, die Stadt wirklich zu entdecken. Für die Fans von Nouvel trug das Aufspüren und Identifizieren seiner Arbeiten zum besonderen Qualität dieser Expo bei. Nouvel ließ seine Expo-Beiträge mehr zu einem Teil der Stadt werden als sie nur zusammenhanglos hinzu zu fügen. Obwohl die Ausstellung nicht so große Beachtung in den Medien fand wie andere seiner Projekte, gehört sie zu seinen einfallsreichsten und überraschendsten Arbeiten. Er bewies hier eine besondere Sensibilität gegenüber sich verändernden Verhältnissen, in denen spektakuläre neue Gebäude möglicherweise weniger zeitgemäß sind als die Fähigkeit, mit einfachen Materialien und Gestaltungsformen einen Raum zu definieren und einem bestimmten Zweck zu dienen.

L'Exposition nationale suisse, qui se tient en principe tous les 25 ans, avait décidé de s'implanter dans la région de Neuchâtel. Les bâtiments devaient être temporaires et situés dans une large mesure sur les lacs de Neuchâtel et de Morat. Jean Nouvel a été choisi pour le projet de la charmante petite cité historique de Morat. Il a conçu une série d'interventions dont la plus visible était un bloc monolithique en acier rouillé posé à quelques encablures de la rive. Une autre création étonnante était l'espace d'exposition occupé par la Fondation Cartier, construite à partir d'empilements de grumes. Par sa référence aux rondins, elle était sans doute plus en rapport avec la Suisse que certains autres éléments des expositions. À l'aide de tentes, de conteneurs et de camouflage militaire, les projets temporaires de Nouvel ont occupé Morat d'une façon et dans un style plus proches de l'installation que de l'architecture. À la différence d'autres villes participant à Expo.02, Morat, à l'instigation de l'architecte, n'avait pas créé de zone fermée mais préféré disperser les divers lieux à proximité du lac, un système de billetterie permettant à chacun de visiter ce qu'il voulait dans l'ordre de ses préférences. Cette dilution de l'Expo, due en partie à la configuration relativement dense de la ville, en permettait cependant une authentique découverte. Pour ceux qui s'intéressent au travail de Nouvel, la recherche et la reconnaissance de ses interventions participaient au plaisir de la visite. Son intervention faisait partie de la ville, plutôt que de se contenter de n'être qu'un simple ajout sans cohérence. Bien que ce travail n'ait pas reçu une couverture médiatique aussi abondante que celle d'autres réalisations récentes de l'architecte, elle fait partie de ses réalisations les plus inventives et les plus étonnantes. Il a montré en particulier qu'il était sensible à des circonstances particulières, que créer une construction qui surprenne était peut-être moins dans l'esprit du moment que la capacité de faire appel à des plans et des matériaux simples pour redéfinir l'espace et répondre à un objectif bien défini.

*Nouvel's contribution to Expo.02 in Morat was not limited to the rusting metal Monolith. He also conceived a number of the lakeside installations.*

*Nouvels Beitrag zur Expo.02 beschränkte sich nicht auf den Monolith aus rostigem Metall. Er entwarf auch etliche der um den Murtensee herum installierten Arbeiten.*

*La contribution de Nouvel à Expo.02 à Morat ne se limitait pas à ce monolithe d'aspect rouillé. Il y a également conçu un certain nombre d'autres installations en bordure du lac.*

# NOX

*NOX/Lars Spuybroek*
*Heer Bokelweg 163, 3032 AD Rotterdam, The Netherlands*
*Tel/Fax: +31 10 477 2853, e-mail: nox@luna.nl*

*Lars Spuybroek*
*Professor of Digital Design Techniques*
*University of Kassel, Germany*
*Tel.: +49 561 804 2352, e-mail: lars@architektur.uni-kassel.de*

Lars Spuybroek is the principal of NOX. Since the early 1990s he has been involved in research on the relationship between architecture and media, and often more specifically between architecture and computing. He was the editor-publisher of one of the first magazines on the subject (*NOX*, and later also *Forum*), and has made videos (Soft City) and interactive electronic artworks (Soft Site, edit Spline, deep Surface). More recently, he has focused more on architecture (HtwoOexpo, Blow Out, V2_lab, wetGRID, D-tower, Son-O-house, Maison Folie). His work has won several prizes and was represented at the Venice Biennale in 2000 and 2002. In 2003 NOX participated in the important international exhibitions "Zoomorphic" at the Victoria & Albert in London and "Non Standard Architectures" at the Centre Pompidou in Paris. NOX is currently finishing the interactive tower for the Dutch city of Doetinchem (D-Tower), "a house where sounds live" (Son-O-house), and a complex of cultural buildings in Lille, France (Maison Folies), as well as working on competitions for the European Central Bank in Frankfurt and the New Centre Pompidou in Metz, France (competition won by Shigeru Ban). Lars Spuybroek has lectured widely. He has taught at several universities in Holland and is a regular visiting professor at Columbia University in New York. Since 2002 he has held a tenured professorship at the University of Kassel in Germany, where he chairs the CAD/digital design techniques department. He is also working on a book, *Machining Architecture*, which is to be published by Thames & Hudson in 2004.

Lars Spuybroek, der Leiter von NOX, beschäftigt sich seit Anfang der 1990er Jahre mit dem Verhältnis zwischen Architektur und Medien, insbesondere zwischen Architektur und Computerwesen. Er war Herausgeber und Verleger einer der ersten Zeitschriften zu diesem Thema, *NOX* (später auch *Forum*), und hat Videos (Soft City) wie auch interaktive elektronische Kunstwerke (Soft Site, edit Spline, deep Surface) produziert. In jüngster Zeit hat er sich mehr auf die Architektur konzentriert, mit Projekten wie HtwoOexpo, Blow Out, V2_lab, wetGRID, D-tower, Son-O-house und Maison Folie. Er wurde mit mehreren Preisen ausgezeichnet und war in den Jahren 2000 und 2002 auf der Biennale in Venedig vertreten. 2003 nahm NOX an den bedeutenden internationalen Ausstellungen „Zoomorphic" am Victoria & Albert Museum in London und „Non Standard Architectures" am Pariser Centre Pompidou teil. Zu den aktuellen Projekten von NOX gehören der interaktive Turm D-Tower für die niederländische Stadt Doetinchem, das Son-O-house, „ein Haus, in dem Geräusche leben", das Kulturzentrum Maison Folies im französischen Lille sowie die Wettbewerbsbeiträge für die Europäische Zentralbank in Frankfurt und das neue Centre Pompidou in Metz (Wettbewerbssieger: Shigeru Ban). Lars Spuybroek hat an mehreren niederländischen Universitäten gelehrt und ist regelmäßig als Gastprofessor an der Columbia University in New York. Seit 2002 hat er eine Professur an der Abteilung CAD/digitale Designtechniken der Universität Kassel inne. Außerdem arbeitet er an einem Buch mit dem Titel *Machining Architecture*, das 2004 bei Thames & Hudson erscheinen soll.

Lars Spuybroek, qui dirige NOX, s'intéresse depuis le début des années 1990 aux relations entre l'architecture et les médias, et plus spécifiquement l'architecture et l'informatique. Il a été rédacteur-en-chef de l'un des premiers magazines consacrés à ce sujet (*NOX*, puis plus tard *FORUM*) et a réalisé des vidéos (Soft City) et des œuvres artistiques interactives (SoftSite, edit Spline, deep Surface). Plus récemment, il s'est davantage impliqué dans l'architecture (HtwoOexpo, BlowOut, V2_lab, wetGRID, D-tower, Son-O-House, Maison Folie). Son travail a remporté plusieurs distinctions et a été présenté aux Biennales de Venise de 2000 et 2002. En 2003, NOX a participé à l'importante exposition « Zoomorphic » au Victoria & Albert Museum à Londres, et à « Architectures non standard » au Centre Pompidou à Paris. NOX termine actuellement une tour interactive pour la ville néerlandaise de Doetinchem (D-Tower), « une maison du son » (Son-O-house) et un complexe d'installations culturelles à Lille, en France (Maison Folie). L'agence a participé à des concours pour la Banque centrale européenne et le nouveau Centre Pompidou à Metz, en France (remporté par Shigeru Ban). Lars Spuybroek donne de nombreuses conférences, a enseigné dans plusieurs universités aux Pays-Bas et est régulièrement professeur invité à la Columbia University à New York. Depuis 2002, il est professeur titulaire à l'Université de Kassel (Allemagne), où il dirige le département des techniques de CAO. Il a rédigé un livre *Machining Architecture*, publié par Thames & Hudson en 2004.

# SON-O-HOUSE

*Son en Breugel, The Netherlands, 2000–2003*

*Client: Enterprise Group. Floor area: 300 m². Costs: € 410 000.*

*These images demonstrate that the apparently complex design of the Son-O-House evolves from the idea of the assembly of simple strips of paper.*

*Diese Bilder demonstrieren, dass sich die komplexe Gestaltung des Son-O-House aus der Idee einfacher, miteinander verflochtener Papierstreifen entwickelt hat.*

*Ces images montrent la conception apparemment complexe de la Son-O-House qui évolue à partir de l'idée d'un assemblage de simples bandes de papier.*

As NOX prinicipal Lars Spuybroek explains, "the Son-O-House is one of our typical 'art' projects which allows us to proceed more carefully and slowly (over a period of three to four years) while generating a lot of knowledge that we apply to larger and speedier projects. Son-O-House is what we call 'a house where sounds live,' not being a 'real' house, but a structure that refers to living and the bodily movements that accompany habit and habitation. In the Son-O-House a sound work is continuously generating new sound patterns activated by sensors picking up actual movements of visitors." More specifically, the structure is derived from a set of movements of bodies, limbs and hands (on three scales) that are inscribed on paper bands as cuts. These paper bands are then stapled together, creating an arabesque of complex intertwining lines that is then made into a three-dimensional "porous structure." An analog computing model is then "digitized and remodeled on the basis of combing and curling rules which results in the very complex model of interlacing vaults which sometimes lean on each other or sometimes cut into each other." Spuybroek goes on to explain that "in this house-that-is-not-a-house we position eight sensors at strategic spots to indirectly influence the music. This system of sounds, composed and programmed by sound artist Edwin van der Heide, is based on moiré effects of interference of closely related frequencies. As a visitor one does not influence the sound directly, which is so often the case with interactive art. One influences the landscape itself that generates the sounds. The score is an evolutionary memoryscape that develops with the traced behavior of the actual bodies in the space."

Lars Spuybroek erklärt: „Das Son-O-House ist eins von unseren typischen ‚Kunst'-Projekten … Es ist kein ‚reales' Haus, sondern eine Konstruktion, die sich an den Lebensäußerungen und Bewegungen der Menschen orientiert, die sich darin bewegen oder wohnen. Im Son-O-House erzeugt eine Soundanlage ständig neue Geräuschmuster, die von den durch Sensoren übertragenen Bewegungen der Bewohner ausgelöst werden." Anders gesagt: Die Form entstand aus einer Serie von Bewegungen von Körpern, Gliedmaßen und Händen, die als Schnitte auf Papierstreifen fixiert wurden. Diese Papierstreifen wurden zusammengeheftet, woraus eine Arabeske aus komplexen, miteinander verflochtenen Linien entstand. Diese wurde dann zu einem dreidimensionalen „durchlässigen Gebilde" geformt. Anschließend wurde ein analoges Computermodell „nach demselben Prinzip wie Haare geflochten werden, digitalisiert und umgeformt, was zu unserem komplexen Modell verschlungener Gewölbe führt, die sich aneinander anlehnen oder überschneiden." Spuybroek abschließend: „In diesem Haus-das-kein-Haus-ist haben wir an strategischen Punkten acht Sensoren installiert, um die Musik indirekt zu beeinflussen. Dieses Soundsystem, das von Edwin van der Heide komponiert und programmiert wurde, basiert auf dem Moiré-Effekt, der durch die Überlagerung eng beieinander liegender Frequenzen entsteht. Anders als bei vielen anderen interaktiven Kunstprojekten kann man hier als Besucher die Musik nicht direkt beeinflussen. Man beeinflusst vielmehr die Umgebung selbst, die den Sound hervorbringt. Dabei stellt die Partitur eine evolutionäre Erinnerungslandschaft dar, die sich mit dem aufgezeichneten Verhalten realer Körper im Raum entfaltet."

Comme l'explique Lars Spuybroek : « La Son-O-House est l'un de ces projets ‹artistiques› typiques qui nous permettent d'avancer plus soigneusement et plus lentement (sur trois ou quatre ans) tout en générant une masse de connaissances dont bénéficieront des projets plus importants et plus pressés … Ce n'est pas une ‹vraie› maison, mais une structure qui se réfère à la vie et aux mouvements corporels qui accompagnent les habitudes et le fait d'habiter. Dans cette maison une centrale sonore génère en continu de nouveaux motifs sonores activés par des capteurs qui enregistrent les mouvements réels des visiteurs. » Plus précisément, cette structure est issue de l'ensemble des mouvements des corps, des membres et des mains (sur trois échelles) qui s'inscrivent sur des bandes de papiers. Celles-ci sont ensuite agrafées ensemble, pour créer une arabesque de lignes entrelacées complexes qui se transforme en « structure poreuse » en trois dimensions. Un modèle de calcul analogique est ensuite « numérisé et remodelé sur la base de lignes qui donnent un modèle très complexe de voûtes entrelacées qui tantôt s'inclinent l'une sur l'autre, tantôt s'entrecoupent ». Spuybroek explique également que « dans cette maison-qui-n'est-pas-une-maison, nous positionnons huit capteurs à des endroits stratégiques qui influencent indirectement la musique. Ce système de sons, composés et programmés par l'artiste sonore Edwin van der Heide, repose sur des effets de moirages d'interférences de fréquences proches. Le visiteur n'influence pas directement le son, ce qui est si souvent le cas dans l'art interactif, mais influence le paysage lui-même qui génère les sons. Le résultat est un paysage mémorisé évolutif qui se développe concurremment au traçage du comportement des corps dans l'espace. »

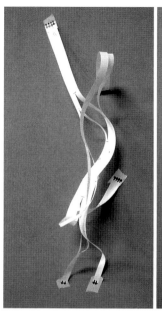

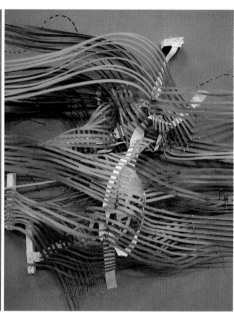

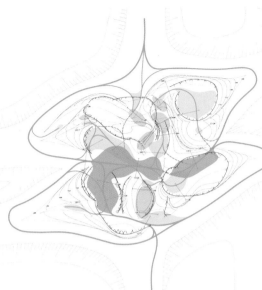

The more finished computer images of the house show its curious shapes that might approach biological forms.

Die Computerdarstellungen des Hauses zeigen die Nähe der merkwürdigen Formen zu Naturgebilden.

Une image de synthèse montre des formes curieuses qui ne sont pas très éloignées de formes biologiques.

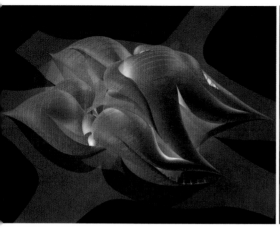

These night views of the Son-O-House give the impression of a living entity, glowing and possibly even moving as its sounds are influenced by visitors' movements.

*Die nächtlichen Ansichten des Hauses lassen an ein lebendiges, im Dunkeln leuchtendes Wesen denken, das sich im Rhythmus seiner Besucher bewegt.*

*Ces vues de nuit de la maison donnent l'impression d'un organisme vivant, irradiant et même mobile puisque les formes sont influencées par les mouvements des visiteurs.*

# PLEXUS R+D

*plexus r + d, Inc.*
*914 Howell Mill Road, Suite 100*
*Atlanta, GA 30318*
*USA*

*Tel: +1 404 815 6776*
*Fax: +1 404 815 9978*
*e-mail: office@plexus-architecture.com*
*Web: www.plexus-architecture.com*

*Park and Observation Tow*

Jordan Williams received his education at Princeton (1992) and the University of Florida (1988). Erik Lewitt attended Princeton (1992) and the University of Florida (1988) as well. The design staff of their firm includes seven persons. Their completed projects include: La Villa office building (with JSA, Jacksonville, FL, 2002); Southern Polytechnic State University Gateway (Marieta, GA, 2001); Husk Jennings Advertising (with JSA, Jacksonville, 2001); Barcelona Residence (Jacksonville, 2001); and Franklins Printing (with Farrington Design Group, Atlanta, 2000). Current work includes: Southern Polytechnic State University Gateway (Marieta, GA, 2004); Beijing Zhongguanchun Life Science Park (with JSA, Beijing, China, 2004); plexus on Ponce (Atlanta, 2004); Midtown West Master Plan (Atlanta, 2004); Atlanta Train Depot (Atlanta, 2004); Piedmont Center (Atlanta, 2004); and Moreland Live/Work (Atlanta, 2004).

Jordan Williams erwarb 1988 den Bachelor of Science an der University of Florida und 1992 den Master of Architecture in Princeton. Auch Erik Lewitt schloss 1988 sein Studium an der University of Florida mit dem Bachelor of Science und 1992 in Princeton mit dem Master of Arts ab. Das Planungsteam ihrer Firma besteht aus sieben Mitarbeitern. Zu ihren realisierten Projekten zählen: das Gebäude für Franklins Printing in Atlanta (2000) – in Zusammenarbeit mit Farrington Design Group –, die Bürogebäude Husk Jennings Advertising (2001) und La Villa (2002), beide in Zusammenarbeit mit JSA und beide in Jacksonville, Florida, sowie die Villa Barcelona in Jacksonville (2001). Zu ihren aktuellen Projekten gehören der Zugang zur Southern Polytechnic State University in Marieta, Georgia (2004), der Wissenschaftspark Beijing Zhongguanchun Life Science Park (mit JSA) in Peking (2004), der Plexus on Ponce (2004), der Masterplan für Midtown West, das Atlanta Train Depot sowie Moreland Live/Work, alle in Atlanta und alle für 2004 geplant.

Jordan Williams et Eric Lewitt ont tous deux étudié à Princeton (Master of Architecture 1992) et à l'Université de Floride (B. Sc. 1988). L'équipe de conception de leur agence compte sept collaborateurs. Ils ont réalisé à ce jour : l'immeuble de bureaux La Villa (avec JSA, Jacksonville, Floride, 2002) ; l'agence Husk Jennings Advertising (avec JSA, Jacksonville, Floride, 2001) ; Barcelona Residence (Jacksonville, 2001) ; l'imprimerie Franklins (avec Farrington Design Group, Atlanta, 2000). Parmi leurs chantiers actuels : le portail d'entrée de la Southern Polytechnic State University (Marieta, Géorgie, 2004) ; le parc des sciences Zhongguanchum (avec JSA, Pékin, Chine, 2004) ; plexus on Ponce (Atlanta, 2004) ; le plan directeur centre ouest (Atlanta, 2004) ; le dépôt ferroviaire d'Atlanta (Atlanta, 2004) ; Piedmont Center (Atlanta, 2004) et Moreland Live/Work (Atlanta, 2004).

# PARK AND OBSERVATION TOWER

*Busan, South Korea, 2003–*

*Client: Bexco. Total floor area: 6 850 m². Costs: not specified.*

This project includes a new park, a facility for the Busan International Film Festival (3 716-square-meter Film and Media Center), an observation tower (1 741 square meters) and a 1 393-square-meter Exhibition and Tourism Center. Busan is the second largest city in Korea and has an ambitious plan to develop itself into an international maritime metropolis. The competition brief for this project provides that the "Busan Tower Complex will be a landmark symbolizing the emerging status of this dynamic and growing port city." The Film and Media Center is carved into Yongdu Hill and is covered by the platform of the Observation Tower. In Korean, the word "yongdu" means the "head of the dragon" and the Yongdu Hill Park is one of the oldest of the city's green areas. The spaces carved out of Yongdu Hill for the Film and Media Center would be left natural "similar to the walls of a stone quarry," while the research, housing and theater facilities would be clad either in translucent curtain wall or metal panels and pre-cast concrete. The Tower would be a steel frame structure with a combination of metal panel and curtain wall cladding, offering both a symbol of the city and a vantage point for viewing day and night. The Exhibition and Tourism Center is to be located at the top of Yongdu Hill Park and connect the Park Level with the base of the Observation Tower. The design calls for an "open and flexible steel frame clad in translucent glass curtain wall."

Der Bauplan für das Projekt umfasst einen neu angelegten Park, ein 3 716 m² großes Film- und Medienzentrum, das gleichzeitig als Spielstätte für das Internationale Filmfestival von Busan dient, eine 1 741 m² große Beobachtungswarte sowie ein 1 393 m² großes Ausstellungs- und Tourismuszentrum. In der Projektbeschreibung für den Architekturwettbewerb hieß es: „Der Busan Tower Complex soll Wahrzeichen und Symbol für die wachsende Bedeutung dieser dynamischen Hafenstadt werden." Ein Teil des Komplexes, das Film- und Medienzentrum, wird in den Yongdu Berg eingebettet und von der Plattform der Beobachtungswarte überdeckt. Der Yongdu Hill Park ist eine der ältesten Grünanlagen der Stadt. Während die Stellen, die für das Film- und Medienzentrum aus dem Berg gebrochen wurden, in ihrem natürlichen Zustand belassen werden, so dass sie wie die Wände eines Steinbruchs aussehen, sollen die für Forschung, Wohnen und Theater vorgesehenen Bauteile entweder mit durchscheinenden Vorhangwänden oder Metalltafeln und großflächigen Betonfertigteilen ummantelt werden. Der Turm besteht aus einer Stahlrahmenkonstruktion mit einer Verkleidung aus Metallplatten und Vorhängwänden und wird somit sowohl zu einem markanten Wahrzeichen für die Stadt als auch zu einem Tag und Nacht sichtbaren Orientierungspunkt. Das Ausstellungs- und Tourismuszentrum befindet sich am oberen Ende des Parks und soll diesen mit dem Beobachtungsturm verbinden. Auch dieser Bauteil soll aus einem offenen und flexiblen Stahlrahmen bestehen und mit einer durchsichtigen Vorhangwand aus Glas umhüllt werden.

Busan, seconde ville de Corée du Sud, s'est dotée d'un ambitieux plan pour devenir une métropole maritime de niveau international. Ce projet comprend un parc, le siège du festival international de cinéma de Busan (Centre du cinéma et des médias de 3 716 m²), une tour d'observation (1 741 m²) et un centre d'expositions et de tourisme de 1 393 m². Le sujet du concours précise que « le complexe de la tour de Busan sera un monument symbolisant le statut émergeant de cette ville portuaire dynamique en plein développement. » Le Centre du cinéma et des médias est creusé dans la colline de Yongdu et recouvert par la plate-forme de la tour d'observation. En coréen, le mot Yongdu signifie « tête de dragon » et le parc de cette colline est l'un des plus anciens espaces verts de la ville. Les volumes creusés seront laissés à l'état naturel « comme les parois d'une carrière », tandis que les équipements de recherche, le théâtre et les logements seront habillés d'un mur-rideau translucide ou de panneaux métalliques et de béton préfabriqué. La tour devrait être une construction à ossature d'acier recouverte d'un habillage combinant mur-rideau et panneaux métalliques, et sera à la fois un symbole pour la ville et un point de vue accessible de jour et de nuit. Le Centre d'expositions et de tourisme sera implanté au sommet de la colline et connectée au niveau du parc à la base de la tour d'observation, « une ossature ouverte et souple en acier habillée d'un mur-rideau de verre translucide ».

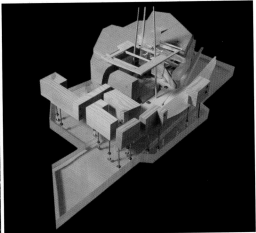

*Taking advantage of the Asian taste for daring new forms in architecture, plexus r+d imagines an astonishing tower and facilities to house a film festival.*

*Sich die asiatische Vorliebe für neue und gewagte Architekturformen zunutze machend, hat plexus r+d einen ungewöhnlichen Turm und Bauten für ein Filmfestival entworfen.*

*Profitant du goût asiatique pour les formes architecturales audacieuses, plexus r+d a imaginé une tour et des équipements étonnants pour abriter un festival du cinéma.*

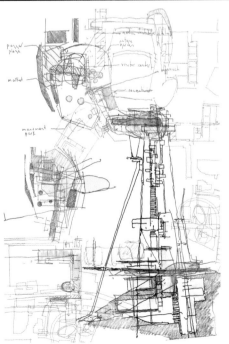

# DIRK JAN POSTEL

*Kraaijvanger.Urbis*
*Watertorenweg 336*
*Postbus 4003*
*3006 Rotterdam*
*The Netherlands*

*Tel: +31 10 498 9292*
*Fax: +31 10 498 9200*
*e-mail: mail@kraaijvanger.urbis.nl*
*Web: www.dirkjanpostel.nl*

Dirk Jan Postel, born in 1957, graduated in architecture from the Technical University of Delft (1986). He has been an associate of the Kraaijvanger.Urbis office for architecture and urban design since 1992. He is a visiting tutor at the Technical University of Delft, and at the Departments of Architecture and Civil Engineering at Queens College, Belfast; Bath School of Architecture; Birmingham School of Architecture; and the University of Central England. He is also the co-founder of GCI, a company for glass consulting and innovation. His work includes: Town Hall (Den Bosch, 1997–2004); Theater (Alphen aan den Rijn, 1999–2005); the Temple de l'Amour II (published here, Burgundy, 2000–01); The British School in The Netherlands (Voorschoten, 1999–2003); Traffic Control Center (Dutch Ministry of Transport, Utrecht, 1998–2000); Bonhoeffer College, Castricum High School (1998–2000); The British School in The Netherlands (The Hague, 1994–1997); 'De Barones' shopping arcade, department store and housing in the center of Breda (with CZWG architects, 1993–1997); The Glass House (Almelo, 1996–97); and the Glass Bridge (Rotterdam 1993–94).

Dirk Jan Postel, 1957 geboren, schloss 1986 sein Architekturstudium an der Technischen Universität von Delft ab. Seit 1992 ist er Teilhaber in dem Büro für Architektur und Stadtplanung Kraaijvanger.Urbis. Außerdem ist er als Gastdozent an der TU Delft und an den Fakultäten für Architektur und Bauwesen der Hochschulen Queens College Belfast, Bath School of Architecture, Birmingham School of Architecture und University of Central England tätig. Dirk Jan Postel gehört zu den Gründern von GCI, einer Beratungsfirma für den Bereich Glas. Zu seinen Bauten zählen: die Glasbrücke in Rotterdam (1993–1994) und – in Zusammenarbeit mit der Architektengruppe CZWG – das Einkaufszentrum mit Wohnungen De Barones in der Innenstadt von Breda (1993–1997), The British School in The Netherlands in Den Haag (1994–1997), ferner The Glass House in Almelo (1996–97), das Rathaus in Den Bosch (1997–2004), das Verkehrskontrollzentrum für das Niederländische Verkehrsministerium in Utrecht (1998–2000), das Bonhoeffer College der Castricum High School (1998–2000), The British School in The Netherlands in Voorschoten (1999–2003), das Theater in Alphen aan den Rijn (1999–2005) und der hier vorgestellte Temple de l'Amour II in Burgund (2000–01).

Dirk Jan Postel, né en 1957, est diplômé en architecture de l'Université technique de Delft en 1986. Depuis 1992, il est associé de l'agence d'architecture et d'urbanisme Kraaijvanger.Urbis. Il est tuteur invité à son université d'origine et aux départements d'architecture et d'ingénierie civile de Queens College à Belfats, à la Bath School of Architecture, à la Birmingham School of Architecture et à l'University of Central England. Il est également cofondateur de GCI, cabinet de consultant et d'innovation dans le domaine du verre. Parmi ses réalisations : un hôtel de ville (Den Bosch, 1997–2004) ; un théâtre (Alphen aan den Rijn, 1999–2005) ; le Temple de l'amour II, publié ici (Bourgogne, France, 2000–01) ; The British School (Voorschoten, 1999–2003) ; un centre de contrôle de la circulation (Ministère néerlandais des transports, Utrecht, 1998–2000) ; le Bohnoeffer College (Castricum High School, 1998–2000) ; The British School (La Haye, 1994–1997) ; le centre commercial, grand magasin et logements « De Barones » au centre de Breda, avec CZWG architectes (1993–1997) : la Maison de verre (Almelo, 1996–97) et le Pont de verre (Rotterdam, 1993–94).

# TEMPLE DE L'AMOUR II

*Talus du Temple, Bourgogne, France, 2000–01*

*Client: Mr. and Mrs. Erik Wolters, Amsterdam. Floor area: 44 m². Costs: € 49 000.*

In the mid-1990s, an 18th-century folly called "Le Temple de l'Amour" located near Avalon in the Burgundy area of France was turned into a small summer residence for a Dutch neurologist. Dirk Jan Postel designed a laminated glass skylight for the house. The opposite end of the site is bordered by the abutment of a demolished railway bridge, and Postel convinced the owner to turn a former gunpowder vault into a guest room. As the architect says, "This construction has a classical, almost Ledoux-like expression, with its large blocks of local limestone." Postel devised a cantilevered roof consisting of a timber stressed skin construction. Laminated glass panels on either side carry its 2 000-kg load. Lateral stability is provided by full height laminated, hardened glass panels. "The aim of the design," says the architect, "is to express the magic of the roof 'floating on nothing'. The detailing is coherent, non-conspicuous, minimal. As if the glass is cut through the ancient stone." This approach to "minimalist historic preservation" won the 2002 DuPont Benedictus Award given for the use of laminated glass in construction.

Mitte der 1990er Jahre wurde ein nahe Avalon im französischen Burgund gelegener Gartenpavillon für einen holländischen Neurologen zu einem kleinen Sommerhaus umgebaut. Für diesen „Temple de l'Amour" aus dem 18. Jahrhundert entwarf Dirk Jan Postel ein Oberlichtfenster aus Schichtglas. Später überzeugte er den Eigentümer, ein ehemaliges Munitionsdepot, das in einem der verbliebenen Gewölbepfeiler einer abgerissenen Eisenbahnbrücke untergebracht war, in einen Raum für Gäste umzuwandeln. Dazu der Architekt: „Diese Konstruktion hat ein klassisches, ein wenig an die Bauten von Ledoux erinnerndes Gepräge, mit ihren großen Blöcken aus hiesigem Kalkstein." Postel entwarf für diesen Bauteil ein auskragendes, in Schalenbauweise gefertigtes Holzdach. Dessen Gewicht von 2 000 kg ruht an den Längsseiten auf Schichtglasplatten, während die Querseitenstabilität durch zwei raumhohe Wände aus gehärtetem Schichtglas gegeben ist. Der Architekt über sein Projekt: „Meinem Entwurf liegt das Ziel zugrunde, die Magie eines Dachs auszudrücken, das ‚auf dem Nichts schwebt'. Die Ausführung ist im Detail kohärent, unauffällig, minimal. Als ob das Glas durch den alten Stein schneiden würde." Dieser Zugang zu einer „minimalistischen Erhaltungsweise historischer Bausubstanz" wurde 2002 mit dem Preis DuPont Benedictus ausgezeichnet.

C'est au milieu des années 1990 qu'une folie du XVIIIᵉ siècle appelée « Le temple de l'amour » située près d'Avalon, en Bourgogne, a été transformée en petite résidence estivale pour un neurologue néerlandais. Non loin, Dirk Jan Postel a conçu ce pavillon en verre feuilleté. Une extrémité du terrain est bordée par la culée d'un pont de chemin de fer détruit, et Postel a transformé l'ancienne chambre d'explosion voûtée en chambre d'amis. Il explique que « avec ses gros blocs de calcaire local, cette construction présente un aspect classique qui fait presque penser à Ledoux ». L'architecte a dessiné un toit en porte-à-faux à charpente à peau contrainte. Les panneaux en verre feuilleté trempé supportent sa charge de 2 tonnes. La stabilité latérale est assurée par des panneaux de verre feuilleté toute hauteur. « L'objectif de ce projet », explique l'architecte, « est d'exprimer la magie d'un toit ‹ flottant sur rien ›. L'exécution est cohérente, discrète, minimale. Comme si le verre reposait sur les blocs de pierre anciens. » Cette approche de « conservation historique minimaliste » a remporté le Prix DuPont Benedictus 2002 pour l'utilisation du verre feuilleté dans la construction.

*The architect imagined a guest house set into the abutment of a demolished railway bridge. As he says, its proportions might even recall the proportions and materials of Ledoux.*

*In dem Gästehaus, das in den Gewölbepfeiler einer ehemaligen Eisenbahnbrücke einfügt ist, finden sich Anklänge an die Proportionen und Materialien von Ledoux.*

*L'architecte a créé une maison d'amis dans la culée d'un pont de chemin de fer démoli, dont les proportions et les matériaux lui rappellent Claude-Nicolas Ledoux.*

A "roof floating on nothing" in fact sits on sheets of laminated glass atop the old railway bridge structure.

Das „schwebende Dach" ruht in Wirklichkeit auf Schichtglasplatten, die auf die alte Bausubstanz der Eisenbahnbrücke gesetzt wurden.

Ce « toit flottant sur rien » repose en fait sur des feuilles de verre feuilleté posées sur la structure de l'ancien pont.

This innovative use of laminated glass won the architect the 2002 DuPont Benedictus Award. Indeed, Postel's project is a demonstration of the great advances that have been made in materials such as glass.

Die innovative Nutzung von Schichtglas brachte dem Architekten den DuPont Benedictus Preis des Jahres 2002 ein. Tatsächlich demonstriert Postels Projekt anschaulich die großen Fortschritte, die in Baumaterialien wie Glas gemacht wurden.

Cette utilisation novatrice du verre feuilleté a valu à l'architecte le Prix DuPont Benedictus 2002. Le projet est une démonstration des avancées réalisées dans des matériaux comme le verre.

# WERNER SOBEK

*Werner Sobek Ingenieure*
*Albstrasse 14*
*70597 Stuttgart*
*Germany*

*Tel: +49 711 76 7500*
*Fax: +49 711 76 75044*
*e-mail: mail@wsi-stuttgart.com*
*Web: www.wsi-stuttgart.com*

*House R 1*

Werner Sobek was born in 1953 in Aalen, Germany. He studied architecture and civil engineering at the University of Stuttgart (1974–1980) and did post-graduate research in "Wide-Span Lightweight Structures" at the University of Stuttgart (1980–1986). He received his PhD in civil engineering at the same University in 1987. He worked as a structural engineer in the office of Schlaich, Bergermann & Partner (Stuttgart, 1987–1991) before creating his own office in 1991. Since 1995 he has been a Professor at the University of Stuttgart where he succeeded Frei Otto as Director of the Institute for Lightweight Structures. His projects include: Ecole Nationale d'Art Décoratif (Limoges, France, 1991–1994); Dome service hall Deutsche Bank (Hanover, 1992–1995); Art and Media Science Center (Karlsruhe, 1992–1997); Facade Interbank (with Hans Hollein, Lima, Peru, 1996–1999); New Bangkok International Airport (Thailand, with Murphy/Jahn, 1995–2004); Private residence R 128 (published here, Stuttgart, 1998–2000), and fair pavilions for Audi and BMW.

Werner Sobek, 1953 in Aalen geboren, studierte von 1974 bis 1980 Architektur und Bauwesen an der Universität Stuttgart und führte dort von 1980 bis 1986 Forschungsarbeiten zum Thema „weitgespannte Leichtbauten" durch. 1987 erwarb er an derselben Universität seinen Doktortitel in Bauwesen. Von 1987 bis 1991 arbeitete er als Bauingenieur bei Schlaich, Bergermann & Partner in Stuttgart, bevor er 1991 sein eigenes Büro in Stuttgart gründete. Seit 1995 ist er als Professor an der Universität Stuttgart tätig, wo er als Nachfolger von Frei Otto Direktor des Instituts für Leichtbauten wurde. Zu seinen Projekten zählen: die École Nationale d'Art Décoratif in Limoges (1991–1994), die Kuppel in der Schalterhalle der Deutschen Bank in Hannover (1992–1995), das ZKM in Karlsruhe (1992–1997), der neue internationale Flughafen in Bangkok (mit Murphy/Jahn, 1995–2004), die Fassade der Interbank (mit Hans Hollein) in Lima, Peru (1996–1999), das hier vorgestellte Wohnhaus R 128 in Stuttgart (1998–2000) sowie Messestände für Audi und BMW.

Werner Sobek, né en 1953 à Aalen, en Allemagne, étudie l'architecture et l'ingénierie civile à l'Université de Stuttgart (1974–1980) et mène une recherche de post-diplôme sur les structures légères de longue portée également à Stuttgart (1980–1986). Il est Ph.D. en ingénierie civile en 1987. Ingénieur structurel à l'agence Schlaich, Bergermann & Partner (Stuttgart, 1987–1991), il fonde la sienne en 1991. Depuis 1995, il est professeur à l'Université de Stuttgart où il a succédé à Frei Otto à la direction de l'Institut des structures légères. Parmi ses projets : École national d'arts décoratifs (Limoges, France, 1991–1994) ; dôme du hall de la Deutsche Bank (Hanovre, 1992–1995) ; Centre des arts et des médias (Karlsruhe, 1992–1997) ; façade d'Interbank (avec Hans Hollein, Lima, Pérou, 1996–1999) ; nouvel aéroport international de Bangkok (Thaïlande, avec Murphy/Jahn, 1995–2004) ; résidence privée, R 128, publiée ici (Stuttgart, 1998–2000) et pavillons de salons pour Audi et BMW.

# HOUSE R 128

*Stuttgart, Germany, 1999–2000*

*Client: Ursula und Werner Sobek. Total floor area: 250 m². Costs: not specified.*

The steep hillside of this 250-square-meter house made construction difficult. An existing 1923 structure was first demolished, and work such as that on the foundation had to be carried out by hand. A great deal of attention was paid to the ease of construction and finishing. The floors, for example, consist of prefabricated plastic-covered wood panels measuring 3.75 x 2.8 meters that are just placed between the floor beams without the use of screws. Aluminum ceiling panels are also clipped in place. The electrical or water lines are placed in aluminum ducts in the walls, never under plaster, to facilitate maintenance. The 11.2-meter, four-story building is made of a bolted steel skeleton with twelve columns arranged on a 3.85 x 2.9 meter grid. The façade is made of triple-glazed panels filled with inert gas and measuring 2.8 meters high by 1.36 meters wide on the north and south – 1.42 meters wide on the west and east. A mechanical ventilation system controls airflow and allows heat to be recovered from exhaust air. Air is blown through a heat exchanger situated below the foundation, taking advantage of the more constant temperature of the earth. Solar panels in the roof run the mechanical ventilation system and heat pump. Werner Sobek has announced that he intended to design only three houses in his life, each one requiring ten years of research. This one, made from twelve tons of steel and twenty tons of glass, was erected in an amazing eleven weeks. A second, teardrop-shaped carbon fiber structure so light it would not need foundations is already in the works.

Die Konstruktion des 250 m² großen Wohnhauses wurde durch seine Lage an einem stark abschüssigen Berghang erschwert. Insgesamt wurde große Sorgfalt auf den glatten Ablauf der Endfertigung verwendet. So bestehen beispielsweise die Böden aus vorgefertigten, 3,75 x 2,80 großen Holzpaneelen mit Kunststoffüberzug, die ohne Einsatz von Schrauben einfach zwischen die Fußbodenbalken eingesetzt wurden. Auch die Deckenplatten aus Aluminium wurden lediglich mit einer Halterung befestigt. Sowohl elektrische Leitungen wie auch Wasserrohre verlaufen durch Aluminiumröhren in den Wänden, liegen aber nicht unter Gipsputz, was die Instandhaltung erleichtert. Die Konstruktion des 11,20 m hohen, viergeschossigen Hauses besteht aus einem verschraubten Stahlskelett mit zwölf Säulen, die innerhalb eines Grundrasters von 3,85 x 2,9 m angeordnet sind. Die Fassade setzt sich aus dreifach verglasten und mit Schutzgas gefüllten Tafeln zusammen, die an der Nord- und Südseite jeweils 2,80 m hoch und 1,36 m beziehungsweise an der West- und Ostseite 1,42 m breit sind. Ein mechanisches Belüftungssystem steuert den Luftstrom und ermöglicht eine Wärmerückgewinnung aus Abluft. Die Luft wird durch einen Wärmeaustauscher geblasen, der unter dem Fundament liegt und die konstante Temperatur des Erdbodens nutzt. Das Belüftungssystem und die Wärmepumpe werden durch Solartafeln angetrieben, die im Dach montiert sind. Werner Sobek hat angekündigt, er wolle in seinem ganzen Leben nur drei Häuser entwerfen, da jedes davon zehn Jahre Forschungsarbeit in Anspruch nimmt. Das hier vorgestellte Haus, das aus zwölf Tonnen Stahl und 20 Tonnen Glas gefertigt ist, wurde in der unglaublich kurzen Zeit von nur elf Wochen errichtet. Ein zweiter Entwurf, eine tropfenförmige Konstruktion aus Kohlenstoff-Faser, die so leicht ist, dass sie keinerlei Unterbau benötigt, ist bereits in Arbeit.

L'escarpement de la pente sur laquelle s'élève cette maison de 250 m² a rendu le chantier difficile. Une grande attention a été portée à la facilité de construction et d'aménagement. Par exemple, les sols consistent en panneaux de bois enduits de plastique de 3,75 x 2,8 m posés entre les solives, sans boulonnage. Les panneaux d'aluminium de la toiture sont simplement clipsés. Les conduites électriques ou d'eau passent par des tuyaux d'aluminium dans les murs, mais jamais sous enduit de plâtre pour faciliter leur maintenance. La maison de 11,2 m de haut et de quatre niveaux fait appel à un squelette d'acier riveté à 12 colonnes disposées selon une trame de 3,85 x 2,9 m. La façade est en panneaux de verre triple épaisseur séparés par une couche de gaz inerte, qui mesurent 2,8 x 1,36 m de haut au nord et au sud, et 2,8 x 1,42 m à l'est et à l'ouest. Un système de ventilation mécanique contrôle l'aération et permet de récupérer la chaleur de l'air usé. L'air est traité par une pompe à chaleur située sous les fondations, pour bénéficier de la température plus constante du sol. Des panneaux solaires en toiture alimentent le système de ventilation mécanique et la pompe à chaleur. Werner Sobek a annoncé sa volonté de ne construire que trois maisons au cours de sa carrière, chacune nécessitant dix années de recherches. Celle-ci, qui a demandé 12 tonnes d'acier et 20 de verre, a été montée très rapidement en 11 semaines. Une seconde construction en forme de goutte et en fibre de carbone, si légère qu'elle ne nécessite même pas de fondations, est déjà en chantier.

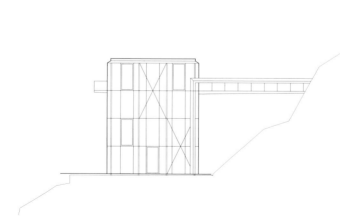

*Making an ecologically sensitive house out of glass is already a considerable challenge. Succeeding in making it esthetically attractive and in harmony with its setting is a triumph.*

*Ein ökologisch sensibles Haus aus Glas zu bauen, ist eine große Herausforderung. Es ästhetisch attraktiv und in Harmonie mit seiner Umgebung zu gestalten, ist ein Triumph.*

*Réaliser une maison d'esprit écologique est un défi considérable, réussir à la rendre esthétiquement séduisante et en harmonie avec son cadre est une performance rare.*

The extreme simplicity of the layout and the entirely glazed walls make the house astonishing to look at from the exterior and allow full views out toward Stuttgart.

Die äußerste Schlichtheit der Anordnung und die zur Gänze verglasten Wände machen das Haus zu einer auffallenden Erscheinung und erlauben einen freien Rundblick.

L'extrême simplicité du plan et les parois entièrement vitrées donnent un aspect étonnant à la maison vue de l'extérieur et permettent une vision panoramique de Stuttgart.

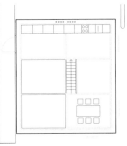

The reduction of this house to its bare minimum does not make it less interesting, quite the contrary. Its highly engineered nature is not at all apparent and that is its success.

Die Reduzierung dieses Gebäudes auf ein absolutes Minimum macht es nicht weniger interessant, ganz im Gegenteil. Dass sein stark ingenieurtechnischer Charakter in keiner Weise spürbar wird, ist ein weiterer Grund für seinen Erfolg.

La réduction de la maison au minimum possible ne la rend pas moins intéressante, bien au contraire. Avoir su faire oublier sa haute technicité est une de ses réussites.

The extreme lightness of the structural elements of the house almost
seems to make the floors hover in
space with no visible means of
support.

*Die extreme Leichtigkeit der Kon-
struktionsteile lassen die Geschoss-
böden fast ohne sichtbare Stützvor-
richtungen im Raum schweben.*

*La légèreté extrême des éléments
structurels donne l'impression que
les niveaux flottent dans l'espace,
sans support visible.*

Conceived on a strict grid system, the house is sparely furnished with couches and chairs designed by Le Corbusier and Breuer.

Das innerhalb eines exakten Grundrasters entworfene Haus ist spärlich möbliert mit Sofas und Stühlen, entworfen von Le Corbusier und Breuer.

Conçu sur une trame rigoureuse, la maison est parcimonieusement meublée de sièges et de canapés modernistes de le Corbusier et Breuer.

# PHILIPPE STARCK

Philippe Starck
18/20, rue du Faubourg du Temple
75011 Paris
France

Tel: +33 1 48 07 54 54
Fax: +33 1 48 07 54 64
e-mail: info@philippe-starck.com
Web: www.philippe-starck.com

*TASCHEN Stor*

Philippe Starck was born in 1949 and attended the École Nissim de Camondo in Paris. Though he is of course best known as a furniture and object designer, his projects as an architect include the Café Costes (Paris, 1984); Royalton Hotel (New York, 1988); Laguiole Knife Factory (Laguiole, 1988); Paramount Hotel (New York, 1990); Nani Nani Building (Tokyo, 1989); Asahi Beer Building (Tokyo, 1989); the Teatriz Restaurant (Madrid, 1990); and his Baron Vert building in Osaka (1990). He has also designed a number of private houses and apartment blocks, for example Lemoult in Paris (1987), The Angle in Antwerp (1991), apartment buildings in Los Angeles (1991), and a private house in Madrid (1991). More recently, he completed the interior design of the Saint Martin's Lane and Sanderson Hotels in London. In 2000, he completed the TASCHEN Store in Paris, and the following year the Clift Hotel in San Franciso.

Philippe Starck, 1949 in Paris geboren, studierte an der dortigen École Nissim de Camondo. Obwohl er vor allem als Designer von Möbeln und Gebrauchsobjekten bekannt wurde, hat er auch Architekturprojekte ausgeführt. Zu diesen gehören das Café Costes in Paris (1984), das Royalton Hotel (1988) und das Paramount Hotel (1990), beide in New York, die Laguiole Messerfabrik in Laguiole, Frankreich (1988), das Nani Nani-Gebäude (1989) und das Gebäude der Asahi-Brauerei (1989), beide in Tokio, das Restaurant Teatriz in Madrid (1990) sowie das Baron Vert Building in Osaka (1990). Darüber hinaus hat Starck auch eine Reihe von Privathäusern und Apartmentgebäuden entworfen, so das Haus Lemoult in Paris (1987), das Haus The Angle in Antwerpen (1991), Wohnbauten in Los Angeles (1991) und ein Haus in Madrid (1991). In jüngerer Zeit führte er die Innenraumgestaltung der Londoner Hotels Saint Martin's Lane und Sanderson durch. Im Jahr 2000 realisierte er die Buchhandlung TASCHEN in Paris und im folgenden Jahr das Clift Hotel in San Francisco.

Philippe Starck, né en 1949, a suivi les cours de l'École Nissim de Camondo à Paris. S'il est surtout connu comme designer de produits et de mobilier, il est aussi l'auteur d'interventions architecturales comme le Café Costes (Paris, 1984), le Royalton Hotel (New York, 1988), l'usine de coutellerie de Laguiole (Laguiole, 1988), le Paramount Hotel (New York, 1990), le Nani Nani Building (Tokyo, 1989), l'Asahi Beer Building (Tokyo, 1989), le Teatriz Restaurant (Madrid, 1990) et le Baron Vert Building (Osaka, 1990). Il a également conçu un certain nombre de résidences privées et d'immeubles d'appartements comme la maison Le Moult (Paris, 1987), The Angle (Anvers, 1991), un immeuble à Los Angeles (1991) et une maison à Madrid (1991). Plus récemment, il a achevé l'aménagement intérieur des hôtels Saint Martin's Lane et Sanderson à Londres. En 2002, il a conçu la librairie TASCHEN à Paris et en 2003 le Clift Hotel à San Francisco.

# TASCHEN STORE

*Los Angeles, California, USA, 2002–03*

Design: Philippe Starck. Art: Albert Oehlen.

The TASCHEN Store is located at 354 N. Beverly Drive, in Beverly Hills. It occupies one-third of an existing art-deco building in the middle of Beverly Hills' commercial district, one block away from Rodeo Drive, and near Frank Lloyd Wright's Anderton Court Shops (1952), Richard Meier's Gagosian Gallery, the Museum of Television & Radio, and a Prada boutique yet to be completed by Rem Koolhaas. The store is one-story with a mezzanine and terrace to the rear. The space is tall and narrow. The main room is four meters wide (including bookshelves) and 30.5 meters long. The coffered wood ceiling is five meters high. There are two long display tables centered in the main room. They were laser-scanned with CAD-CAM software on the basis of a small-scale model made by Starck's office. They are metalized with bronze finish. There is also a similarly made bar table that is located underneath a glass ceiling (the glass floor of the mezzanine). To each side of the bar table are lavender colored upholstered niches with built-in banquettes. At the rear of the main room is an all-glass mezzanine room. Glass wall panels are art glass made of layers of sandblasted, laminated glass with a drip-motif design. They were made by Pictet in Paris. There is a glass "coffee bar alcove" located at the rear of the main sales room. Walls, ceilings, bar counter and shelves, are all finished in lavender-hued mirrored glass that is engraved with a pattern designed by Starck. Kanner Architects were the local office in charge of the project (Executive architect) and TASCHEN called on German artist Albert Oehlen to produce twenty works for the bookshop. These computer generated images constitute a sequence of collages inspired by the publisher's titles.

Die Buchhandlung TASCHEN findet sich unter der Adresse 354 N. Beverly Drive in Beverly Hills. Sie nimmt ein Drittel eines Art déco Gebäudes ein, das im Zentrum des Geschäftsviertels von Beverly Hills liegt, einen Häuserblock vom Rodeo Drive entfernt und in der Nähe von Frank Lloyd Wrights Anderton Court Shops (1952), Richard Meiers Gagosian Gallery, dem Museum of Television & Radio sowie einer derzeit von Rem Koolhaas gestalteten Prada Boutique. Das eingeschossige Geschäft hat einen Mezzaninraum mit kassettierter Holzdecke und an der Hinterseite eine Terrasse. Der hohe und schmale Hauptraum ist 4 m breit (einschließlich der Bücherregale), 30,5 m lang und 5 m hoch. Die beiden langen, in der Mitte des Raums aufgestellten Büchertische wurden mit einer CAD-CAM Software und Laserscanner nach einem kleinformatigen Modell angefertigt. Sie sind mit einer Metallschicht bedeckt und bronziert. Ein als Coffee-Bar dienender Tisch ähnlicher Machart steht am hinteren Ende des Verkaufsraums unter einer Glasdecke, die gleichzeitig den Glasboden des Mezzanins bildet. Zu beiden Seiten dieses Tisches befinden sich lilafarben ausgepolsterte Nischen mit eingebauten Sitzbänken. Die Wände des vollständig aus Glas konstruierten Mezzaninraums bestehen aus sandgestrahltem Schichtglas mit Tropfmotiv-Design. Sie wurden von der Pariser Firma Pictet angefertigt. Die Oberflächen sämtlicher Wände, der Decke, Bar-Theke und Regale sind mit lavendelfarbenem Spiegelglas, das mit einem von Starck entworfenen Gravurmuster verziert wurde. Die architektonische Leitung des Projekts lag bei dem in Los Angeles ansässigen Büro von Kanner Architects. TASCHEN gab speziell für die Buchhandlung 20 Arbeiten bei dem deutschen Künstler Albert Oehlen in Auftrag. Seine computergenerierten Darstellungen bilden eine Serie von Collagen, zu denen sich der Künstler von den Buchtiteln des Verlags inspirieren ließ.

Au 354 N. Beverly Drive, la Librairie TASCHEN occupe le tiers d'un bâtiment de style Art-déco du quartier commercial de Beverly Hills, à un bloc de Rodeo Drive et non loin des Anderton Court Shops de Frank Lloyd Wright (1952), de la Gagosian Gallery de Richard Meier, du Musée de la télévision et de la radio et d'une boutique Prada en cours d'achèvement par Rem Koolhaas. Le volume haut et étroit se déploie sur un seul niveau, mais avec une mezzanine et une terrasse à l'arrière. La salle principale mesure 4 m de large (y compris les rayonnages) et 30,5 m de long. Le plafond de bois à caissons est à 5 m de haut. Le centre de l'espace est occupé par deux longues tables de présentation métallisées de finition bronze, réalisées par commande numérique à partir d'une maquette à petite échelle fournie par l'agence de Starck. On trouve un bar de traitement similaire sous un plafond de verre qui est le sol de la mezzanine. De chaque côté de ce bar ont été installées les banquettes dans des niches rembourrées de couleur lavande. La pièce en mezzanine, à l'arrière, est entièrement en verre. Les panneaux qui recouvrent les murs sont en couches de verre feuilleté sablé avec un motif de couture. Elles ont été réalisées par les ateliers Pictet à Paris. Au fond de l'espace de vente est installé un « bar à café en alcôve ». Les murs, les plafonds, le bar et les rayonnages sont tous en verre miroir de nuance lavande gravé d'un motif dessiné par P. Starck. Kannen Architects ont été les architectes exécutifs et TASCHEN a fait appel à l'artiste allemand Albert Oehlen pour une suite de vingt œuvres réalisées par ordinateur, collages inspirés des titres publiés par l'éditeur.

*Inspired by titles in the TASCHEN catalogue, works by Albert Oehlen animate the space that Philippe Starck has created.*

*Die von Büchern aus dem Programm des TASCHEN Verlags inspirierten Arbeiten von Albert Oehlen beleben den Innenraum.*

*Inspirées de titres du catalogue TASCHEN, des œuvres d'Albert Oehlen animent l'espace créé par Philippe Starck.*

Leonardo da Vinci

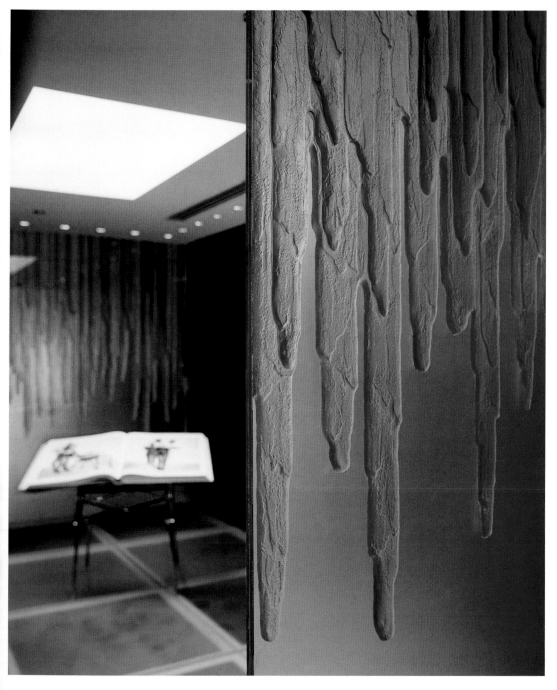

Furniture by Starck blends with un-usual surfaces, creating a surprising backdrop for books that have in themselves often attained the status of cult objects.

Einrichtungsgegenstände von Starck verschmelzen mit ausgefallenen Oberflächen zu einem ungewöhn-lichen Hintergrund für Bücher, von denen einige bereits selbst den Sta-tus von Kultobjekten erlangt haben.

Le mobilier de Starck se mélange à des effets de surface inhabituels, créant un fond surprenant pour des livres qui sont eux-mêmes souvent devenus des objets-cultes.

Philippe Starck's own monograph published by TASCHEN forms a décor (lower left) while other books take their place in an environment where design and publications accompany each other like equivalent forms of expression. Starck's décor borders on the kitsch, which in the environment of Los Angeles is hardly an accident. The designer amuses himself even as he accomplishes the essential commercial task he set out to deal with.

Die von TASCHEN veröffentlichte Monografie von Philippe Starck bildet ein eigenes Dekor (unten links), während die anderen Bücher in einem Umfeld präsentiert werden, in dem sich Design und Druckwerke wie gleichwertige Ausdrucksformen ergänzen. Starcks Innenraumgestaltung grenzt an Kitsch, was im Kontext von Los Angeles kaum ein Zufall sein dürfte. Der Designer löst seine im Grunde rein kommerzielle Aufgabe mit Amüsement und Ironie.

La monographie de Philippe Starck publiée par TASCHEN forme un décor (en bas à gauche) tandis que d'autres livres trouvent leur place dans un environnement ou le design intérieur et les livres s'accompagnent mutuellement, comme des formes d'expression équivalente. Le décor imaginé par Starck frise le kitsch, ce qui n'est pas un hasard dans le contexte de Los Angeles. Le designer s'amuse, même lorsqu'il répond aux exigences de tâches commerciales.

# JYRKI TASA

*Jyrki Tasa*
*Architectural Office*
*Nurmela-Raimoranta-Tasa Ltd.*
*Kalevankatu 31*
*00100 Helsinki*
*Finland*

*Tel: +358 9686 6780*
*Fax: +358 9685 7588*
*e-mail: tasa@n-r-t.fi*

*House Moby Di⬤*

Born in Turku, Finland, in 1944, Jyrki Tasa graduated from the Helsinki University of Technology in 1973. He set up an architectural office with Matti Nurmela and Kari Raimoranta in Helsinki the same year. He has been a professor at the University of Oulu since 1988. He has won 20 first prizes in architectural competitions. He won the Finnish State Prize in Architecture and Planning in 1987. His most significant work includes the Malmi Post Office, the Kuhmo Library, the Paavo Nurmi Stadium in Turku, the Into House in Espoo, the BE Pop Shopping Center in Pori, and the Moby Dick house published here. All of these projects are located in Finland.

Jyrki Tasa, 1944 im finnischen Turku geboren, schloss 1973 sein Studium an der Technischen Universität Helsinki ab. Im selben Jahr gründete er zusammen mit Matti Nurmela und Kari Raimoranta ein Architekturbüro in Helsinki. Seit 1988 lehrt er außerdem an der Universität von Oulu. Jyrki Tasa ist im Laufe seiner Karriere aus 20 Architekturwettbewerben als Sieger hervorgegangen und 1987 wurde ihm der Finnische Staatspreis für Architektur und Bauplanung verliehen. Zu seinen wichtigsten, alle in Finnland realisierten Bauten, gehören das Postamt in Malmi, die Bibliothek in Kuhmo, das Paavo Nurmi Stadium in Turku, das Haus Into in Espoo, das Einkaufs-zentrum BE Pop in Pori sowie das hier vorgestellte Haus Moby Dick.

Né en 1944 à Tuku, en Finlande, Jyrki Tasa est diplômé de l'Université de Technologie d'Helsinki en 1973. Il crée son agence d'architecture avec Matti Nurmela et Kari Raimoranta à Helsinki la même année. Il enseigne à l'Université d'Oulu depuis 1988 et a remporté 20 premiers prix de concours architecturaux. Il a reçu le Prix d'architecture et d'urbanisme de l'État finlandais en 1987. Parmi ses réalisations les plus marquantes, toutes en Finlande : la poste de Malmi, la bibliothèque de Kuhmo, le stade Paavo Nurmi à Turku, la maison Into à Espoo, le centre commercial BE Pop à Pori et la maison Moby Dick publiée ici.

# HOUSE MOBY DICK

*Espoo, Finland, 2002–03*

Client: a four person family (private). Total floor area: 570 m². Costs: not specified.

Few houses appear as different as this one when seen from one side (below) or the other (right). Elevations show better how this surprising transition is accomplished.

Wenige Häuser wirken so unterschiedlich, wenn man sie von verschiedenen Seiten (unten und rechts) betrachtet. Die Aufrisse machen die Ausführung der Übergänge deutlich.

Peu de maisons présentent autant de différences d'une façade (ci-dessous) à l'autre (à droite). Les élévations expliquent cette surprenante transition.

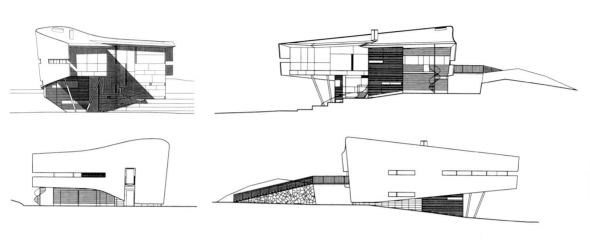

Built for a four-person family, this 570-square-meter "biomorphic" house is approached via a stone stairway and a steel bridge leading to the first floor above ground level. At the entrance level, there are a living room, library, master bedroom, and two balconies. The ground floor contains the children's spaces, a guestroom, and a garage, while a sauna, fireplace, and gym are in the basement of the house. A two-story-high winter garden, three translucent glass and steel bridges and a staircase forming the spatial core of the house all participate in the open movement of the residence. The stairway offers views into every area of the house. The curving exterior of the structure, evoked by its name "Moby Dick," contrasts with the rectangular interior walls. Made with concrete-filled steel pillars, concrete-steel composite slabs and a steel and wood roof, the house is mostly clad with plywood or pine. The house is equipped with a heat pump and floor heating system.

Der Zugang zu dem für eine vierköpfige Familie gebauten „biomorphen" Haus erfolgt über eine Steintreppe und eine Stahlbrücke, die zum ersten Stock führen. Auf dieser Ebene liegen ein Wohnraum, die Bibliothek, das Elternschlafzimmer und zwei Balkone. Das Erdgeschoss enthält die Räume der Kinder, ein Gästezimmer und eine Garage, während Sauna, Kamin und Fitnessraum im Souterrain untergebracht sind. Ein Wintergarten mit doppelter Raumhöhe, drei durchscheinende Brücken aus Glas und Stahl und ein Treppenaufgang bilden den räumlichen Kern des Gebäudes und tragen in ihrer Gesamtheit zu seiner offenen, rhythmischen Gestaltung bei. Die geschwungenen Fassaden, von denen das Haus den Namen Moby Dick hat, kontrastieren mit den rechtwinkligen Innenwänden. Die Konstruktion besteht aus Stahlsäulen mit Betonfüllung, Betonstahlplatten und einem Dach aus Stahl und Holz. Die Außenverkleidung ist hauptsächlich aus Sperrholz oder Kiefernholz gefertigt.

On accède à cette maison biomorphique de 570 m², construite pour une famille de quatre personnes, par une allée pavée et une passerelle d'acier menant directement au premier niveau au-dessus du rez-de-chaussée. Il contient le séjour, une bibliothèque, la chambre principale et deux balcons. Le rez-de-chaussée regroupe les espaces pour les enfants, une chambre d'amis et un garage, tandis que le sous-sol comprend un sauna, une cheminée et une salle de gymnastique. Le jardin intérieur sur deux niveaux, trois murs de verre translucide, des passerelles et un escalier en acier constituent le noyau de cette maison et assurent une circulation ouverte. La façade incurvée, qui justifie le nom de « Moby Dick » contraste avec les murs intérieurs orthogonaux. L'ensemble a fait appel à des piliers d'acier remplis de béton, des dalles de béton armé, un toit en bois et acier. La façade est habillée pour l'essentiel de contreplaqué ou de pin.

*Contrary to what the closed entrance façade might imply, the house is bright, open and light its in articulation.*

*Im Gegensatz zu dem, was man von der geschlossenen Eingangsfassade erwarten könnte, ist das Haus hell, offen und von lockerer Eleganz.*

*Contrairement à ce que la façade d'entrée fermée laisse entendre, la maison est très ouverte et d'articulation légère.*

Daylight floods the interior space where wood and glazing form the major surfaces. Plans below show the rather unusual disposition of the structure.

Das Tageslicht durchflutet den Innenraum, in dem Holz und Glas vorherrschen. Die Grundrisse unten zeigen die ungewöhnliche Anordnung des Gebäudes.

La lumière naturelle inonde l'intérieur, traité essentiellement en bois et en verre. Les plans ci-dessous montrent le plan assez curieux de la maison.

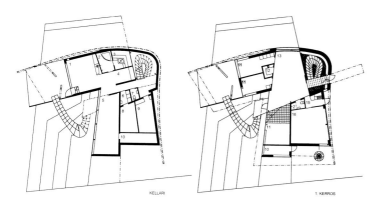

KELLARI

1. KERROS

An unusual irregular spiral staircase connects the interior levels of the house, and the architect uses a full palette of materials to surprise and delight the inhabitant or visitor.

Eine auffallend unregelmäßige Wendeltreppe verbindet die Geschossebenen des Hauses. Die volle Palette von Materialien überrascht Bewohner wie Besucher.

Un curieux escalier irrégulier relie les niveaux intérieurs. L'architecte a fait appel à une palette variée de matériaux pour surprendre et ravir l'occupant ou le visiteur.

# AKIRA YONEDA

*Akira Yoneda Architect/Architecton*
*1-7-16-612 Honcho*
*Shibuya-ku, Tokyo 151-0071*
*Japan*

*Tel: +81 3 337 40 846*
*Fax: +81 3 536 52 216*
*e-mail: a-tecton@pj8.so-net.ne.jp*

*Bloc*

Akira Yoneda was born in Hyogo, Japan in 1959. He received his BE (Bachelor of Engineering) degree from the University of Tokyo in 1982 and Masters of Architecture degrees from both the University of Tokyo (1984) and the Harvard University Graduate School of Design (1991). He worked for the Takenaka Corporation, Design Department, in Tokyo (1984–1989) before creating his own firm, Architecton, in Tokyo (1991). His work includes: Kyokuto Kaihatu Kogyo Miki Plant Office (Miki, Hyogo, 1996); White Echoes/House (Nerima-ku, Tokyo, 1998); ambi-flux/House (Minato-ku, Tokyo, 2000); nkm/House (Arakawa-ku, Tokyo, 2001); Beaver House (Koto-ku, Tokyo, 2002); connoid/House (Meguro-ku, Tokyo, 2002); Bloc/House (Kobe, Hyogo, 2002); and the White Base/House & Studio (Koganei, Tokyo, to be completed in 2004).

Akira Yoneda, geboren 1959 in Hyogo, Japan, erwarb 1982 seinen Bachelor of Engineering an der Universität Tokio und jeweils einen Master of Architecture an der Universität Tokio (1984) und an der Harvard University Graduate School of Design (1991). Von 1984 bis 1989 arbeitete er in der Designabteilung der Firma Takenaka Corporation in Tokio und gründete 1991 sein eigenes Büro, Architecton, in Tokio. Zu seinen Arbeiten zählen: das Bürogebäude der Fabrikanlage Kyokuto Kaihatu Kogyo in Miki, Hyogo (1996), das Haus White Echoes in Nerima-ku (1998), das Haus ambi-flux in Minato-ku (2000), das Haus nkm in Arakawa-ku (2001), das Beaver House in Koto-ku (2002), das Haus connoid in Meguro-ku (2002), alle in Tokio; ferner das Haus Bloc in Kobe, Hyogo (2002) und das Haus mit Atelier White Base in Koganei, Tokio, das 2004 fertig gestellt sein soll.

Akira Yoneda, né à Hyogo, Japon, en 1959 est Bachelor (ingénierie) de l'Université de Tokyo (1982), et Master of Architecture de l'Université de Tokyo (1984) et de la Harvard University Graduate School of Design (1991). Il travaille pour le département de design de la Takenaka Corporation (Tokyo, 1984–1989) avant de créer son agence, Architecton, à Tokyo en 1991. Parmi ses réalisations : Usine et bureaux Kyokuto Kaihatu (Miki, Kogyo, 1996) ; White Echoes House (Nerima-ku, Tokyo, 1998) ; Ambi-flux House (Minato-ku, Tokyo, 2000) ; nkm House (Arakawa-ku, Tokyo, 2001) ; Beaver House (Koto-ku, Tokyo, 2002) ; Connoid House (Meguro-ku, Tokyo, 2002) ; Bloc/House (Kobe, Hyogo, 2002) et la White Base, maison et studio (Koganei, Tokyo ; 2004).

# BLOC

*Kobe, Hyogo, Japan, 2001–02*

Client: private. Floor area: 242 m². Costs: not specified.

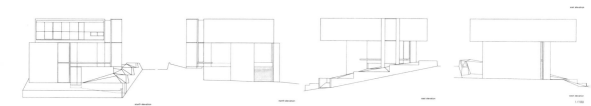

The unusual volume of the roof or upper volume of the Bloc House is emphasized by its green color. The "bloc" seems to hover above its intentionally less substantial looking base.

*Der ungewöhnliche Charakter des oberen Bauteils, gleichzeitig Dach des Gebäudes, wird durch seine grüne Farbe noch verstärkt.*

*Le volume inhabituel de la partie supérieure, ou toit, de la Bloc House est mis en valeur par sa couleur verte.*

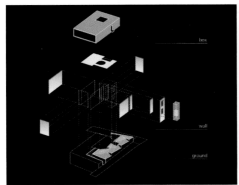

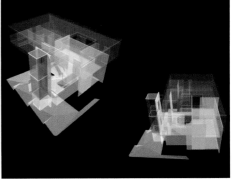

Despite being radically different from its neighbors, the Bloc House somehow does fit in, given Japanese tolerance for unusual or quirky architecture.

Obwohl radikal anders als seine Nachbargebäude, wirkt das Bloc House nicht unpassend, bedenkt man die Toleranz der Japaner für ungewöhnliche Architektur.

Radicalement différente de ses voisines, la Bloc House s'y intègre cependant, et ce d'autant plus que les Japonais acceptent facilement les formes architecturales bizarres.

Built with Masahiro Ikeda, this 242-square-meter house is set on a 276-square-meter site. It is a steel frame structure designed for an elderly client who lost her "European style" house in the 1995 earthquake. It has a spectacular view of the harbor of Kobe and the Inland Sea beyond. The house consists of "white planes" on the first and second levels, with a large green slab floating above. The maximum overhang of this block (10 meters) gives an unusual appearance to the house, which surprisingly enough does not seem "top-heavy." Rather the overhanging volume looks light because the glass and support walls below are unusually thin. Particularly at night, the "Bloc" that the house is named after looks like it is hovering above the port. The residence area of the client is actually contained in this green volume that is symbolically intended to recall the shoreline beyond. The section below is for the occasional visit of her adult children, and also includes a library and entrance hall.

Das 242 m² umfassende Wohnhaus, das Yoneda zusammen mit Masahiro Ikeda realisierte, steht auf einem 276 m² großen Grundstück, und besteht aus einer Stahlrahmenkonstruktion. Das Haus, von dem aus man einen fantastischen Blick auf den Hafen von Kobe und das Binnenmeer dahinter hat, ist auf den ersten beiden Ebenen aus senkrechten, weißen Flächen zusammengesetzt, über die ein ausladender, grüner Riegel gelegt wurde. Dieser bis zu 10 m vorspringende Teil verleiht dem Gebäude ein auffallendes Äußeres, dennoch wirkt es überraschender Weise nicht „kopflastig". Besonders nachts wirkt der „Block", als würde er über dem Hafen schweben. Mit seiner grünen Farbgebung soll außerdem die hinter diesem Wohngebiet liegende Küstenlinie symbolisiert werden. Der darunter liegende Bereich des Hauses ist für die gelegentlichen Besuche der erwachsenen Kinder der Hausherrin gedacht und enthält zudem eine Bibliothek und einen Eingang mit Vorraum.

Construite en collaboration avec Masahiro Ikeda, cette maison de 242 m² à ossature en acier occupe un terrain de 276 m². Elle offre une vue spectaculaire sur le port de Kobe et la mer intérieure du Japon. Elle se compose au premier et au second niveau, de « plans blancs » surmontés par une grande dalle verte. Le porte-à-faux maximum de cet élément (10 m) contribue à l'aspect étonnant de cette maison qui ne semble pas pour autant écrasée. Le volume en porte-à-faux semble même léger grâce à la minceur des murs de soutènement et des parois de verre qui le soutiennent. Ce « Bloc » pour reprendre le nom de la maison semble flotter au-dessus du port, en particulier la nuit. Contenant la partie résidentielle, il veut symboliquement rappeler la ligne de la côte. La partie inférieure est prévue pour le séjour des enfants du propriétaire et comprend également une bibliothèque et le hall d'entrée.

*Communication between the upper and lower levels of the house creates opportunities for a hovering lightness that is willfully asymmetric.*

*Der Dialog zwischen den oberen und unteren Ebenen schafft Momente einer schwebenden und eigenwillig asymmetrischen Leichtigkeit.*

*La communication entre les niveaux supérieurs et inférieurs accentue les effets de légèreté en suspension et de parti pris asymétrique.*

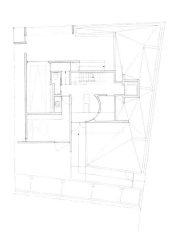

Plans show the lower and then upper level of the house with its dominant upper block.

*Die Grundrisse zeigen die untere (links), mittlere und obere Geschossebene mit ihrem dominanten „Block".*

*Plans des différents niveaux de la maison, dont celui de la « dalle » qui domine la composition.*

A clever use of light and dark as well as the green tone imposed by the coloring of the upper block create a complex orchestration of floating, opaque elements with frequent openings.

Der intelligente Einsatz von Hell und Dunkel sorgt für ein komplexes Zusammenspiel fließender, opaker Elemente und häufig wiederkehrender Öffnungen.

L'utilisation intelligente de la lumière et de l'ombre crée une orchestration complexe d'éléments opaques et flottants entrecoupés de fréquentes ouvertures.

# CARLOS ZAPATA

*Wood + Zapata Inc.*
*444 Broadway*
*New York, NY 10013*
*USA*

*Tel: +1 212 966 9292*
*Fax: +1 212 966 9242*
*Web: www.wood-zapata.com*

*Quito Hous*

Carlos Zapata obtained his Master of Architecture degree from Columbia University and his Bachelor of Architecture at the Pratt Institute. He was a Vice President of Ellerbe Becket (New York, 1986–1991) before creating the Carlos Zapata Design Studio in Miami in 1991. He has also been a Principal of Wood and Zapata Inc. in Boston since 1996. Current work includes the new 63 000-seat Chicago Bears Stadium at Soldier Field (Chicago); Concourse J., Miami International Airport (Miami, for United Airlines), as well as private houses in Montauk, New York and Golden Beach, Florida. Completed projects include the Hamilton Square Specialty Market and 800-car (10-story) Parking Garage (Philadelphia, PA); Chicago Bears Field House and Indoor Practice Facility (Lake Forest, Illinois); the Quito House in Miravalle, Ecuador, published here; the Landes House (Golden Beach, Florida) and JPBT Advisors Headquarters (Miami, Florida).

Carlos Zapata erwarb seinen Bachelor of Architecture am Pratt Institute in New York und seinen Master of Architecture an der Columbia University. Von 1986 bis 1991 war er Vizepräsident der Firma Ellerbe Becket in New York, bevor er 1991 das Carlos Zapata Design Studio in Miami gründete. Seit 1996 ist er außerdem Direktor von Wood and Zapata Inc. in Boston. Zu seinen aktuellen Projekten gehören das neue, mit 63 000 Sitzen ausgestattete Stadium der Chicago Bears am Soldier Field in Chicago, die Halle J am Miami International Airport für United Airlines sowie Wohnhäuser in Montauk, New York, und Golden Beach, Florida. Zu seinen fertig gestellten Bauten zählen: der Spezialitätenmarkt Hamilton Square und ein zehngeschossiges Parkhaus mit 800 Plätzen in Philadelphia, das Field House und eine Trainingshalle für die Chicago Bears in Lake Forest, Illinois, das hier vorgestellte Quito House in Miravalle, Ecuador, das Haus Landes in Golden Beach, Florida, sowie die Zentrale von JPBT Advisors in Miami.

Carlos Zapata, Bachelor of Architecture du Pratt Institute et Master of Architecture de la Columbia University, a été vice-président de Ellerbe Becket (New York, 1986–1991), avant de fonder le Carlos Zapata Design Studio à Miami en 1991. Il dirige également Wood and Zapata Inc. à Boston, depuis 1996. Parmi ses travaux récents : le nouveau stade des Bears de Chicago, 63 000 places (Soldier Field, Chicago) ; le Hall J de l'aéroport international de Miami pour United Airlines et des résidences privées à Montauk, New York et Golden Beach (Floride). Il est également l'auteur du Marché d'Hamilton Square et de son parking de 800 places (Philadelphie, Pennsylvanie) ; du club des Bears et du stade d'entraînement couvert (Lake Forest, Illinois) ; de la Quito House (Miravalle, Équateur), publiée ici ; de la Landes House (Golden Beach, Floride) et du siège de JPBT Advisros (Miami, Floride).

# QUITO HOUSE

*Miravalle, Quito, Ecuador, 1998–2002*

*Client: private. Total floor area: 743 m². Costs: not specified.*

*With its forward leaning façade and surprising terrace, this house would stand out in any environment.*

*Das mit seiner nach vorn geneigten Fassade und stegartigen Terrasse überraschende Haus würde in jeder Umgebung auffallen.*

*La façade inclinée vers l'avant et l'étonnante terrasse de cette maison se feraient remarquer dans n'importe quel environnement.*

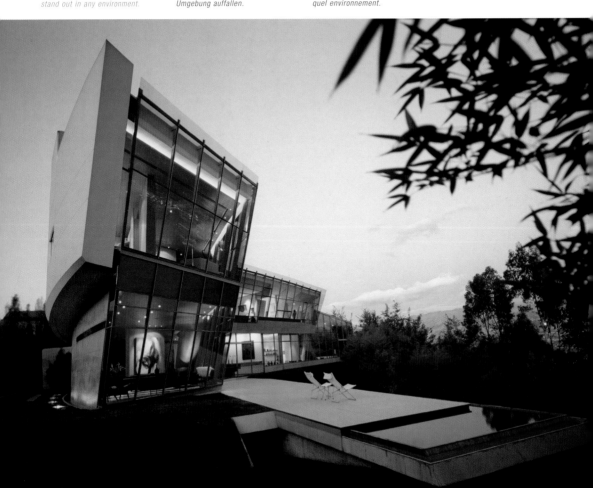

*With its cantilevered volume and oblique columns the house appears to be ready to slide backward, or to take off.*

*Mit seinem auskragenden Baukörper und den schrägen Säulen wirkt das Haus, als würde es gleich nach hinten kippen oder auch abheben.*

*Le volume en porte-à-faux et les colonnes obliques donnent l'impression que la maison va glisser vers l'arrière ou s'envoler.*

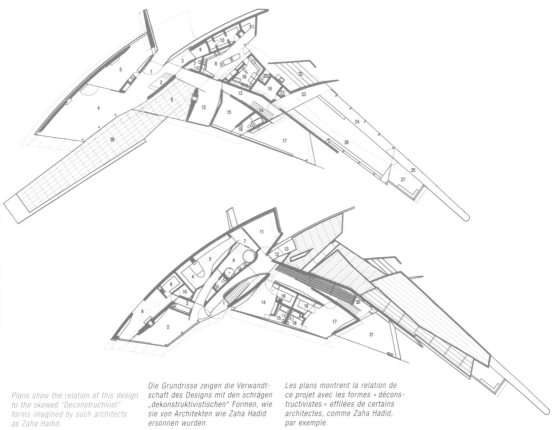

*Plans show the relation of this design to the skewed "Deconstructivist" forms imagined by such architects as Zaha Hadid.*

*Die Grundrisse zeigen die Verwandtschaft des Designs mit den schrägen „dekonstruktivistischen" Formen, wie sie von Architekten wie Zaha Hadid ersonnen wurden.*

*Les plans montrent la relation de ce projet avec les formes « déconstructivistes » effilées de certains architectes, comme Zaha Hadid, par exemple.*

Built on an inclined, 5 000-square-meter site very close to Quito with a 180° view of the valley of Miravalle and the Andes Mountains, this 743-square-meter house is part of a development with 80 other parcels of land. The main materials are poured-in-place concrete, stucco, glass, granite, zinc, stainless steel, and local wood. The architects write, "the house is an assembly of fluid, energetic, puzzle-like fragments which together fuse with the terrain and accentuate its natural contours. The resulting composition is therefore brought together with a powerful gesture inherent in the terrain itself." Two V-shaped floors are split apart by the main staircase opposite the entrance. The first wing of the first floor contains a living room adjacent to a family room and separated from it by a movable translucent wall. The second wing of the first floor contains a formal dining room, with an informal dining room adjacent to it. A movable wall allows the two dining rooms to become one for special functions. An interior garden next to the main entrance, the guest bathroom, the kitchen area, the laundry with exterior patio, a guest room with bathroom shared by a playroom and storage space are also located here. The children's wing contains two bedrooms with their respective bathrooms. The second wing of the second floor contains the master bedroom, a painter's studio adjacent to it, and the master bathroom adjacent to an open private garden.

Das Wohnhaus hat eine Gesamtnutzfläche von 743 m² und steht auf einem 5 000 m² großen, leicht abschüssigen Grundstück nahe Quito mit Aussicht auf das Tal von Miravalle und die umliegenden Berge der Anden. Es ist zusammen mit 80 weiteren Parzellen Teil eines Bauprojekts. Die Baumaterialien für dieses Gebäude sind Gussbeton, Gipsputz, Glas, Granit, Zink, rostfreier Stahl und lokales Holz. Die Architekten über ihren Entwurf: "Das Haus ist eine Zusammenstellung fließender, energetischer, puzzleartiger Fragmente, die zusammen mit dem Terrain verschmelzen und dessen natürliche Konturen akzentuieren. Die endgültige Komposition ist folglich aus einer vom Terrain selbst ausgehenden, kraftvollen Geste entstanden." Im Innern bildet die gegenüber dem Eingang liegende Treppe die Trennlinie zwischen den beiden V-förmigen Geschossen. Der vordere Trakt des unteren Stockwerks enthält zwei Wohnbereiche, die sich durch eine durchscheinende Schiebewand voneinander abgrenzen lassen. Im hinteren Trakt befinden sich ein großes und ein kleineres Esszimmer, die sich wiederum durch Öffnen einer Schiebewand für besondere Anlässe zusammenlegen lassen. Ebenfalls in diesem Teil des Hauses liegen ein Wintergarten neben dem Haupteingang, der Küchenbereich, ein Gästezimmer mit Bad, ein Spielzimmer, mehrere Neben- und Versorgungsräume und ein Patio. Der von den Kindern bewohnte Teil enthält zwei Schlafzimmer mit dazugehörigen Badezimmern. Im Obergeschoss sind das Elternschlafzimmer, daran angrenzend ein Maleratelier und ein Badezimmer untergebracht, das sich zu einem kleinen Garten hinaus öffnet.

Construite près de Quito sur un terrain de 5 000 m² bénéficiant d'une vue à 180° sur la vallée de Miravalle et les Andes, cette résidence de 743 m² fait partie d'un lotissement de 80 parcelles. Les principaux matériaux sont le béton coulé sur place, le stuc, le verre, le granit, le zinc, l'acier inoxydable et le bois de la région. Pour l'architecte : « Cette maison est un assemblage de fragments de puzzle, fluides et énergétiques qui fusionnent avec le terrain et font ressortir son profil naturel. La composition qui en résulte est un geste puissant inhérent au site. » Deux niveaux en V séparés par l'escalier principal s'ouvrent de chaque côté de l'entrée. La première aile du premier niveau contient un séjour adjacent à un salon familial dont il est séparé par un mur translucide. La seconde aile de ce niveau contient une salle à manger de réception et une salle à manger familiale, qu'un cloisonnement mobile permet de réunir en certaines occasions. La même zone comprend également un jardin intérieur près de l'entrée principale, une chambre d'invités, la cuisine, la lingerie et son patio extérieur, une salle de jeux, une salle de bains et un espace de rangement. L'aile des enfants contient deux chambres et leurs salles de bains respectives. La seconde aile du second niveau est occupée par la chambre principale, un atelier de peinture adjacent et la salle de bains principale ouvrant sur un jardin privatif.

*The forward tilting glazed façade of the house allows unusual interior spaces to be created with a combination of ample light and a certain amount of protection from the bright sky.*

*Die vornüber geneigte Glasfassade des Hauses erlaubt eine ungewöhnliche Innenraumgestaltung und bietet sowohl reichlich Tageslicht als auch Schutz vor direkter Sonneneinstrahlung.*

*La façade vitrée inclinée de la maison permet de créer des volumes intérieurs inhabituels qui combinent un généreux éclairage naturel à un certain degré de protection solaire.*

Skewed walls or stairways animate interior spaces and a warm color scheme gives the whole a friendly, open appearance.

Die abgeschrägten Wände und Treppen beleben die Innenräume, während die warme Farbgebung dem Ganzen eine freundliche, offene Note verleiht.

Les murs penchés et les escaliers animent les volumes intérieurs. La coloration chaleureuse confère à l'ensemble un aspect amical et ouvert.

One might imagine a rectilinear modernist design as seen through the deforming effect of a wide-angle lens in the picture above, but it is the architecture itself that leans forward.

Bei der Abbildung könnte es sich um ein durch ein Weitwinkelobjektiv verzerrtes, modernistisches Design handeln, doch es ist die Architektur selbst, die sich vornüber neigt.

On pourrait presque imaginer un projet moderniste déformë par un objectif grand angle : en réalité, c'est la maison elle-même qui a décidé de se pencher en avant.

A swimming pool is largely sheltered by the house and participates in its unusual combination of materials and skewed angles.

Der Swimmingpool ist größtenteils vom Haus geschützt und trägt zu der ungewöhnlichen Kombination von Materialien und schrägen Winkeln bei.

Une piscine participe à l'esprit d'ensemble par un mariage inhabituel de matériaux et les profils des murs et du plafond.

# RENÉ VAN ZUUK

*Rene van Zuuk Architekten BV*
*De Fantasie 9*
*1324 HZ Almere*
*The Netherlands*

*Tel: +31 36 537 9139*
*Fax: +31 36 537 9259*
*e-mail: mail@renevanzuuk.com*
*Web: www.renevanzuuk.com*

*De Verbeelding Pavilion*

**RENÉ VAN ZUUK** received a Master of Sciences degree from the Technical University of Eindhoven (1988) and created his own firm in 1993. He has a design staff of five persons. Prior to that date, he worked for Skidmore, Owings Merrill in London and Chicago (1988–89) and at Facilitair Bureau voor Bouwkunde Rotterdam, Hoogstad, van Tilburg Architecten (1989–1992). His notable completed projects include: ARCAM Architectural Center (Amsterdam, 2003); Art Pavilion "De Verbeelding," (Zeewolde, 2001); Center for Plastic Arts "CBK" (Alphen aan de Rijn, The Netherlands, 2000); Educational Farm "Griftsteede" (Utrecht, 1999); 4 Canal Houses (Java Island, Amsterdam, 1997); Lock House "Oostersluis" (Groningen, 1995); Villa van Diepen (Almere, 1995); and 8 Bridges (Nieuwsloten, The Netherlands, 1993). Current work includes: Blok 16 housing and fitness complex (Almere, 2003); bridge for bicycles and pedestrians (Almere, 2003); bridge keeper's house (Middelburg, The Netherlands, unbuilt); and office building "Zilverparkkade" (Lelystad, The Netherlands, 2004).

**RENÉ VAN ZUUK** erwarb 1988 den Master of Sciences an der Technischen Universität Eindhoven und gründete 1993 seine eigene Firma, wo er heute mit fünf Mitarbeitern tätig ist. Davor hat er für Skidmore, Owings & Merrill in London und Chicago (1988–89) und im Facilitair Bureau voor Bouwkunde Rotterdam, Hoogstad, van Tilburg Architecten (1989–1992) gearbeitet. Zu seinen wichtigsten, alle in den Niederlanden realisierten Bauten zählen: acht Brücken in Nieuwsloten (1993), die Villa van Diepen in Almere (1995), das Haus Oostersluis in Groningen (1995), vier Kanalhäuser auf der Java-Insel in Amsterdam (1997), das Schulbauernhaus Griftsteede in Utrecht (1999), das Center for Plastic Arts CBK in Alphen aan de Rijn (2000), der Kunstpavillon de Verbeelding in Zeewolde (2001) und das ARCAM Architectural Center in Amsterdam (2003). Zu den aktuellen Projekten van Zuuks gehören die Wohnanlage mit Fitnesscenter Blok 16 (2003), eine Fußgänger- und Fahrradbrücke, beide 2003 in Almere entstanden, das bislang unrealisierte Haus des Brückenwärters in Middelburg sowie das Bürogebäude „Zilverparkkade" in Lelystad (2004).

**RENÉ VAN ZUUK**, Master of Sciences de l'Université technique d'Eindhoven (1988), crée son agence en 1993. Son équipe de conception compte cinq collaborateurs. Auparavant, il avait travaillé pour Skidmore, Owins Merrill à Londres et Chicago (1988–89) et chez Facilitair Bureau voor Bouwkunde Rotterdam, Hoogstad, van Tilburg Architecten (1989–1992). Parmi ses réalisations les plus remarquées, toutes aux Pays-Bas : Centre d'architecture ARCAM (Amsterdam, 2003) ; Art Pavilion « De Verbeelding » (Zeewolde, 2001) ; Center for Plastic Arts CBK (Alphen aan de Rijn, 2000) ; ferme d'enseignement Grifsteede (Utrecht, 1999) ; 4 maisons de canal (Java Island, Amsterdam, 1997) ; Lock House Ooosterluis (Groningue, 1995) ; villa van Diepen (Almere, 1995) et 8 ponts (Nieuwsloten, 1993). Plus récemment, il a achevé : le Blok 16, logements et salle de remise en forme (Almere, 2003) ; un pont piétonnier (Almere, 2003) ; une maison de pontonnier (Middlebourg, non construit) et l'immeuble de bureaux Zilverparkkade (Lelystad, 2004).

# DE VERBEELDING PAVILION

*Zeewolde, The Netherlands, 2001*

*Client: Stichting de Kunstbaan. Floor area: 375 m². Costs: € 425 000.*

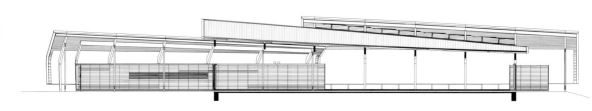

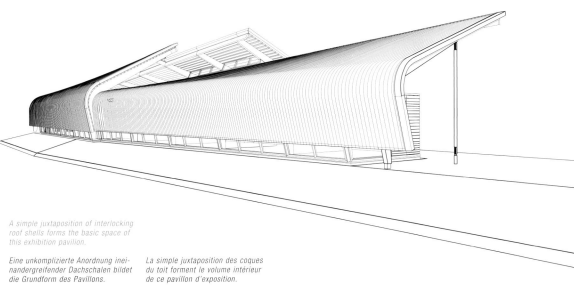

A simple juxtaposition of interlocking
roof shells forms the basic space of
this exhibition pavilion.

Eine unkomplizierte Anordnung inei-
nandergreifender Dachschalen bildet
die Grundform des Pavillons.

La simple juxtaposition des coques
du toit forment le volume intérieur
de ce pavillon d'exposition.

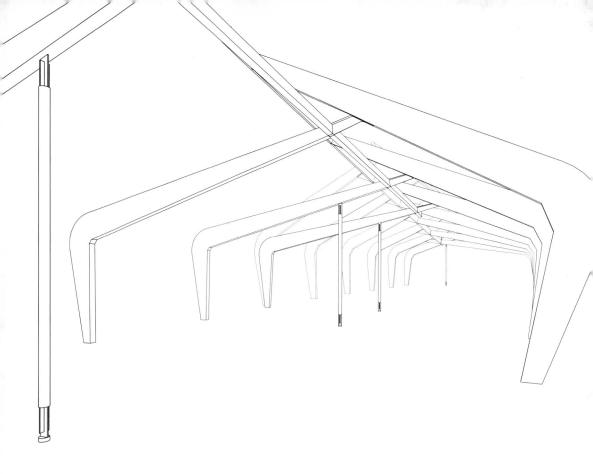

Located on a small peninsula in a moat, the shape of this house was influenced by a neighboring work by the American sculptor Richard Serra. His concrete wall called "Sea Level" was at the origin of the long form of Zuuk's structure. Meaning "the imagination," the De Verbeelding Pavilion makes use of structural elements that are frequently found in local barns, but since there are exhibition spaces in the structure, it had to meet usual requirements than other rural buildings. A glass strip in the roof provides interior lighting and the "light and pleasant space" wanted for this international center for landscape art. A glass plinth also brings light reflected off the water into the building. A glass wall also offers a view over the water to toward Richard Serra's sculpture.

Der Pavillon liegt auf einer kleinen Landzunge, die sich in eine Dammgrube erstreckt. Seine Form wurde von einer Arbeit des amerikanischen Bildhauers Richard Serra inspiriert. Auf dessen in unmittelbarer Nachbarschaft errichtete Betonwand mit dem Titel „Sea Level" geht die lang gestreckte Gestalt von Zuuks Arbeit zurück. Der Pavillon wird „de Verbeelding" genannt, was „die Imagination" bedeutet. Bei dieser Konstruktion wurden Baumaterialien verwendet, wie man sie auch in den für diese Region typischen Scheunen findet. Da Zuuks Bauwerk jedoch für Ausstellungen konzipiert ist, musste es gleichzeitig sehr speziellen Erfordernissen entsprechen. So sorgt beispielsweise ein in das Dach integriertes Glasband für die Beleuchtung der Innenräume und für das „leichte und angenehme" Raumgefühl, das für dieses internationale Zentrum der Land-Art gewünscht wurde. Auch ein Glassockel bringt Licht, das vom umliegenden Wasser in das Innere reflektiert wird, während man durch eine Glaswand einen Ausblick über das Wasser auf die Skulptur von Richard Serra hat.

La forme de cette maison posée sur une petite avancée de terre sur un plan d'eau, a été influencée par une œuvre voisine du sculpteur américain Richard Serra, « Sea Level », qui est en fait un mur de béton. Ce pavillon qui porte le nom d'« Imagination » fait appel à certains éléments structurels que l'on trouve fréquemment dans les granges de la région. Cependant, l'organisation d'expositions a imposé des contraintes techniques autres que celles de simples bâtiments agricoles. Un bandeau de verre dans le toit capte l'éclairage naturel et participe à ce concept « d'espace léger et plaisant » que voulait le Centre d'art du paysage dans lequel il se trouve. Une plinthe de verre apporte à l'intérieur la lumière réfléchie par la surface de l'eau. Un mur de verre ouvre une perspective par-dessus l'eau vers la sculpture de Richard Serra.

*Like interlocking fingers the roof elements close over what becomes the interior space, almost as though the architecture itself were created by its covering.*

*Die sich wie Finger verschränkenden Dachteile definieren den Innenraum, so als würde die Architektur selbst von ihrer Ummantelung hervorgebracht.*

*Comme des doigts croisés, les éléments de la toiture se referment sur ce qui devient alors le volume intérieur. L'architecture est créée par sa couverture.*

Opening in a simple unadorned manner onto its watery environment, the pavilion is at once innovative and quite simple in its conception.

Der Pavillon, der sich auf schmucklose Weise zu seiner sumpfigen Umgebung hin öffnet, ist ebenso innovativ wie einfach in seiner Konzeption.

S'ouvrant en toute simplicité sur son environnement lacustre, le pavillon est à la fois novateur et assez simple de conception.

# CREDITS

## PHOTO CREDITS

**18** © Atelier Hitoshi Abe / **19, 21–23** © Daici Ano / **24** © Acconci Studio / **25–33** © Hufton + Crow/VIEW / **34** © Adjaye Associates / **35–41** © Lyndon Douglas / **42–47** © Steffen Jänicke / **48–53** © Paul Warchol / **54** © Shigeru Ban / **55, 57, 59–61** © Hiroyuki Hirai / **62** © Christian Kandzia / **63, 68** © Roland Halbe/Martin Schodder / **65–66** © Christian Kandzia / **67** left © Christian Kandzia / **67** right © Martin Schodder / **70** © Giorgio von Arb / **71, 73–77** © Roland Halbe/artur-photo / **78** © Cook/Fournier / **79–83** © Paul Raftery VIEW / **84** © Charlee Deaton / **85, 87–93** © Undine Pröhl / **94** © dECOi Architects / **95** © Robert Such / **100** © Neil M. Denari Associates / **106** © Mark LaRosa / **107–109, 111–113** © Paul Raftery/VIEW / **110** © Diller + Scofidio / **114** © Olafur Eliasson / **115–119** © Paul Raftery/VIEW / **120–121, 124–125, 127–129** © Hiro Sakaguchi / **130** © Valerie Bennett / **131, 133** bottom**–134,136–137** © Sue Barr/VIEW / **133** top, **138** top and bottom left © Satoru Mishima / **141** © James Haig Streeter / **138** bottom right © Kenchiku Bunka / **142** © Thomas Mayer / **143** © Peter Aaron/Esto / **145–153** © Christian Richters / **154** © Gigon/Guyer / **155–159** © Christian Richters / **160** © Marcus Wee / **161–169** Earl Carter / **170** © Alexander Gorlin / **171–179** © Ron Pollard / Peter Aaron/Esto / **180** © Gould Evans / **181, 183–189** © Timothy Hursley / **190** © Steve Double / **191, 195** top, **196–197** © Hufton + Crow/VIEW / **192–194, 195** bottom left to right, **198–203** © Christian Richters / **204** © Margherita Spillutini / **205** © Tim James/VIEW / **207–211** © Christian Richters / **212** © Toyo Ito / **213–214, 217** © Nick Guttridge/VIEW / **215, 216** bottom © Raf Makda/VIEW / **216** top © Peter Cook/VIEW / **218** © Luca Vignelli / **219, 221–223** © Erich Ansel Koyama / **224** © Anish Kapoor / **225–229** © Dennis Gilbert/VIEW / **230** © Rem Koolhaas / **231, 233, 235–237** © Christian Richters / **238** © Roland Kirishima / **239, 241–243** © Satoshi Asakawa / **244** © Studio Daniel Libeskind / **246, 247** bottom, **248, 253** © Hufton + Crow/VIEW / **247** top, **249** top right to bottom left and right, **250–252** © Peter Cook/VIEW / **247** top left © Chris Gascoigne/VIEW / **254** © Luca Vignelli / **255–259** © Scott Frances/Esto / **260–262, 265** © Alan Karchmer/Esto / **266** © Reyer Boxem / **267–275** © Christian Richters / **276** © Cezar Coelho / **277–278** © Nick Guttridge/VIEW / **279** top, **280** bottom, **281** © Chris Gascoigne/VIEW / **279** bottom, **280** top © Raf Makda/VIEW / **282** © Jean Nouvel/Lewis Baltz / **283, 285–287** © Paul Raftery/VIEW / **288** © Joke Brouwer / **290–291** © NOX/Lars Spuybroek / **294** © plexus r+d / **298** © Kraajvanger–Urbis / **299, 301–303** © Christian Richters / **304** © Wilfried Dechau / **305–313** © Roland Halbe/artur–photo / **314** © Philippe Starck / **315–321** © TASCHEN GmbH / **322** © Studio 17 / **323–329** © Jussi Tiainen / **330** © Akira Yoneda / **331–337** © Koji Okumura / **338** © Wood + Zapata Inc. / **339–345** © Undine Pröhl / **346** © Rene van Zuuk / **347–349, 351** © Christian Richters

## CREDITS PLANS / DRAWINGS / CAD VISUALIZATIONS

**20–23** © Atelier Hitoshi Abe / **26, 29, 31** © Acconci Studio / **41** © Adjaye Associates / **56, 58, 60–61** © Shigeru Ban Architects / **65, 67, 69** © Behnisch, Behnisch & Partner / **72, 75, 78, 80, 85** © Santiago Calatrava / **81–82** © Peter Cook / **86, 89** © Praxis Design / **96–99** © dECOi Architects / **101–105** © Neil M. Denari Associates / **108–109** © Diller + Scofidio / **122–123, 127, 131** © Masaki Endoh and Masahiro Ikeda / **144–145, 149** © Gehry Partners / **157, 159** © Gigon/Guyer / **162, 165** © Sean Godsell Architects / **173, 177** © Alexander Gorlin Architects / **182–183, 189** © Gould Evans / **206** © Herzog & de Meuron / **220** © Jones Partners Architecture / **240** © Kengo Kuma & Associates / **260, 264** © Richard Meier & Partners, Architects / **269, 271, 275** © Meyer en Van Schooten Architecten B.V. / **289, 291–293** © NOX/Lars Spuybroek / **295–297** © plexus r+d / **300, 302** © Kraajvanger–Urbis / **307–308** © Werner Sobek Ingenieure / **325, 327** © Jykri Tasa Architectural Office / **332–333, 335** © Akira Yoneda Architect / **341** © Wood + Zapata Inc. / **348–350** © René van Zuuk Architekten BV